IN THE REDEEMING CHRIST

In the Redeeming Christ

TOWARD A THEOLOGY OF SPIRITUALITY

by F. X. Durrwell, C.SS.R.

translated by ROSEMARY SHEED

SHEED AND WARD - NEW YORK

Originally published as *Dans le Christ
redempteur*, 1960, by Editions Xavier
Mappus, Le Puy, Lyons and Paris

Library of Congress Catalog Card Number 63-8545

NIHIL OBSTAT: JOANNES M.T. BARTON, S.T.D., L.S.S.
  CENSOR DEPUTATUS
IMPRIMATUR ✠ GEORGIUS L. CRAVEN,
  EPUS SEBASTOPOLIS VIC. CAP.
WESTMONASTERII, DIE 3IA JAN. 1963

The nihil obstat and Imprimatur are a declaration that a
book or pamphlet is considered to be free from doctrinal or
moral error. It is not implied that those who have granted
the Nihil obstat and Imprimatur agree with the contents,
opinions or statements expressed.

Contents

Foreword

Though in our time we have witnessed a flowering of theological, biblical and liturgical studies, there is one complaint we still hear; we have no theology of the spiritual life.

Yet our age has certainly produced some spiritual writings; books on asceticism and mysticism have been published in various countries, and works of spirituality abound.

We have become demanding readers. Too demanding, perhaps. Is it not too much to expect an author to give us "The Theology of the Spiritual Life"? One can describe the beginnings of Christian sanctification, its growth, its expression; one can write a history of the different schools of spirituality, an inventory of their doctrines and methods. But a true and total theology of the spiritual life can only be given within the framework of a study of theology as a whole.

For the doctrine of our sanctification is the doctrine of our eternal salvation—because man is saved only by being sanctified in God—and we know that the doctrine of salvation is co-extensive with theology itself.

The science of theology, of course, extends its search for knowledge beyond man's salvation, and seeks to penetrate into the inmost life of God. But the doctrine of salvation also reaches this point, for it is precisely in that life of God that man's salvation lies. There is no Christian truth that is not related to man's salvation; theology knows nothing about God which does not also concern the salvation of man; it is the science of revelation, and God has revealed himself only in the history of salvation, for the purpose of salvation, as being himself our salvation. In all its depths theology is influenced by this origin and goal, it is filled with the mystery of salvation. To separate these two—the science of God and the science of our salvation—would be to condemn ourselves to having no true knowledge of either.

The centre and fullness of this mystery of salvation is Christ the redeemer, the Son of God in his death and resurrection. It is in the crucible of Easter that Christ brings about man's salvation in himself, that the Church is born and continues to be born, baptized forever in the death and resurrection of the Son of God. This is the point at which revelation finds its goal, its fullness and therefore its source, this pasch when the incarnate Word of God is delivered for us. In his death and glorification, Christ is at once the source and fullness of revelation, and the source and fullness of salvation. We may say indeed that the theology of the Redemption as set out by a Christian thinker in its true dimensions—though the dimensions of this mystery have always exceeded the power of man's mind to compass them—would be at once a total synthesis of Christian theology, and the longed-for work on the spiritual life.

In an earlier work on Christ's resurrection,[1] I tried to outline the major features of a theology of Christ in his death and glorification. In doing so, I was also formulating the essential principles of the spiritual life. This book can add little to them; it can only formulate the same laws, make them clearer, stress certain things, and suggest practical applications of them. It will not even attempt to set out the full doctrine of the Christian life; it will pass over a great many aspects of it, and not give reasons for many of its statements, since the earlier book provides full justification for

[1] F. X. Durrwell, *The Resurrection*, New York, Sheed and Ward, 1960.

them. It makes no claim to be anything more than a collection of notes about the spiritual life.

Any study of spirituality must in fact have some such humble title, unless it is offered as part of a *summa* of the whole mystery of redemption. But in the present case, the word "notes" suggests something even more modest; it indicates an avowedly fragmentary work, whose chapters have no strictly logical arrangement.[2]

The one ambition this book has is that of *never* seeing the Christian life except in relation to Christ the redeemer who is its centre. This anxiety never to forget the central point must be the excuse for a certain necessary monotony, for a constant returning to the same principles.

When one has finished such a work, one tries to get away from one's own ideas, to listen once again to the original sound of the spring which flows at the heart of the Church, in her Scriptures and her liturgy; and one finds that one has developed only one or two of its many notes, and that the book one has written could have been written in a hundred other ways.

This one, such as it is, is dedicated to her who is the model, in the Church, for all Christians, the Virgin Mary, who lived the mystery of the redeeming Christ in its untarnished fullness. I dedicate it also to her who in our own time has been the humblest, and certainly the best, spiritual writer, St. Thérèse of Lisieux, who was predestined, in her turn, to live the marriage of the Church and her redeemer in the depths of its mystery.

May their prayers make every page reveal something of the Lord's face.

[2] Some appeared previously as articles in *Masses ouvrières* and *La Vie spirituelle*.

PART I

PRINCIPLES OF CHRISTIAN LIFE

1

Redemption and Personal Sanctification

In St. John's Gospel, Christ generally makes a brief comment on all his actions: "Know you what I have done to you . . . being your Lord and Master?" (John 13.12-13)—for every action has a meaning. At Cana he refers to the hour when all "the signs" will be accomplished, when the true transformation of water into wine will take place: "My hour is not yet come" (2.4). After the multiplication of the loaves, he proclaims mankind's true bread come down from heaven. Before curing the man born blind, he declares that he is the light of the world. Before raising Lazarus, he speaks of the resurrection of eternal life.

So, when the hour is about to strike, when all Christ's life is to come to its fulfilment, he says a solemn prayer. We call it the High-Priestly Prayer. We might equally call it the commentary on Christ's Mass on Calvary, and on every other Mass, or the *Memento* listing the intentions for which this unique sacrifice, which the other Masses said every day merely make present to us, was offered.

The intentions of that Mass, of every Mass, were expressed by Christ in these words: "For them do I sanctify myself, that they also may be sanctified in truth" (John 17.19).

"I sanctify myself"

Was he not already holy? "That which shall be born of thee shall be Holy, Son of God" (Luke 1.35). He was, and in a sense, his holiness was so perfect that it could not be increased.

But our word "sanctify" does not give all the richness of the word Christ used. It would be better translated, "I consecrate myself to God." And, as the phrase is used in the Bible, this would mean, "I consecrate myself to God in immolation, I vow myself to God by a total renunciation of myself."

To give anything to God, that thing must be withdrawn from all profane use, taken out of this world far from God, and borne into the very sanctuary of divine holiness. The sanctification spoken of by Christ meant both immolation and giving to God. In the Old Testament, the word "sanctify" was a sacrificial word; a victim was sanctified by being taken out of its profane existence and placed in the sphere of God's holiness.

"I sanctify myself," said Christ; I die to myself that I may only be to God; I leave this earthly existence to enter the holy, immortal life of God.

Though he was consecrated from the beginning, he sought a more total consecration, a more complete union with God. He often repeated, "I go to my Father." Between him and the Father there was a distance (though not of a spatial kind) that must be overcome; he must return to his Father, not by a movement in space but by a sanctification, by dying to this world of sin and rising in God. And in this *Vade ad patrem,* this personal sanctification of Christ, the redemption of mankind took place.

Christ in the world of sin

In biblical thought, the unredeemed world is a world cut off from God and his life and given over to death. It is closed in upon itself in an autonomy of wretchedness, a kind of gaol (Gal. 3.22;

Rom. 11.32), with sin, death, the law and the powers of nature personified, in St. Paul's dramatic thinking, as its warders. And behind all these powers is the shadow of another, the "prince of this world" of despair.

Lacking the Spirit, who is the lifegiving holiness of God, shut up in a universe of sin, man has no way out into life. Any movement must be along the way of all flesh—to damnation and death. No road could lead him away from damnation, because damnation was built into his very existence, in his flesh doomed to sin and death. "Unhappy man that I am, who shall deliver me from this body of death?" (Rom. 7.24).

To save me from "this world" and its damnation, is it enough that Christ should die for me? How can anyone die in my place, when I bear sin and death within my very existence? He may shed his blood as a ransom for my sin, but this cannot save me from my hopeless condition. For it is not just a question of cancelling a debt; condemnation is built into my nature, and the redemption must be accomplished in a physical transformation, since man's trouble is primarily in the physical sphere: "All do need the glory of God" (Rom. 3.23), do need the Holy Spirit who is the life-giving holiness of God.

Christ began by entering into our wretchedness himself; he shared with man that existence which Scripture calls existence according to the flesh. A natural existence not animated by the glorious holiness of God. A frail existence filled with mortal weakness, as far from God as the distance between us and God's infinite power of life. The existence of the sinful Adam's sons. He came into human existence with a body of "death" similar in every way to our "sinful flesh" (Rom. 8.3), and appearing to be not the Son, but one of the descendants of Adam who sinned: ". . . taking the form of a servant, being made in the likeness of [other] men, and in habit found as a man" (Phil. 2.7). Become sin for us (2 Cor. 5.21), subject to death and to the Law (Gal. 4.4), made lower than the angels (Heb. 2.9), Christ was, by his very existence, placed within the unredeemed world.

He was still Son of God. But there were within him quite
considerable elements which God's glorifying holiness did not
enter; not only his body, but all the faculties which brought him
into contact with us, were so incompletely possessed by the life
of God that Christ could suffer fear and anguish, that the Son of
the immortal God could succumb to death.

The drama of man's redemption must be completely enacted in
Christ's own person. He must cry out to his Father his anguish,
and his own longing for the salvation that man can find only in
the undying life of God: "Who in the days of his flesh, with a
strong cry and tears, offering up prayers and supplications to him
that was able to save him from death" (Heb. 5.7). He must go to
the Father, and in order to rejoin him in his life-giving holiness,
must step in bloodshed out of the existence of sinful mankind: "I
sanctify myself," I renounce my earthly being and dedicate myself
to the holiness of God.

It was a total renunciation of everything which did not as yet
live by God in the man Jesus. A radical impoverishment whereby
he lost not merely the goods of this world but the life of this world.
A fundamental purification, immolating not just the leanings of the
flesh, but sinful flesh itself. An absolute obedience, which did not
simply lay aside the desires of carnal nature, but actually immolated that nature in a desire to be totally possessed by God.

That is how Christ went to the Father, through dying to himself.

Christ in the Holiness of God

He went to the Father. He did not die for the sake of dying but
in order to live to his Father. "I sanctify myself" meant "I immolate myself," but first of all, "I pass into the possession of God."
His death was a gift of love bearing him outside himself and this
world into the embrace of God. "I lay down my life that I may
take it up again," said our Lord (John 10.17); I die to rise again;
not into a life of this world, that is immolated forever, but into the
holiness of God: "His death was a death to sin once and for all;

his life is a life unto God" (Rom. 6.10). In his death, he was caught up by the hand of God to whom he was abandoning himself, by the glorifying hand of God which is the Holy Ghost: "He was enlivened in the spirit" (I Peter 3.18) who is the power, the glory and the life-giving holiness of God.

The Resurrection was for Christ the entry into the life of the Son, and Easter may be called a birthday. It was then, after all, that St. Paul thought of the Father as saying the solemn words, "Thou art my Son, this day have I begotten thee" (Acts 13.33). Once born, like us, into slavery, son of a man-doomed-to-death, henceforth "constituted the Son of God in power, according to the spirit of sanctification, by the resurrection from the dead" (Rom. 1.4). This was a completely different kind of birth: he was born into divine life by entering into the bosom of the Father. Even the life of his body is now grace, is the life of that Spirit who so filled him that one can now say: The Lord is spirit, "a quickening spirit" (2 Cor. 3.17; 1 Cor. 15.45).

Christ is "sanctified" forever; he is consecrated to God in his death to himself and in the life-giving holiness of the Father. The Epistle to the Hebrews describes at some length what happened in this sacrifice, comparing it with that offered by the Jewish high priest who, once a year, left the profane world, and taking with him the blood of goats and bulls, went through the veil into the Holy of Holies; whereas Christ passed through the veil of his own flesh (Heb. 10.20), that is through his damaged body, and entered with his own blood not into an earthly sanctuary, but into the very bosom of God (9.11-12).

Christ fixed forever in his redemptive act

Christ will never leave behind that immolation and that new life; his existence is fixed forever at the moment of the Redemption. The five wounds he showed his disciples are not merely the receipt for our ransom inscribed upon his body, but the wounds of a death from which he will never recover. He did not rise to the life he had

had before, to this world, to this time; in that sense he did not rise at all. He died once for all. The life of glory is a perpetuation of his death; the fire of the Spirit which consumes him keeps him as an eternal holocaust. The Lamb of God stands in glory and is surrounded by hymns of triumph, but he is still slain (Apoc. 5.6).

He is fixed to his death and resurrection not as in that state that follows the redeeming act; he remains fixed in the act itself, in the unrepeatable moment of his death and glorification. Having come, at the moment of his death, to the high point of his movement towards the Father, of his gift of love, he is received at that same moment with the welcome of divine glorification: "Father, into thy hands I commend my spirit" (Luke 23.46). And this glorifying embrace is eternal, an action without any sequel: "This day have I begotten thee," says the Father, as he extends to the soul and then to the body of the Saviour the glory, formerly hidden, of the eternal generation of the Son. On one hand, the glorifying action of the Father, the eternal generation, is always happening; Christ remains forever fixed at the moment of his glorification. But on the other hand, that ever-actual glorifying action coincides with Christ's death, and thus keeps the Saviour forever at the moment of his death to the world, at the high point of his giving of himself to the Father.

Death "to the world" takes place in Christ simultaneously with God's action in raising him divinely. The Redemption is in him as something happening now, in the moment of its taking place. From now on salvation, which is a dying to the world and a rising again, is at the disposal of all mankind in Christ: "And being consummated [in his death and glory], he became, to all that obey him, the cause of eternal salvation" (Heb. 5.9).

He had entered the doomed world, taking flesh "in the likeness of sinful flesh" (Rom. 8.3); then, with that same body, he made the breakthrough of our deliverance. He is "the beginning, the first-born from the dead" (Col. 1.18), "the prince of life" (Acts 3.15) who has achieved the redemption of all things in his own person.

It now remains for men to find this "redemption, that is in Christ Jesus" (Rom. 3.24).

"That they also may be sanctified in truth"

Why did Christ first become one of us, sharing with us that existence of remoteness and weakness? Why did he consecrate himself to God by dying to himself? It was for us, answers St. Paul, that he died and rose again (II Cor. 5.15). Before he died Christ said, "I go away and I come" (John 14.28). He went not for the sake of leaving, not even in order to come again, but quite simply to "come." His "coming" was now beginning, that coming to redeem which had so often been promised: "When the Son of Man shall come . . ." On earth he had been with men; but, like a grain of wheat remaining alone, he had been outside them, even outside his intimates, living as we do a life according to the flesh, closed in upon itself in the autonomy of its own weakness. Now he is dead to the flesh and its limitations, he lives in the Spirit who is the power of God, he is infinite openness and total outpouring; he communicates himself, enters within men's hearts, draws them towards him and contains them within him. The grain has become the laden ear of wheat, bending under its load; Christ has become the Church; the multitude of mankind has become the body of Christ, in which is salvation.

The Church as Christ's body in the redemptive act

From the standpoint of purely juridical considerations, one could work out a theology of the Redemption in which man would not need to unite himself to Christ nor be sanctified in him in order to be saved. Christ would have "ransomed" us, cast onto the scales of justice the price of our pardon, his blood, his life; he would have died in our place. Once this price was paid, God would not need to raise Christ again for us (2 Cor. 5.15); we should not need Christ any more. We should not need the Church, Christ's visible presence

on earth; nor the sacraments, which are our means of contact with
him. It would be enough to believe in the pardon won for us and to
accept it, to have the faith by which man could shelter behind the
wall of merits that protects man from God. Man would be
pardoned and would have no need to be sanctified in Christ.

Yet St. Paul says, "If Christ be not risen again . . . you are yet in
your sins" (1 Cor. 15.17). Redemption is not, then, simply a question of expiation by death, of payment of ransom, of buying us
back. It was a personal sanctifying of Christ whereby he passed
from life according to sin into the holiness of God; a drama played,
from first to last, in the single person of Christ. And if it was
entirely a drama personal to Christ, men have no share in the
Redemption unless his drama becomes theirs. His death on Calvary
profited Christ alone; the object of that death, the complete and
only object of its merits, was Christ's resurrection; it sanctified no
one, at first, except Christ himself. The Redemption is nothing but
the pasch of Christ; it *is* the Redeemer himself in his death and
resurrection: a "redemption, that is in Christ Jesus" (Rom. 3.24).

To find this salvation that is no mere pardon but the life-giving
holiness of God, man must identify himself with him in whom alone
God has made that holiness blaze forth, must identify himself with
Christ risen from the dead, must become the body of that Christ
whom God raised from the dead.

The Church, identified with Christ, finds this salvation of the
Resurrection because she is incorporated into the Saviour, not in
this or that moment of his life—Bethlehem, Nazareth, the roads of
Palestine—nor yet in a heavenly existence subsequent to the act of
redemption, but in the act of redemption itself. She is the body
of Christ in one precise, and henceforth eternal, moment, in the
moment when the Redemption takes place, in the moment of his
death on the Cross, when Christ was glorified by the Father.[1]

The Church's union with Christ implies not simply a communion

---

[1] The Christian may also unite himself to the events of Christ's life on
earth, for they are all related to the death which is made redemptive,
eternalized and accessible to men in all ages by the glory of God.

of being and of life, but a mysterious communion in his own death and glorification. The idea of the Mystical Body includes equally the identification with Christ in a single body, and the sharing in a single redemptive act; and it would be an incomplete theology of the Mystical Body that did not see the Church as the body of paschal Christ, in other words, of Christ in the act of dying and being glorified.

Man's salvation results from his communion in both the death and glory of Christ simultaneously. It is the effect of the divine action which raises up the man Jesus and at the same time raises all those who are in him. But we only benefit from that raising in our communion in Christ's death, for God only glorified Christ in his death, in the total oblation by which he gave himself over to the action of his Father.

Christ's body, which is also the Church, is therefore not a static reality; Christian life is a movement, a never-ceasing activity. We are united to Christ in an action—in his total death to self which opened out into a divine life, in the heroism of his redemptive love. Only there, on this summit of charity, where he gives himself to the Father for mankind, does Christ unite himself to the Church and make her his own body.

St. Paul indeed calls the Church Christ's pleroma, the receptacle of his fullness; she adds nothing to the perfection of Christ, but simply receives it. Yet she is not passive. For Christ himself, who gives her that fullness, is in action, in the intense act of his redeeming charity; he is the Christ of the Pasch, whose existence is wholly a giving of himself. Could she be identified with him passively? The Church is the body of Christ in the redemptive act, one with him in that act.

Redeemed man is thus not simply man pardoned, not even man re-created, brought to life, but man giving himself, identified with Christ in total self-giving. Such is the grace of God: it gives man the power to give himself, it frees him from his sin, saves him and re-creates him by making him a being wholly given. It makes him like God in charity—imperfectly in this world, until the day of the

revelation of the sons of God (Rom. 8.19) when all men, in Christ
the Redeemer, will be like him who exists in a single act, like God
who is love. That is how Christ himself attained to salvation[2]—
how he was revealed as the Son of God, when he had sacrificed
himself, and glory had established him forever in the fullness of
self-giving.

The Church "sanctifies herself" in Christ

The men who live in Christ lead a paschal existence; they are
always going forward, as pilgrims going by way of death to the
divine life, pilgrims in Christ who is the way by which they "go to
the Father." In the Fourth Gospel, which so often alludes to
Christ's "passage," which gives the phrase "*Vado ad patrem*,"
Christ says, "I am the Way" (John 14.6). That way leads from
death to life, and it lies through the body of the Saviour: "A new
and living way which he hath dedicated for us through the veil,
that is to say, his flesh" (Heb. 10.20). Having gone up to the Father
by the ladder of the Cross, Christ draws all things to himself, and,
in him, takes them up, by their sharing in his own death, to the
very bosom of the Father.

Christians set out on the road in the early morning. In the
morning of their lives, at baptism, they unite themselves to Christ,
become one body with him (Gal. 3.27), and participate in his death
and resurrection: "Buried with him in baptism, in whom also you
are risen again" (Col. 2.12). In the morning of life's day, they
eat Christ's body, and become him more and more, as the Eucharist
makes him present to them—in his death and glorification.

Then, throughout that long day, they realize, even in their own
"members which are upon the earth" (Col. 3.5), the death
mystically wrought in the sacrament. They die to the world with
Christ by all their renunciations, by faith, charity and hope, by
chastity and poverty, by dedication and obedience to God. Right
up to the final death, the death of the body, at which the death of

[2] A salvation which he had to win for us in his own person.

baptism, their eucharistic communions, and all the lesser deaths of every day, are consummated, and they complete their death with Christ (2 Tim. 2.11) "out of this world towards God."[3]

Such is the life of Christians: "Ought not Christ to have suffered these things, and so enter into his glory?" (Luke 24.26). An austere life, a way of exodus, unceasingly departing! Yet one in which one does not die for the sake of dying, in which one leaves constantly to arrive. All our deaths are paschs. The way that lies through the body of Christ is "new and living."

"A faithful saying: for if we be dead with him, we shall live also with him" (2 Tim. 2.11). For the death of the Saviour is redemptive, opening out into divine life. In the Christ of glory, death dwells together with life, and is but one aspect of glory. You cannot take part in Christ's death without being caught up in God's action to raise the dead. We talk of death, but what we ought to say is "the gift of self." All our many deaths in Christ have but one name—divine charity. "I sanctify myself," said Christ; that is, I give myself to God. Love is all that is necessary. "The charity of Christ presseth us" (2 Cor. 5.14), and carries us out of ourselves towards the Father. The only true Christian renunciation is the renunciation that goes with love.

The sanctification of the Church is the redemption of the world

Christ prayed "that they also may be sanctified in truth." Strictly personal, yet infinitely open, Christ's sanctification possesses the power to redeem all things.

When the Church sanctifies herself in her individual members, she is, in her turn, co-operating in the redemption of the world. For she unites herself to the body of Christ, is transformed into him, and communicates in her saviour's own death and resurrection. The body she becomes is indeed Christ's, and the death and resurrection in which she dies and rises again are his. And the body, the death and the resurrection are directed towards the

[3] Ignatius of Antioch, commenting Rom. 2.2.

salvation of the whole world. Every believer who sanctifies himself takes part in the mystery of universal redemption. It is his privilege that he cannot save himself alone; his personal sanctification is also an apostolate, a work of redemption in Christ.

In the same way, there can be no true apostolate without personal sanctification. There are not two redemptions, one effected by Christ, the other by his apostles. There is only one, strictly personal to Christ, effected in his death and resurrection. The apostle can place it at the disposal of the world by realizing it in himself. The apostle is not above his master, and, by the grace of his master, he is not below him either. The work of redemption is not something exterior to him, an alien grace merited by Christ and which the apostle simply passes on like a worker on an assembly line. For him as for his master, redemption is a living work which is accomplished in a personal sanctification, in a death to self and a resurrection in God. Thus Christ exalts the person of the apostle and magnifies him in proportion as he demands that the apostle die to himself, for it is in the apostle's own person that the salvation of others is worked out.

The prime law of the apostolate, then, is a law of communion in Christ and in his mystery of redemption. Everything else—the law of incarnation, for instance, or external activity—is secondary, though not subordinate; it can only follow from this first law.[4]

⁴ It is sometimes said that the first law of the apostolate is the law of the Incarnation, because the Son of God had to start by becoming incarnate in order to save the world. But this is somewhat ambiguous. The incarnation of the Son of God only became effectively redemptive in the Resurrection, when Christ had left this world of sin by dying. During his life on earth, Christ remained alone, enclosed in the limits of his fleshly nature. He could not then communicate himself to others; our salvation could not be realized in him yet. But once dead and risen in the Holy Spirit, he communicates himself, draws all mankind into himself, and bestows upon them the salvation effected in his own person.

The apostle has not got to imitate the Son of God's coming into this world of sin. He is in it by birth. He must share in the Redemption at the moment of its redemptive efficacy, by uniting himself to the man Jesus in his death to the world of sin and his resurrection in God. Thus, like Christ, he will be in a position to penetrate to the very heart of the world he must

St. Paul and the other Apostles knew this: the success of their apostolate depended on their share in the Saviour's death. Christ had said, "They are not of the world" (John 17.14), and they considered themselves as set apart: "I am separated unto the gospel of God" (Rom. 1.1). But as soon as they were sanctified in Christ, redemptive graces flowed out from them, those same rivers of the Spirit which flowed from the belly of the risen Christ (John 7.37-9). All that is said of Christ in glory, that he "rose again for our justification" (Rom. 4.25), that he became "a quickening spirit" (1 Cor. 15.45), that he "is made for us wisdom, and justice, and sanctification, and redemption" (1 Cor. 1.30)—all this could be said in a lesser but perfectly real way of Christ's disciples. "We who live are always delivered unto death for Jesus' sake, that the life also of Jesus may be made manifest in our mortal flesh. So then death worketh in us, but life in you" (2 Cor. 4.11-12).

Christ alone is the Redeemer, his death and resurrection alone are redemptive. But he is only present in the world through his Church, which is his body still present in the world; his death and resurrection only reach the world in as much as they are realized in the Church. The apostle, the Church's representative in her essential and unique role as redeemer, must be the presence of Christ among men, must make present his mystery of death and resurrection "that they also may be sanctified in truth." The Christian's salvation lies in his personal sanctification. There too begins the salvation of others.

---

save, and to bring it salvation. Only the man who has died to himself and risen in the charity of the Holy Spirit can be present to others and bring them salvation.

It is, of course, essential to the apostolate that it be present among men. By his death and resurrection, Christ has left this world, and now has no natural contact with it. His Church and his apostles are the sacraments of his presence in our history, by which he weaves the Redemption into the fabric of the world. It is because the Church is a sacrament that the apostle has a duty to be present at the heart of the world. But the Church is the sacrament of the dead and risen Christ. That is why I say that the first requirement of the apostolate is communion in the redemptive mystery.

2

The Justice of God Is
Man's Holiness

God is coming to judge the world. His judgement on the world
is already given. These and similar statements are to be found
throughout the preaching of the New Testament. Indeed the
judgement of God forms the major theme of that preaching, as
much as, or even perhaps more than, it was of the Old Testament
prophets. The Gospel, the good news of salvation, proclaims the
justice which has come to the world in Christ. Such a message is
full of paradox. It heralds stern justice, yet claims to be good news.
"The Lord shall judge his people. It is a fearful thing to fall into the
hands of the living God" (Heb. 10.30-31). Yet St. Paul rejoices
at "the superabundance of the justice" of God (Rom. 5.17), and
his heart feeds on "the hope of justice" (Gal. 5.5). These texts
clash together, apparently contradictory, and the Christian who
reads them is likely to feel torn by conflicting feelings.

Yet God is one, and can only be adored in spirit and in truth
with a mind that is also one. It is essential, therefore, that we go
more deeply into this central theme of Gospel preaching, to get
to the root at which the elements that appear so diverse on the
surface come together. If the proclamation of justice is truly good
news, must we not believe that the justice of God is exercised
simply to save men, that the result of his stern judgement is nothing

other than the salvation of sinners? If so, we shall then discover that the true name for fear of the Lord is hope.

I. *THE JUSTICE OF GOD COMES INTO THE WORLD THROUGH CHRIST*

1. THE ANNOUNCEMENT OF THE JUDGEMENT

Like a cathedral doorway with a judgement scene above it, the Gospel opens by proclaiming the day of God's justice. This first announcement re-echoes through the whole Gospel message. And finally, to conclude his preaching, Christ once again paints for us a great fresco of the Last Judgement—like the picture in the cathedral's apse (Matt. 24-25). The whole Gospel, the good news of salvation, seems to proclaim God's justice imposed on the world. From the opening of the Gospel, then, this is how salvation appears. In the eyes of Simeon, the child presented in the Temple came as the judge who was to divide Israel into two camps, one destined for disaster, the other for resurrection: "This child is set for the fall, and for the resurrection of many in Israel" (Luke 2.34).

John the Baptist heralded the advent of the Last Judgement in the imminent coming of God. His message was tragic. His voice trembled with fear of that terrible day, fear of justice close by. He speaks of anger, of the axe ready to cut the tree, of the reaper of the Last Day, the cleansing of the floor, putting the wheat into barns, casting out the chaff and burning it with unquenchable fire. He promises baptism with the Holy Ghost and with fire, God's great judicial action to purify Israel, sanctifying some in the holiness of God, burning the rest, for "our God is a consuming fire" (Heb. 12.29).

This power of God coming, this justice that sweeps all before it, is not simply something that will be imposed on the world once the work of redemption is complete; according to John, that work consists wholly in the judgement, it is accomplished in the Holy Ghost and fire on the appointed day. He sees the redemption of Israel as none other than the judgement of the Last Day.

John always had before his eyes this vision of grandeur and fear up till the day when he met Jesus of Nazareth, meek and humble, in whom the justice of God appeared in the guise of a man dedicated to dying for the salvation of others: "Behold," he then says, "the Lamb of God, who taketh away the sins of the world" (John 1.29). But Christ himself again takes up the theme of justice and judgement: "Do penance, for the kingdom of God is at hand" (Matt. 4.17). He demands that we be converted if we would escape condemnation when the Kingdom comes. Christ has, of course, come to save us: "I am come not to lose but to save" (cf. Luke 9.23 ff.). Yet he also says he has come as a dispenser of justice, and that salvation will take place in judgement: "For judgement I am come into this world" (John 9.39). His coming, the whole redeeming incarnation right up to the last day, is a trial and a judgement.

What Christ says in so many words in the fourth gospel, he describes in parables in the Synoptics. The fishes caught in the net are to be sorted out. The wheat and cockle grow either for God's barn or for burning. The ten virgins are separated for ever into two groups, five and five. Those unworthy of the feast are cast out of the lighted house into the outer darkness. "Think you that I am come to bring peace?" Christ has come with the sword of God's justice, to divide.

The threat of judgement weighs upon all men, and no one can escape it. The Pharisees who thought themselves privileged, in a special category of justice, expected to evade the great trial, but John the Baptist warned them that they could not: "Ye brood of vipers, who hath shewed you to flee from the wrath to come?" (Matt. 3.7). Nineteen men were crushed under the tower of Siloe in Jerusalem. When his disciples told him this, Christ said, "Except you do penance, you shall all likewise perish" (Luke 13.5). In the new House of Israel, the Son of Man will appoint leaders, just as in the people of old, stewards with the job of distributing the daily measure of wheat to the other servants of God. Are they too under threat of judgment? "And Peter said to him, Lord, dost thou speak this parable to us, or likewise to all?" And Christ asks him "Who is the faithful and wise steward, whom his lord setteth over his family," is it not you? Happy that servant if he has been found faithful at his master's coming! But if he gets drunk, and begins to strike the menservants and maid-servants, then when his master comes, he "shall separate him, and shall appoint him his portion with unbelievers" (Luke 12.41-6). This is the parable of the leaders of the new Israel, popes, bishops and priests. On more than one judgement scene on a cathedral tympanum we find a bishop or monk in the forefront of the damned.

Having come for this, for the judgement of God in the world, having always proclaimed that judgement, when Christ came to the high point of his life, to "his hour," he solemnly declared that henceforth God's justice would invade the world: "Now is the judgement of this world" (Luke 12.31). He stood before the Sanhedrin, he submitted to the judgement of men, "Nevertheless I say to you, hereafter you shall see the Son of man sitting on the right hand of the power of God, and coming in the clouds of heaven" (Matt. 26.64).

2. THE CARRYING-OUT OF THE JUDGEMENT

From that time, Christ "is coming;" at that moment there is spoken in him the last judgement, which imposes God's justice on the world. The coming upon the clouds which will make "all the tribes of the earth mourn" (Matt. 24.30), the great eschatological drama, the tribunal of the last judgement, begin in that hour: "From now on you shall see the Son of man coming in the clouds of heaven." Our Lord had said a few days earlier, "The judgement of this world is now." The only judgement he can have meant was the same judgement the gospel always speaks of—the last judgement. From the moment when Christ died and rose again, God's judgement—the last judgement—was in the world. Christ, who dies and whom the Father raises up, is himself the trial whereby the world is judged and the sentence pronounced upon it.

(a) The end of this world

It was not for nothing that the sun was darkened and the earth quaked—"the earth trembled and was still when God arose in judgement" (Ps. 75.9-10)—that darkness fell upon the earth, that the dead rose; all these signs were foretold for the great and fearful day by the Prophets. Not for nothing was the veil of the Temple rent from top to bottom, as a sign that the Temple, which was itself a symbol of this world, was destroyed.

From that moment "this world," the world of sin, was virtually finished ("the fashion of this world passeth away" (I Cor. 7.31)), just as from that moment the Temple collapsed of which Christ had said, "Destroy this temple [made with hands] and in three days I will rebuild it [not made with hands]" (John 2.19-21; Mark 14.58; Heb. 9.11). In his eschatological discourse Christ had already made it clear that the end of the world coincides with the destruction of the sanctuary (Matt. 24): both perished in Christ's death.

In Christ, come "in the likeness of sinful flesh" (Rom. 8.3), "made sin for us" (2 Cor. 5.21), who died according to the flesh, God solemnly condemns sin and "sinful flesh." In Christ, he "hath condemned sin in the flesh" (Rom. 8.3). He has condemned sin and sinful flesh not simply in Christ, but in all mankind. "For me," says St. Paul, "the world is crucified" (Gal. 6.14). What is this world that he sees as crucified? It is not simply the spirit of the world, or the maxims of the world. It is the world itself as sin has made it, the world "according to the flesh," lacking the Spirit. Christ on earth was part of it, for he lived an existence "according to the flesh," belonging to "this world." But by his death he passed out of that existence according to the flesh, passed out of "this world." From that time forward the world of old was like a building without its keystone, and St. Peter urges us, "Save yourselves from this perverse generation" (Acts 2.40), lest we be buried in its ruins.

Nothing, of course, looked different after Christ's death. This world of sin seemed quite healthy, it bore an air of triumph, the tree appeared strong. But its roots were cut, Christ had withdrawn from it, and, as St. Paul's prophetic eye could see, "the fashion of this world passeth away." When the veil of the Temple was rent, they continued to immolate paschal lambs; for forty years the splendours of the ancient liturgy went on—a permanent temptation to the faith of the Christians who came from Judaism (Heb. 10), just as the power of the world threatens the faith of believers in our own day. Yet, Christ having moved out of the power of the Law by his death, the veil of the Temple having been torn, the mystery of the Temple was laid open, and "the house left desolate" (Matt. 23.38). The Jewish pasch went on being held, and the Temple was already collapsing in ruin over its sacrifices.

(b) A new creation in justice

At the same time as the world of sin is condemned in Christ's flesh, there is inaugurated in the body of Christ in glory a new world of holiness and justice, the new creation foretold by the Prophets, of which the first creation was no more than a kind of rough sketch. The stone rejected by the builders now became the "head of the corner" of a new house (Acts 5.11; I Pet. 2.6-8). The destroyed temple of Jerusalem was rebuilt on the third day, the mysterious temple of a new people. Christ's resurrection on the first day of a new cosmic week was the true birth of the world: a new mankind, the world of "the resurrection of the dead" (Rom. 1.4; I Cor. 15.21), "a new creation" in Christ (2 Cor. 5.17; Gal. 6.15), rose through the Holy Spirit, the creative force of God, in whom Christ rose from the dead.

(c) Two worlds

Since then there are two worlds, two worlds enmeshed together
even in our hearts: one with the imprint of sin, which Christ has
left, a world without a future, with no value for eternity, going only
to destruction; the other, created in the glorified Christ, in whom
God's creative wisdom is expressed and carried out, the final plan
for the world intended from the beginning (Eph. 1.4-10). This is
the world of God's justice—in other words, of his holiness: "He
is made unto us [following upon his death] wisdom and justice
and sanctification" (1 Cor. 1.30). Those who belong to it are not
of "this world," are not under condemnation ("There is now therefore no condemnation to them that are in Christ Jesus" Rom. 8.1),
but live in the justice of God, for Christ "rose up again for our
justification" (Rom. 4.25).

From that moment on, Christ draws the first creation to himself
to change it into the new creation; he seeks to transubstantiate it
into himself. He calls sinners, and if they thirst for justice in all
humility, he justifies them in the justice with which he himself has
now been filled.

That is how the last judgement is in the world; some accept to
enter the new creation in the glorifying justice of God; others
stubbornly remain in the now condemned world of sin, a world
headed for doom. The separation of the Last Day is already happening. "Hereafter," said Christ, "you shall see the son of man
coming in the clouds of heaven" (Matt. 26.64). In his death and
glorification, he is the dispenser of God's justice on the Last Day,
giving to some the new creation, resurrection and justification, but
only eternal condemnation to the world he has left.

After Christ's death, the Apostles took up the role of preaching
justice which John the Baptist and Christ had filled. They did not
now foretell a justice that was to come; they proclaimed that it was
already in the world, for, "him God raised up . . . to be judge of
the living and of the dead" (Acts 10.40,42). The whole Gospel,

that is to say, the whole mystery of the Redemption, is the revelation of divine justice. "The gospel . . . is the power of God unto salvation to every one that believeth . . . for the justice of God is revealed therein" (Rom. 1.16-17). In the past God had tolerated the extreme wickedness of the world, for it was "the time of forbearance" of evil, until the fullness of time. But now "he shows his justice and that he is the just [God], and the justifier of him who is of the faith of Jesus Christ" (Rom. 3.26). He saves men from their sins by subjecting them to his justice.

II. *THE JUSTICE OF GOD IS THE SALVATION OF MEN*

One line of prophecy shows the Day of the Lord as a day of redemption, another as the final condemnation; both lines come together in Christ's pasch. The justice which God exercises in Christ saves whoever submits to it, and damns whoever rejects it.

1. THE JUSTICE OF JUSTIFICATION

To those men who want salvation, God exercises a judgement of justification. He judges them by justifying them, by pouring into them the new life, the life of resurrection which *is* God's justice, his life-giving holiness. This is how it is exercised in Christ who, by his death, offered himself to God's justice; he "was justified in the Spirit" (1 Tim. 3.16), brought to life in holiness, in the Holy Spirit of God. The Fourth Gospel was to say that those who believe in Christ will not be judged, meaning that they will not be condemned; judgement for them consists in passing from death to life, from darkness to light (John 3.17-21; v, 24). God carries out his justice by communicating it to them.

This judgement is no mere pronouncing of sentence. Every word of God is an action, a sentence which carries itself out. The sentence of justice pronounced in Christ is a creative act, it is the

life-giving holiness of the Spirit which raises up Christ and creates
the world of divine justice. The faithful are judged in this sentence
of justifying life, they "are quickened with Christ" (Eph. 2.5).
The justice which is in God becomes the salvation of man, the
fullness of life which provides his happiness. Blessed are they
who thirst after justice! This judgement is pronounced in us for
the first time in baptism. Then each man is created anew in Christ,
rises with him, and enters with him into the world of justice.
God impresses his justice upon him by the gift of his life-giving
holiness. Baptism is an eschatological rite, the beginning of the
resurrection of the dead, the first realization of the Last Judgement.
A Christian who is humble and believing is always submitted to
this judgement which justifies, re-creates and vivifies. The justice
of God is always advancing in him, from justification to justification, from an imperfect life to a more intense life, from resurrection
to resurrection. It is at once a case of being tried by justice and a
process of vivifying justification, of resurrection.

Man is thus judged, justified, vivified, by his encounters with
God in Christ. These encounters are many: in the sacraments, in
every cross, in every fellow man, especially the poorest, in the
Church which is the sign of Christ upon the world; right up to the
last and total encounter, when Christ "will come" at the Last
Judgement. How glorious will that judgement be, when God's
justice takes total possession of every believer! How glorious that
epiphany of our Judge and Saviour which the early Christians
longed for so impatiently: "We look for our Saviour" (Phil. 3.20).
Then will the final judgement be pronounced, in a total justification, in a complete resurrection.

How wonderful, then, is this justice of God in Christ, effected
in the sinner who seeks salvation. A justice of justification, a justice
which is communicated, a justice which gives life, which raises
man up in holiness. God's justice and holiness are none other than
the Spirit. And the power which raises up Christ and the faithful
in him is none other than the Spirit. And the new life communicated to us is none other than the Spirit poured into our hearts.

The Spirit is love. It is in the Holy Spirit that God judges the world, through him that divine justice is imposed upon the world; it is in love that the world is judged. So totally true is it that God is love—his justice is love.

Sinful man may rejoice in God's justice and long for it, that justice which is exercised by giving itself. "We wait for the hope of justice" (Gal. 5.5), said the first Christians. Hope and justice: they said the two words in one breath and saw no opposition between them. It was with great longing that they awaited the Day of Judgement.

2. THE JUSTICE OF DAMNATION

However, there are men for whom this judgement of justification, this justice of self-giving love, becomes reprobation, a justice of condemnation. For such men close themselves to the love of God which justifies. They refuse to go from the darkness into the lighted place, which is the risen Christ, the house of God's glory, and they remain outside in "the world" Christ left, in the exterior darkness where there is weeping and gnashing of teeth. "They are already judged [condemned] because they loved darkness rather than light" (John 3.18), the exterior darkness.

The vision we are offered by faith is apocalyptic. The division of the Last Day is made in us at every moment of history, and heavenly life and everlasting death are already in the world. On one side are the unbelieving, the disobedient, all who refuse God's holiness; on the other the believing, those whose humble and faithful hearts are open to justice.

One day God will impose for good the justice that he wills, will extend the Easter mystery to the whole world, drawing all men in the creative force of the new world which raises up Christ in the justice of God. Those who reject him may try to barricade themselves against justice, but they cannot make history go backwards: in Christ the whole world is involved in dying to its old form and rising again. Men will only exist by the redemptive power of God

in Christ; mankind will be dominated by the life-giving justice of
God.

For those whose being is in accord with that justice, who receive
it in faith and humility right to the very depths of their souls, it
will be what it is in God and in the risen Christ: holiness of the
Spirit, eternal love, beatifying life. But in those who "have not
submitted themselves to the justice of God" (Rom. 10.3), that
same force of everlasting justification will produce only a rejected
life, a life held at bay, which men cannot receive, and which is
unable to develop: a frustrated life whose very essence is denied,
so as to make it no more than an unsatisfied need for holiness and
love. An existence in which life and death are joined together forever—a life coming from Christ, and a refusal of that life coming
from man's inmost self.

There will be a resurrection of life and a resurrection of damnation "because [Christ] is the son of man" (John 5.27), lord of the
last days who brings salvation to all, both to those who accept it
and those who refuse. He will be the centre of the new world;
both heaven and hell come from him. Blessed are they who are
poor in spirit, who hunger and thirst after justice, who receive the
sanctifying will of God. The Kingdom is theirs in the justice of
God.

III. *ACCEPTING THE JUSTICE OF GOD*

The essential is to submit to God's judgement, to "receive the
abundance . . . of justice" (Rom. 10.3; 5.17) which has burst into
the world through Christ. Man's forgiveness is there, and there
too is his sanctification and salvation.

1. ACCEPTING

The Redemption is a pasch, as we have said (Chap. 1), a personal sanctification of man. With Christ, man goes out of this
world to God. He goes, and it might look almost as though in the

drama of his salvation he himself is the leading actor. He enters upon the way with Christ, he sanctifies himself, by a tremendous effort he turns towards God. Yet, in the preaching of justice, salvation appears not as resulting from man's effort but as a gift from God. This gift is simply God's justice being imposed on the world, God's sovereign will, declared in Christ, to which man must consent.

How can man work out his salvation himself, if salvation is simply God, God's Spirit given to men? How can he find it as the term of his own efforts? Since salvation consists in the holiness of God communicated to us, there is no connection between it and our efforts. Man goes, and his salvation takes place in his going, from this world to the Father, in a great effort; God comes to man, and salvation lies wholly in that coming, in the entry of God's justice into man's hearts. These two aspects of the Redemption do not clash, but in fact make each other clear. We see man's necessary effort for what it is: even at its fiercest, it is no more than an effort to accept salvation; man's supreme gift of himself to God is no more than a total submission, a consent to God's saving justice.

Man works out his salvation by accepting it; he is saved from sin by God's justice which he receives. All he must do is to submit to God's justice which has come into the world in Christ, all he must do is to accept that justice. Man's forgiveness is there, there are his sanctification and final salvation. "It is not of him that willeth, nor of him that runneth, but of God that sheweth mercy" (Rom. 4.16) and that saves us by "abundance . . . of the gift and of justice" (5.17). Our justice before God does not come from ourselves, like that "justice of my own," gained from observing the Law, which St. Paul rejects (Phil. 3.9). It is only ours because of the acceptance we give it, "the power of God unto salvation" (Rom. 1.16) to which we consent. "You are saved not by your works . . . for we are his workmanship" (Eph. 2.8-10).

By an inborn pride from which only grace can wean him, man continues to declare himself against God. He sets himself up on a kind of pedestal, by claiming an autonomy which he does not possess. He behaves as though he were master even when he tries to give honour to his God. He places himself at God's disposal, as though he existed of himself; he presents his goods to God as though they really belonged to him. He treats his works as though they were of value in themselves, and offers them to God with the idea that they give him some right to a divine value in exchange, a right over the things of heaven. Yet the only way in which he can give anything to God is to accept *his* gift, to submit to *his* salvific will. Such was Christ's own sacrifice, and it was the only true one, offered in Spirit and in truth. After the sacrifices of the Old Testament, in which men were by way of giving something to God, and which God did not accept (Heb. 10.5 ff.), came Christ; he subjected himself even to death (Phil. 2.8), offered himself up to his Father's will, and accepted the glory of God, the gift of justice, the Holy Spirit of the Resurrection. That is how he merited, by accepting the life of the Spirit in dying to the flesh. That is how he expiated, as, dying to "sinful flesh," he accepted justice. That is how man, from afar off, went to the Father in Christ; fleshly man, closed in upon himself, was opened out in the Holy Spirit. He was opened in the very depths of his being to God's justice. God's judgement, which saves the world, takes place simultaneously in death and in a rush of life, in a death which opens Christ to life. God and man both have their part in the work of redemption, and man's part consists in accepting God's. Christ's death alone would not have accomplished salvation, would not have carried out justice: "If Christ had only died, you would be still in your sins" (1 Cor. 15.17). But every sin was expiated, all guilt effaced, all justice done, at the instant when Christ, abandoning himself to the Father, was filled with the holy glory of God. Expiation is to be found in grace and in being open to grace, in God who raises up the man Jesus, and in the man Jesus who, by his death, lays himself open to that glory.

He did not suffer humiliation, torture and death, then, to throw them into the balance as a counterweight to sin. He did not let himself be destroyed to appease the anger of justice; he did it to accept justice, to submit to glory, to make his own the will of the Spirit and receive his life-giving holiness. Dead to himself to be brought to life in God that sinful man might be "justified in the Spirit" (1 Tim. 3.16), and that, "made sin for us" on the cross (2 Cor. 5.21), he might also become the justice of God for us (1 Cor. 1.30).

That is why St. Paul does not say simply that Christ died for us, but "for us died and rose again" (2 Cor. 5.15; Rom. 4.25). The death had no value in itself, only in its relation to the glory; it was redemptive by its object, its only object, the one object of its merit—the Resurrection: the filling of the man Jesus with the justice of God. Where there had been the carnal man, refusing God, closed to the Spirit, there was now the Saviour in whom mankind accepted justice.

This teaches us the glorious fact that our redemption lies in God's justice and the reception we give it. It is therefore a question of accepting with Christ in order to be saved in him, with a tremendous and humble will towards God, with great longing.

How, then, can we think to expiate our sins by using our actions to make reparation for the infringements of God's rights? God in himself has never been harmed by sin, for sin can not reach God, nor touch him at all in himself. Sin injures God only in the heart of man, closing that heart to God's will to save him; it deprives man of God's glory (Rom. 3.23). How can we expiate that sin except by opening our heart—with a tremendous and humble will towards God, with great longing?

How can we think to counterbalance our sins and win salvation by casting a weight of merits and good works on to the scale? Neither our merit nor our sin is anything in itself. Merit in us is a capacity for, and a receiving of, grace; sin is a refusal. That is why no one's merit, even Christ's, can efface the sin of anyone else.[1]

[1] Christ did of course merit for us. He accepted the justice of God as a representative of mankind. Our redemption is effected, we are henceforward justified (Rom. 5.18), our sins are effaced. That is the marvel of the epiphany of God's merciful justice in Christ: the treasures of justice are

To be saved, we must open ourselves with him to the life-giving justice of God, with a tremendous and humble will to good and with great longing.

Can suffering as such expiate sin, satisfy outraged justice, restore a balance? What suffering could do this? There is no parallel between the justice of God and the suffering of man; they are realities of a different order, unable to make contact in themselves. The reign of God's justice does not lie in any balance— it is precisely a reign in which man is wholly possessed by God's Justice. Suffering is redemptive for man when it is an acceptance of God.

To make up for sin, which is a refusal, and to satisfy God's justice offended by the refusal, all that is wanted is acceptance. There is no other means, and by this one means all justice is accomplished. The forgiveness of sins is in grace: the Prodigal Son ceased to be a sinner in his father's arms. When man, having sinned, despairs of God, he becomes fixed in rejection, fixed in sin. But God makes total reparation if one opens one's heart to him in a tremendous will to good and with great longing.

It is not a question of reconciling God with us, but us with God,[2] and of submitting to his will to save us. Man must return again to childhood, the childhood of Christ who is begotten by his Father and receives everything from him. He must be small before God, believe in his love and his redemptive justice, and entrust himself to that justice. If he is small and if he accepts, he is created anew in Christ. Then there will be a great torrent of riches flowing

---

put at our disposal. But we only get the advantage of them when we accept them within ourselves as Christ accepted them in himself. We must unite ourselves to Christ in that acceptance—in other words, in his death to himself.

Though Christ's redemptive merit cannot be distinguished from his redemptive act, and we can only share in that merit by communicating in that act, the Protestant theology of justification considers the merits of Christ as a reality, a thing in itself, behind which, without receiving justice, one may shelter against God's anger.

[2] St. Augustine, *Tract. in Joh.*, 110, 6. *PL*, 35 (1924).

from his heart, flowing out to meet other men, seeking to penetrate them and give them life too. The believer in turn will become a source of justice among men, to join them to the new creation that is in Christ.

How generous is God's justice working upon men, that justice which is the Holy Spirit, the eternal happiness of mankind! Yet how dreadful too, how harsh to selfishness, is that justice which, because it is love, must bring to death the worthless men that we are. For there lies the true death of sinful man, when he accepts God's love and its demands for holiness—so hard a death that only Christ could achieve it, and he now seeks to extend it to us.

2. ALWAYS ACCEPTING

Many are the occasions when the justice which wants to create the world anew knocks at our door. It knocks when we hear it announced in preaching, and by the grace of faith which that announcement holds. Man opens his heart and receives this word, and with it justice (John 5.24; 1 Thess. 2.13). But whoever shuts his heart to this word is judged by it, because he is shutting it to justice.

It knocks in the Eucharist, and the Eucharist too is a tribunal—a tribunal of love, a trial of redemptive, justifying justice. "Judge me, O God," says the priest at the foot of the altar; in other words, "Come to my help, O God, my salvation!" By the Eucharist man is joined to the body of the risen Christ, to the new creation, to the kingdom of justice. But for anyone who receives it without uniting himself to that body, the Eucharist becomes a condemnation; he has shut himself to God's justice in that body, "he eateth judgement to himself" (1 Cor. 11.29).

God's justice comes in the sacrament of penance, and that too is a tribunal. Once again, a tribunal of love and mercy where justice acts upon the man who has sinned by giving itself to him. But that justice becomes condemnation if anyone comes to the

Sacrament who does not truly want it, and who remains closed to it.

God's justice knocks at man's door through his neighbour, for the neighbour asks him to open his heart to charity, and charity is the justice of God. Thus it is his neighbour who sets a man at the right or left hand of the Judge, who determines whether he stands with or against the justice of God.

God's justice knocks at man's door in death, the final and decisive time of judgement. For death offers man his last opportunity to encounter his saviour and his saviour's death, in which alone God's judgement for the salvation of the world is declared. It is only there, in that place and at that time, in Christ and in his death, that man comes into contact with the life-giving justice of God. Divine justice raises up Christ alone, and raises him only by his death—therefore only those are raised who are united with him and share in his death. God offers every one of us encounters with Christ and his death throughout our lives—in the grace of faith, in the sacraments, in suffering, in all the vicissitudes of life in which Christians are crucified with Christ. But the believer's existence is always fixed at that hour: "With Christ I am nailed to the cross" (Gal. 2.19). But a special chance, and the last one, is offered to man in death. If, at that moment, he persists in his refusal to die with Christ, if he sets his heart against the justice of God in Christ, he dies outside justice, he dies the death that is simply the condemnation of sin. From then on there is no way to unite himself to Christ in his death, and man will encounter God's justice no more. Hell will be the impossibility to die to self, the irrevocable rejection of God's justice.

Thus each day of our lives is parousia and judgement, in which we are sanctified or damned. One day Christ will come for the last time, and the case will be concluded: "Wherefore, as the Holy Ghost saith: *Today if you shall hear his voice, harden not your hearts* . . . Take heed, brethren, lest perhaps there be in any of you an evil heart of unbelief, to depart from the living God . . .

Today, if you shall hear his voice, harden not your hearts" (Heb. 3.7-15).

They were right, the Prophets, John the Baptist and the Apostles, to proclaim as dreadful the judgement of God. Man should be afraid, for it is God who effects salvation: "With fear and trembling work out your salvation. For it is God who worketh in you, both to will and to accomplish, according to his benevolent designs" (Phil. 2. 12-13). Man can find no assurance in himself, in mankind, or in the world, nor even in his struggle for virtue and his good works. He must fear. But what he must fear is that he may fail to believe in the gift of God's justice, may fail to hope, may fail to accept with joy and trust God's redemptive love. "Live in fear . . . knowing that you were redeemed . . . with the precious blood of Christ" (1 Pet. 1.17-19). The only truly Christian fear is called hope; it is giving oneself to the God who saves.

"A sign" (Apoc. 12.1) has been given us, a paradigm of the judgement pronounced by God and man's acceptance of justice: our Lady. She was always submitted to God's justifying judgement, always accepted it, from the first moment of her life until her death. And the fullness of justice, the Last Judgement, is already complete in her. Though she is, like every other creature, subject to the final judgement, she will not be judged with the rest at the end of the world, for she has already undergone the Last Judgement, wholly filled as she is even in her body by the justice of God. In our Lady's salvation God's justice already celebrates its final triumph.

For us, our Lady is a living hope, an eschatological cause for rejoicing, an evidence of God's justice and a proof that that justice is love. Mary's merit was that she believed, that she was "humble," that she "hungered" for justice (Luke 1.52-3), and that she accepted justice when it came. At once the summit and centre of the communion of saints, she now helps all believers to assent to God.

PART II

THE SACRAMENTS OF CHRISTIAN LIFE

3

The Sacrament of Scripture

The sacraments exist to make contact between men and the Word of God at the point when that Word is pronounced for our salvation: in the man Jesus and in his action redeeming us. Their name, "sacraments," means "mysteries," because by them the mystery of "the redemption that is in Christ Jesus" is accessible to mankind.

Holy Scripture, too, is a kind of sacrament—not one of the seven, of course, yet comparable to them because intended like them to link us with the word of salvation in the redeeming Christ. That once-spoken word came from the Father, and with it have come many words to us, like circles spreading out from the Word falling into the sea of mankind, all round it in time, spreading to the beginnings of centuries and the ends; or the echoing and re-echoing of the word spoken in the redeeming Incarnation. These words are at work for God's designs of which Christ is the fullness; they are intended to lead men to the centre from which they grow and which by growing they extend—to the mystery of salvation which is in Christ. One may say that Scripture is also, in its own way, a sacrament to incorporate us into the redeeming Christ.

I. *HOLY SCRIPTURE, THE PRESENCE*
OF THE REDEEMING CHRIST

From patristic times, theology has related the two mysteries of
Scripture and the Incarnation. There exists a real analogy between
them. As Bossuet said: "He [the Word] took a kind of second
body, I mean, the word of his Gospel."[1] Through the action of the
Holy Ghost in the Virgin Mary, God's own thought—his Word—
was clothed in human nature, with its imperfections, and dwelt
amongst us. Through another action of the Holy Ghost, in the
sacred writers, in the womb of their intellect, God's thought was
introduced into humanity, taking the form of human thought, and
dwelt amongst us.

This divine thought, conceived from all eternity, eternally one,
holy and infinite, God has conceived in time, in the imperfection
of the things of time, fragmentary, complex and limited. He has
conceived it through the minds of men, which are limited both in
themselves and by the restrictions of the time and place in which
they function. The Word has put off its glory, taken the form of
a servant, and come to dwell amongst us.

In the office for the Blessed Sacrament, the Church sings her
happiness at possessing the incarnate Word in her midst in the
Eucharist: "Neither is there nor has there been any other nation
so great, that hath gods so nigh them, as our God is present to all
our petitions." The words are taken from Deuteronomy (4.7), and
were used by the Jews to express the pride they felt in having a
God who spoke to them, and whose thought and will for them they
possessed in the sacred scrolls they carried with them. "For what
other nation is there so renowned that hath ceremonies, and just
judgements, and all the law, which I will set forth this day before
your eyes?" (4.8). This praise, which we now sing of the Incarna-

---

[1] Bossuet, *Second sermon pour le deuxieme dimanche de carême: Sur la
Parole de Dieu.*

tion and the Eucharist, was first uttered to glorify Scripture, which was a sort of first incarnation of God's thought.

Having sung at length the divine origins of Wisdom and its eternal prerogatives, "I came out of the mouth of the Most High . . . From the beginning, and before the world, I was created . . .," Ecclesiasticus concludes: "All these things are the book of life and the book of the covenant of the Most High . . . who filleth up wisdom as the waters of Phison, and as the Tigris in the days of the new fruits" (24.5,14,32,35). In Scripture God's wisdom is already incarnate, flowing in the sacred book like a river between its banks. Israel made that divine presence an object of worship. The tables of the Law were placed in the Ark; in the synagogues, the Bible, contained in a cupboard facing the people, was the only object of worship. No one touched it till he had washed his hands, and then with much reverence.

Similarly, there is an intense presence of God in the books of the New Testament, but closer and more evident. Before becoming human in the thoughts and words of men, God's wisdom, which wrote the New Testament, took human flesh, and it is that incarnate Wisdom, Christ in his glory, who dwells amongst us in the books of the New Testament. For it is he who is the author of the New Testament. "The members [the Apostles] wrote what the Head inspired them to. Christ dictated to them, as to his hands, which of his words and actions he wanted us to know about."[2]

One text in St. John shows us that the opened side of Christ in glory is the source whence the books of the New Testament flow:

If any man thirst, let him come to me, and let him that believeth in me drink. As the Scripture saith: *Out of his belly shall flow rivers of living water.*

From Christ's belly the rivers will flow—we should translate this Hebrew phrase by saying they will flow from Christ's heart. And

[2] St. Augustine, *De consensu Evangeliorum*, bk. 1, cap. 35. PL,34(1070).

"this he said of the Spirit which they should receive who believed in him"; he said it of the Holy Spirit whose tremendous out-pouring in the last days had been spoken of by the Prophets. From Christ's sacred body where the soldier's lance struck him, as from the rock of Sinai, would flow the rivers of the New Testament, all the graces of the Kingdom, and also those of Scripture—the graces by which Scripture would be inspired, by which it would be read and understood, by which it would give life to the world. All these rivers will flow from that open side on the day of his redeeming glory. Until that day, "the Spirit was not given, because Jesus was not yet glorified" (John 7.27-9). "O heart of my beloved," cried St. John Eudes, "I adore you as the source of all the holy words in this book." The Evangelists came, and each drank from that spring. "He drank the rivers of the gospel from the sacred fount of the Lord's heart," we say of the Apostle John in the office for his feast.

The New Testament is not Christ's book because it tells his story; it is his book because it is from him, born out of the wound in his heart, born like a child. Every word of Scripture is a grace of the Spirit of Jesus, a thought of everlasting life which flowed from his heart along with his blood: "And there came out blood and water," the water of the Spirit with the blood of immolation. With their sure instincts, the saints felt this redeeming presence in the New Testament. St. Ignatius of Antioch wrote: "I take refuge in the Gospel as in the flesh of Jesus Christ."[3] Other saints were to love to hide in Christ's heart, but St. Ignatius sought his refuge in the Gospel, in the revelation of the Christian mystery, for that gospel was like a sacrament of the redeeming Christ, like a field in which, as St. Jerome said, the treasure was hidden, the treasure of Christ himself.

In Christian worship, Holy Scripture is forever linked with that supreme sacrament of Christ's body and the redemption, the Eucharist; the same name is used for both: "This chalice," Our Lord said, "is the New Testament"; this book also we call the New

[3] St. Ignatius of Antioch, *Philad.* 5,1.

Testament; chalice and book, each in its own way, contain the
New Covenant, the mystery of our redemption in Christ. The
analogy is tremendous: "I think myself that Christ's body is [also]
his gospel," says St. Jerome, "the bread of Christ and his flesh is
the divine word and heavenly doctrine."[4] The early Church,
struck by the resemblance between these two sacraments of Christ's
presence, placed together, as on "two tables"[5] side by side, the
Bread of Christ and the Book, invited the faithful to sit equally at
both, to feed upon their Saviour and upon the salvation that was
in him.

II. *COMMUNION IN CHRIST THROUGH SACRED SCRIPTURE*

For, in every form, Christ's presence among men has that same
purpose. By his very being and in everything he does, Christ is
always the Redeemer; his presence is there to create a communion
of salvation with men. This Scripture does; it, too, establishes a
communion, different from the Eucharist but real none the less, a
communion of thought between two people who love each other
and talk together, one of whom is Christ.

Whenever we read his Scriptures with faith, Christ speaks. It
was long ago that he inspired his Apostles, and centuries have
passed since. But though the human writing of the Book was something that happened in the past, the inspired words still live in the
moment when they are spoken by Christ. "This was written for us,
and preserved for us; it is recited for us and will also be recited for
our descendants, right up to the end of time."[6] The redeeming
action of Christ in glory knows no succession of time; he speaks
to the heart of the Church in eternity. The thoughts formulated by
the Apostles and put into writing at a given moment of history are

---

[4] *Tract. de Ps. cxlv.*, in *Anecdota Maredsolana*, III, II, pp. 301, 291.

[5] *Imitation of Christ*, bk. iv, ch. 11.

[6] St. Augustine, *In Jo., tract.* 30; *PL*,35(1632).

addressed to the Church of all the ages in an eternal present. Men are coming into existence now, are now reading Christ's word with faith, are hearing Christ speaking to them now.

Because Scripture is an everlasting word, always being said, the epistle to the Hebrews introduces all its quotations from Scripture by saying, "The Holy Ghost saith," "The Holy Ghost doth testify" (Heb. 3.7; 10.15)—all in the present tense.

Christ speaks to us at this moment, but not like a friend far away communicating by letter; "God is not far from every one of us" (Acts 17.27) and "Christ dwells in our hearts" (Eph. 3.17). We sit at his feet and listen to him: "We must listen to the Gospel as to Christ amongst us,"[7] "the Gospel is the very mouth of Christ,"[8] a sacrament of his words to us. There is no human intermediary between his word and our mind; the sound we hear is actually his voice. According to St. Thomas, God has two far from equal ways of teaching us: he speaks through an intermediary in human books or religious instruction, but "he speaks directly to our minds in sacred Scripture."[9] Tired of hearing only a distant echo of Christ's voice from human lips, saints like St. Thérèse of Lisieux resolved to read nothing but Scripture.

This communion with Christ in thought is even closer than that between two people speaking together. When we look for the truth hidden in the text of Scripture, Christ can communicate the meaning of his words directly to our minds. I can read a given human book, and learn a philosophical truth from it. But what I get from its words depends on my perspicacity; I understand it only in proportion to my intelligence. The author may be dead, but even were he alive, he could not communicate to his reader the same understanding of the truth he is expressing that he has himself. The writer's thought comes to me not directly, but through signs, through words which I must interpret. But when we hear the words of Scripture, "the Master is in our hearts"[10] and communicates the

[7] St. Augustine, *In Jo., tract. 30; PL,*35(1632).

[8] St. Augustine, *Sermo LXXXV,*1; *PL,*38(520)

[9] *In 2 Tim.,* c.3. lectio 3.

[10] St. Augustine, *Sermo* 85,1. *PL,*38(520).

same understanding of the truths they express that he himself has; he arouses in us his own sentiments: "Let the word of Christ dwell in our hearts in all its riches" (Col. 3.16). It is a wonderful communion of mind and heart—the communion of Mary of Bethany, of the disciples on the road to Emmaus.

This communion, too, is effective, giving eternal life. Of Scripture as of the Eucharist it can be said, "Pinguis est panis"—it is a substantial bread. For Christ lives now only in his redemptive act, given to God for mankind, immortal in his death for them, and forever an instrument of God's action in raising up to eternal life. Every presence and every action of Christ works redemption. When he appeared in the evening of Easter Day, he sent the Apostles out to forgive sins. In the same way he made them write the pages of the New Testament for the remission of sins and the salvation of men.

By we know not what hidden influence, Scripture bestows a spirit of life on those who read it with faith. "Was our heart not burning within us, whilst he spoke?" (Luke 24.32); "The word of God is living and effectual" (Heb. 4.12), it is the "sword of the spirit" (Eph. 6.17). If ordinary human words, noble or degraded, can transform a man by their psychological dynamism, how much more must the word of God penetrate and pierce to the very depths of the soul, for it is "more piercing than any two-edged sword; and reaching unto the division of the soul and the spirit, of the joints also and the marrow" (Heb. 4.12).

It is not merely that God's word contains the thoughts of Christ, lofty and profound, which can stir up man's heart; but it is spoken for *me* and for *my* salvation; it is spoken by my saviour, in the grace of the Holy Spirit which flows from his pierced side. The Gospel is a message of redemption, a sacrament of salvation, in which "the Holy Ghost works in efficacious words."[11]

"Attend unto reading" (1 Tim. 4.13). For "the holy scriptures

[11] Paschasius Radbert, *De Corpore et Sanguine Domini*, 3,2; *PL*,120 (1276).

can instruct thee to salvation, by the faith which is in Christ Jesus. All scripture, inspired of God, is profitable to teach, to reprove, to correct, to instruct in justice, that the man of God may be perfect, furnished to every good work" (2 Tim. 3.15-17).

Scripture is the treasure of "the man of God"; it is that rich treasure from which the householder "bringeth forth new things and old" (Matt. 13.32) to accomplish "every good work." That good work is first of all accomplished actually in the heart of the man of God; the word is planted there, grows there and bears fruit there ("the word of truth . . . bringeth forth fruit and groweth" [Col. 1.5-6]); it gives consolation there, too, that joy which glows where there is salvation, whereby we are born to the hope of the Last Day: "For what things soever were written were written for our learning: that through patience and the comfort of the Scriptures, we might have hope" (Rom. 15.4).

The Fathers seem to have been unable to find images strong enough to describe the banquet of redemption offered on the table of Scripture. The Gospel, according to St. Jerome, is true food and true drink;[12] Scripture is an ocean of fulness, says St. Ambrose, a cup from which we drink Christ, a cup that is a river whose waves delight the city of God.[13] It is the cure for all our ills: "Take and drink; all sickness of soul finds its remedy in Scripture."[14] The Eucharist, says St. John Chrysostom, makes us as fierce lions in face of the devil. Also, says St. Athanasius, Scripture puts our adversary to flight, for "in Scripture the Lord is present, and the demons, who cannot bear his presence, cry: I beg you, do not torment us before our time. They burn simply from seeing the Lord present."[15]

Thus the banquet of Scripture feeds and strengthens just as does the eucharistic banquet of Christ's immolated flesh; and like it, it has its joys, "the chaste delights of Scripture" spoken of by St.

---

[12] *In Eccle.; PL*,23(1039).
[13] St. Ambrose. *In Ps.* 1,33; *PL*,14(940).
[14] St. Augustine, *In Ps.* 36,1,3; *PL*,36(357).
[15] *Ep. ad Marcellinum,* 33; *PG*,27(44ff).

Augustine,[16] "the comfort of the Scriptures" which gives us hope (Rom. 15.4), that great comfort which made the Maccabees say, "We needed none of these things, nor any one, having for our comfort the holy books that are in our hands" (I Macc. 12.9).

Scripture and the Eucharist are the life-force and the joy of the Church, because they are for her a communion in the body given and blood shed for us. Other than that banquet, there exists only what this life can offer us: "We have in this world only this one good thing: to feed upon his flesh and drink his blood, not only in the [eucharistic] sacrament, but in the reading of Scripture."[17]

Despite its own efficaciousness, Scripture does not enter into any kind of competition in our souls with that other sacrament of presence and communion, the Eucharist; it does not supplant it, or make it unnecessary. The central point of Christian worship is the incarnate Word in his eternal sacrifice. Scripture comes to us from that centre, and must canalize our minds and hearts towards it. It is by the Eucharist that Christ is present to us in the reality of his body, in the reality of his immolation and his glory. So Scripture must collaborate with the Sacrament to unite believers with the redeeming Christ.

In the Mass, the splendour of Scripture comes to surround the sacred body of Christ on all sides, as the royal purple of the incarnate Word in his immolation, as the veil of the Holy of Holies in which the eternal sacrifice is offered—a veil which is not there to hide but to reveal the way into the sanctuary. It was in this way, through the veil of the Scriptures, that the world of the Old Testament was brought to Christ.

Many non-Catholic Christians read Scripture more assiduously than many Catholics, but do not feed on the Eucharist. Among a lot of them there is a profound tendency not to accept the incarnation of the Word in its ultimate reality, but to prefer what seems to be a worship of God's transcendence—to prefer, at least in prac-

---

[16] *Conf.*, 11,2; *PL*,32(810).
[17] St. Jerome, *op. cit.*

tice, the spoken Word to the personal Word, to remain in the Old Testament, on the threshold of the fulness of the Incarnation. Many Catholics have a tremendous devotion to the Eucharist, but neglect Scripture. Many of them, perhaps, do not therefore know the personal Word as well as they might, and are not in the best possible dispositions to receive him in the Eucharist. For the secret of opening one's heart to that one Word is contained most fully in Scripture.

III. *NECESSARY DISPOSITIONS FOR A FRUITFUL READING OF SCRIPTURE*

God allows us to "taste his good word" (Heb. 6.5), but we do not always appreciate its savour. This bread is no more acceptable every day to all tastes than was the manna in the desert, or is the Eucharist. Our soul must be disposed to receive God's word.

To read in faith

We must have ears to hear the Word of God which are not the ears of the body: "Let him that hath ears, hear what the Spirit saith to the churches" (Apoc. 2.7). The ears to hear are the ears of faith. It is faith which opens the word of God to us. "The word of God worketh in you who have believed" (1 Thess. 2.13).

Like every heavenly reality offered to us during our life on earth, Scripture has two facets—one accessible to the senses, the other visible to faith alone. It was so with Christ, whom his enemies saw with their eyes and nailed to the Cross, but whom his believers adored. It is thus with the Church, whose human face can be seen by all, but whose mystery is hidden for many. It is thus also with the Eucharist which to some is simply bread, and to others the body of the glorified Christ.

There are various ways of approaching Scripture, and not all of them lead to an encounter with Christ. Scholars without faith can make Scripture an object of investigation; but there is no critical apparatus that can bring them to the heart of Scripture, to the point of meeting with Christ. It has been said that Scripture is a locked house with the key inside. To enter it one must live in it, one must be in Christ, in his house which is the Church. One must be inside faith. This is yet one more sphere in which it is true that "whosoever hath, to him shall be given" (Luke 13.18).

"My sheep hear my voice," said our Lord (John 10.16). Those outside may hear the words, but only the flock hear the voice, the voice which reveals the person. Thus it was on Easter morning that one of Christ's sheep recognized the Lord by the sound of his voice. There are the words, there is the voice; the first express ideas, the second a person. The words of Scripture can be compared with ordinary human words, but the voice is incomparable because the person it reveals is unique. While the believer listens to the succession of words, behind the closed doors of his soul he hears the voice, and the word reveals himself. Only faith has ears to hear the voice; it alone establishes contact with Christ. When he hears the voice, and feels that contact with our Lord, the believer knows that the words are addressed to him. Each sheep is called by his name, the encounter is personal, and becomes a dialogue. "Mary," said Christ, and Mary answered, "Rabboni!"

By the light of faith Scripture is seen to have a dimension that no other book has. It is not invariably the finest of all literature. Not all its lines contain profound ideas, and even the most striking may have had their edges blunted by long use. One can hardly deny that there are human books superior to some parts of Scripture. But to the believer, these words offer a dimension of mystery, a stirring resonance: for it is the Lord who speaks them. One may recall how Mozart once played the clavichord in the house of a rich burgher of Prague. At the end his host, greatly impressed, said, "Would that I were the Emperor! I should give you a pat on the shoulder, and say, 'You really have played well, Mozart!' That would be enough for you. But who am I to be able to reward you?" Similarly, the word which of itself would be but a pebble on the roadway, is a diamond when spoken by the Lord.

To read in the light of Easter

The Christ whose voice Scripture makes us hear is the Lord of Easter, the Christ of faith. He became the author of that book in the light and fire of the glory of his raising by the Father. The rivers of the Spirit, of all the charismata of the New Testament, the gift of scriptural inspiration, all flow from his pierced side after his return to his Father. The Apostles and Evangelists understood this, and wrote "in that day," in the light of Easter. Even Christ's life on earth was told from the point of view of his resurrection, in faith in the glorified Christ. The thought of his death and resurrection is the golden thread which binds together the separate pages of the Gospel and makes it a book.

Again, it was the risen Christ, source of the Spirit, who opened the minds of his disciples on the road to Emmaus, and interpreted the Scriptures to them.

Just as Magdalen could no longer catch hold of the glorified Lord with her bodily hands, so scholars cannot hear him with their human minds. He is accessible only to faith. He can only be seen, touched and heard by his disciples, those who eat and drink with him after the Resurrection (Acts 10.40).

To him who believes, our Lord's face appears even in the pages of the Old Testament. It is Christ, dead and risen again, who gives the whole Bible its unity and meaning. If it is divorced from the glorified Christ it is a dead letter, a story written in sand, a set of laws which cannot give life. "The letter killeth, but the spirit quickeneth" (2 Cor. 3.6). "The letter" here is the realities of the Old Testament considered in themselves, and all the things of this world. "The spirit" means reality in its fullness, the reality of heaven, of which all other realities are but fleeting shadows. The reality of heaven comes at the end, according to the promise given in the Old Testament; it is none other than the very Spirit of God, in whom all will be consummated, all be made one and living.

Now the risen Christ "is the Spirit" (2 Cor. 3.17). He is the solid body whose shadow was cast right back to the beginning of the world (Col. 2.17). The reality of all things is in him, and without him all is shadow and death. In him all becomes spirit and life. For he has been "enlivened in the Spirit" (1 Pet. 3.18), in the total outpouring of the Holy Ghost. He has been so completely transformed in the spirit, that he himself has become a "quickening spirit" (1 Cor. 15.45), and that we may speak of the body of the glorified Christ as in a sense the body of the Holy Ghost.[18] In his redeeming glory, he has become the centre of creation (Col. 1.16). "And I, if I be lifted up, will draw all things to myself" (John 12.32); he draws to himself not only all men, but all things, making himself the centre of nature and history, of the Old Testament and the New, lord of the past and the future; Elijah and Moses, prophecy and the Law, the whole of the Old Covenant, all turn their faces towards the transfigured Christ. He is God's "Amen" (2 Cor. 1.20) to the promise of the Old Testament, and to all the promises contained in the first creation, "because in him it hath well pleased the Father that all the fullness [of the universe] should dwell" (Col. 1.19).

The unbeliever looking at the Bible sees only the dead letter, the disparate elements; his eyes are bound. The believer reads with uncovered eyes, and has only to open the Old Testament to find himself face to face with Our Lord in glory; he feels himself "transformed into the same image from glory to glory, as by the action of the Lord who is the Spirit" (2 Cor. 3.14-18).

A simple and living faith

The believer opens the sacred book with respect, just as in the synagogue at Nazareth, Christ stood up to read the prophecy of Isaiah (Luke 4.16), filled with veneration for the Word of his God and Father. Faith reads with a simple and sincere heart. "How should one read the sacred Scriptures?", someone asked Padre

[18] St. Ambrose, *De Mysteriis*, 9,58; *PL*,16(409).

Nadal, one of the first Jesuits. "Like a good old grandmother," he replied. Timothy had read Scripture at the knees of his grandmother and his mother, with these women's faith: "I call to mind that faith which is in thee which also dwelt first in thy grandmother Lois and in thy mother Eunice . . . . From thy infancy thou hast known the holy scriptures, which can instruct thee to salvation, by the faith which is in Christ Jesus" (2 Tim. 1.5; 3.15).

It is an obedient faith: "And they shall all be taught of God" (John 6.45), God's pupils, desiring to "do truth" (John 3.21). We must read Scripture with the hope of finding there our marching orders: "Good master, what shall I do that I may receive life everlasting?" (Mark 10.17). For it is Christ's essence to redeem, and no-one enters into communion with him unless he wants to be saved by him. The Fathers used to say that Scripture was a letter sent by God from his kingdom far away, to draw us to him.

A loving faith

A letter from God must be read with loving faith. Kierkegaard said people should read the Bible not so much as critics and scholars, but "before God," as a man would read a letter from his fiancée. For to understand one must love. St. Paul asks that the eyes of our heart be enlightened (Eph. 1.18). It is the heart that sees, it is love that knows; in the biblical sense of the word, knowledge is mutual possession: "Blessed are they who know by the delight they have experienced, with what gentleness, what allurement, the Lord deigns to explain the Scriptures to us in prayer and meditation . . . He does it when he lights up our hearts with the beams of charity."[19]

To read prayerfully

If Christ is to come and eat with his own, he must find in them "a large dining-room furnished" (Mark 14.15). It is the work of

[19] St. Bernard, *Sermo in feria secunda Pasch.* 20; *PL*,184(976).

prayer to prepare hearts for his coming, by the longing it expresses. Every parousia of Christ comes as an answer to longing: "Come, Lord Jesus!"

"In truth," said St. Augustine to the *studiosi venerabilium litterarum,* "to understand Scripture, what is essential is to pray."[20] He gave an example of this himself:

Let your Scripture be my chaste delight . . . Give me freely the time I need to meditate on the secrets of your law; close not to them that knock. It was not for nothing that you willed so many mysterious pages written. Have not these forests too their stags who take refuge and comfort there, come and go in them, feed, sleep and ruminate there?—O Lord, perfect your work in me! Reveal those pages to me! Behold, your word is my joy; indeed your word is a joy higher than all pleasures.[21]

In a letter to Gregory the wonderworker, his "most dear Lord," Origen wrote:

Well then, my son and lord, give yourself above all to the study of Holy Scripture, but you must give yourself. It requires great attention to read of the things of God, to say or think nothing unfitting.

And, giving yourself to read the things of God with the dispositions of faith pleasing to him, knock that the things contained in them may be opened, that that door may be opened of which Christ said, "The doorkeeper will open to him." Giving yourself to that reading, seek with sincerity and with an unshakable faith in God what is hidden from so many: the meaning of the sacred books.

Do not be content with seeking and knocking, for it is prayer above all that is needed for the understanding of the things of God. Our Lord urges us to it, saying not only, "Knock and it shall be opened; seek and you shall find," but also, "Ask and you shall receive."

It is my paternal love, that I dare say this to you.[22]

We address that prayer to Christ, whose heart is the source of all the words in Scripture. We address it to our Lady representing

---

[20] *De Doctrina Christiana,* 3,37; *PL,*34(80).

[21] *Conf.* 11,2; *PL,*32(810).

[22] *Ep. ad Gregorium; PG,*11(92).

the whole of the believing Church for which the sacred books are written, that Church which weighs and compares together the words of God. Her own heart was the most fertile field in which the seed of redemption is sown. Of the Gospel of St. John, Origen declares: "No one can understand it who has not leant on the breast of Christ and received Mary as his Mother."[23]

The Scripture as the source of prayer

Prayer prepares a place for the Lord in the reader, makes ready for an intimate communion. But reading Scripture, in its turn, rouses a desire for his coming and invites to prayer. "Sacred Scripture is a calling towards our heavenly home, it transports the reader from the desires of this world to the love of higher things. The more one meditates upon it the more one loves it."[24]

Every sacrament of the Church is a pasch celebrated with Christ, and a parasceve (preparation for the Pasch), an actual parousia (presence) and a preparation for the Coming. Thus the Eucharist is now the true banquet of the end of time, the pasch in the Kingdom, and it is also still the manna of the Exodus, which supports and helps us on in our journey to the Promised Land. So it is with the mystery of Scripture. Christ comes and talks to the faithful, but only in the inn at Emmaus, in the half-light of the upper room, under the veil of the letter. He celebrates the pasch in darkness. But the night is past midnight, the dim light of the coming day (Rom. 13.12) fills the Church with longing and hope. The faithful bear within them the word of God "as a light that shineth in a dark place, until the day dawn, and the day star arise in your hearts" (2 Peter 1.19), ". . . the root and stock of David, the bright and morning star" (Apoc. 22.16). In this world every communion in the pasch is a mystery of hope as well as a beginning of possession, a banquet which satisfies yet gives rise to hunger. As

[23] *In Ev. Joh.* 1; *PG*,14(32).
[24] St. Gregory the Great, *Moralia,* 20,1; *PL*,76(135).

she folds up the letter her Saviour has sent, the betrothed girl sighs, "Come, Lord Jesus!" It is upon this longing that Scripture finishes on the last page of the Apocalypse (Apoc. 22.20), upon this that our reading of Scripture concludes.

4

The Mass in Our Lives

Only one man was able to pass from this world of sin and death into the eternal life of God. None before him and none since. From sin to salvation, from death to life, there is no bridge for any but that one man: Christ. He alone could effect human redemption. He did it in his own person, in his death and glorification.

If any other man is to be saved, is to pass in his turn from this world to God, he must participate in that one great act in which salvation lies. In his death and resurrection, Christ is the bridge and the passage. The man whom he wills to save, he must first place upon that bridge; he must literally take him into his own redemptive humanity, must make him share in his own passage, in his own death in which he is glorified.

But how can I be united to Christ in his redeeming act? He died far away two thousand years ago; how can I join him in that one redeeming act? Were I to go to Palestine, I should not find him now. I might kiss the ground where Christ's blood was shed, but I still should not find him. I cannot become contemporary with his death and resurrection. And even had I been contemporary with Christ, even had I been present at his agony upon Calvary, I could not have attached myself to his redeeming pasch, which bore him from this world to the Father. For his pasch was personal to him. Redemption was simply his own death. And one man's death cannot be another's.

There is no redemption except in Christ and for him.

I. *THE MEANING OF THE MASS*

Before he celebrated his own pasch, Christ created a mysterious means of sharing in his death and resurrection—a paschal sacrament that could introduce men into his redeeming act. He took bread into his holy hands and said: "Take ye and eat; this is my body given for you." The Eucharist is Christ's body in the act of redemption, in that unique and personal act which happened once and for all in history, under Pontius Pilate, at the gates of Jerusalem, but which comes mysteriously into our time and place so as to become ours.

The Mass makes present Christ's body and his redeeming act

The Redemption is in Christ, personal to him, as it were takes substance in him. For it to be communicated to us, Christ must in some way enter our substance; our personality must be laid open to his. The Mass is our Saviour himself communicating himself to us: "Take ye and eat; this is my body." This food is not Christ's body as it might have been at any moment of his life on earth, but Christ's body in the act of redeeming us. When Christ asks us to this meal, he says, "Take and eat, this is my body given for you." He does not simply say, "This is my body," but "my body given for you." The body of Christ is communicated to us as "given," as dead to this world and glorified in God. When he consecrates the chalice, Christ says: "This chalice is my blood [at this moment] shed" (cf. Luke 22.20).

In the eucharistic discourse he promises: "The bread that I will give is my flesh [given] for the life of the world" (John 6.52). St. Paul reminds the Corinthians: "As often as you shall eat this bread, and drink the chalice, you shall show the death of the Lord" (I Cor. 11.26). That death which St. Paul speaks of and Christ speaks of, is Christ's death, the one and only death, *sub Pontio Pilato*. The Mass is Christ present in his one and only redeeming act, the sacrifice of Calvary becoming a reality of our lives too.

"How can it be a sacrifice?" ask Protestants. There is only one sacrifice of Christ: "By his own blood he entered once into the holies, obtaining eternal redemption" (Heb. 9.12). "By one oblation he hath perfected forever them that he hath sanctified" (Heb. 10.14). That is one of the key ideas of the Epistle to the Hebrews: the sacrifices of the Old Testament had constantly to be renewed because they were always ineffective, incapable of "sanctifying" man, of immolating him to himself and bringing him into the life-giving holiness of God. Christ, on the other hand, has offered a single sacrifice, perfect and sufficient, the sacrifice of the end of time, which fulfills and crowns all mankind's longing for salvation and sacrificial actions. By his death, Christ entered once for all into the sanctuary of divine life, and takes with him all his followers.

The Protestants are therefore quite right in their dogged affirmation of the absolute uniqueness of Christ's sacrifice. There is but that one, which took place once and for all, never repeated, never repeatable. Yet the Church believes that the Mass is a sacrifice. She believes it because of Scripture, and because of her own uninterrupted and most ancient tradition, through which the Holy Ghost speaks, "for the Spirit is the truth" (1 John 5.6). She is faced with two apparently contradictory truths: the fact that Calvary is unique, and the fact that the Eucharist is a sacrifice. Like the faithful spouse, she accepts, even before she can understand it, the word of the Lord she loves. She believes it: there is no sacrifice but that of the Cross, and every Mass is a sacrifice.

Of these two truths, the prime and essential one is the uniqueness of Christ's sacrifice; the Church must hold this in all strictness. The Mass cannot be another sacrifice, a reproduction or repetition, a second, third or hundredth sacrifice following the one offered under Pontius Pilate. If it is a sacrifice, it must be that one and only one, made two thousand years ago, never repeated, never repeatable, but mysteriously brought into our lifetime.

There are millions of hosts, but one body of Christ. There are millions of Masses said, but only one sacrifice of Christ, offered on

Calvary, which enters into our lives: "Just as everywhere it is only one body that is offered, and not many bodies, so there is but one sacrifice."[1] The millions of Masses offered through the ages in all parts of the world, are Christ present in the midst of his Church, in the unique moment of his sacrifice on Calvary.

When the priest says the words of consecration, he pauses in wonder at this *mysterium fidei*. For it is doubly a mystery—the mystery of Christ's unfathomable sacrifice, and the mystery of that sacrifice made present to us. Between the sacrifice of Calvary and the sacrifice of the altar the only difference is in the way it is present. The Mass is the one and only Tree of the Cross planted in our midst that we may eat its fruits.

A *mysterium tremendum,* said the early Christians, a fearful mystery. They were right. Christ is present to us in the most majestic moment of history, the moment of his sacrifice in which the world of sin dies, and the world of the last days is created in God's love. We sing, "Holy, Holy, Holy!" not only to acclaim the Lord coming in glory, but to adore the Godhead entering our lives at that moment.

A fearful mystery of faith, but a mystery of joy too. It is what gives the Church her exultant joy and her hope; it is her one treasure. Christ at the moment of the Redemption is in her midst, and with him all the riches of that redemption. We need only the faith to believe.

. . . That the Church may become Christ's body and take part in his redeeming act

Why should Christ, with his redemptive act, make himself present in every time and place? In order that the Church may, in every time and place, take part in his redemptive act. For, in order to be saved, the Church must unite herself to her saviour, must die together with him, and rise with him.

What good would Christ's death have done me if he had been

[1] St. Thomas, *Summa,* pt. 3, Qu. 83, art. I, ad lm.

content simply to die for me? No one can die for me, die in my place. Sin is in me, in my body, in my whole being. I am a sinner by my nature. If I am to be saved from my condition of sin and death, the Saviour must take me into himself, must make me die in him to my life of sin and death, must transfer me into his holy and immortal risen life.

Thus our Saviour makes himself present in all times and places, here, this year, today, in order that I who live here today may today be caught up by him, may die to myself in Christ's own death, may be raised up by the divine action that raises Christ. That is Christ's purpose in placing himself, with his sacrifice, in our time and in our lives: to join the whole Church to his body, and turn her into his own sacrifice, that she may be Christ on earth in his redeeming sacrifice—one body in him, one death with him, and one resurrection.

The Mass is celebrated like a meal. We consume the body of Christ in his death and glorification. This meal makes us Christ's body. "Because there is but one bread, we all form one body, all we who have partaken of that bread" (1 Cor. 10.17). We become Christ's body not simply in faith and charity, but literally.[2] If we are to be saved, we must become Christ's body, for redemption is in that body and nowhere else. But the Mass is not just the presence of the Body and the meal of the Body; it is the presence of Christ in his sacrifice, and the meal is a participation in that sacrifice. Our Saviour takes us into himself and absorbs all our existence into his redeeming act.

Thus the Eucharist is a food which kills and brings to life, puts the man of this world to death and resurrects him into the life of God. Caught up in Christ's sacrifice, in his single sacrificial act, the Christ of all ages, the Church throughout the world becomes the very body of her Saviour in his redeeming act. She herself becomes Christ's sacrifice still present forever in the world until the parousia.

The Christ who redeems us, permanently risen, and by that resurrection fixed forever in death, is a heavenly reality, and cannot

[2] St. John Chrysostom, *In Mt., Hom. LXXXII; PG,* 58 (753ff).

be present, in his own form, to the world he is going to save. He enters our sphere by means of the eucharistic sign, and makes the Church his own body present to the world, containing salvation for the world. Thus the Mass is celebrated in order that the Church may become the Mass, the one sacrifice of Christ still forever present on earth. In order that all Christians may become martyrs, either actual or virtual.[3] In order that the whole world may become the Golgotha of Christ's death and resurrection, that the whole world may be saved. Until the parousia, the Church, through all her members who believe, hope and love, will be the redeeming Christ on earth, in his death and his risen life; she will be so in order that salvation may be accomplished in all men as it has been accomplished in Christ. Our Lord would not have instituted the Mass, he would not have needed to, if it were not for the purpose of making the unique redeeming sacrifice effective in us all.

II. *THE CELEBRATION OF MASS*

Our eucharistic liturgy, then, must not be thought to consist simply in movements, in singing, signs and outward worship. To attain its goal, it must bring about by those actions and signs, our participation in Christ and his act redeeming us.

We celebrate Mass by dying and rising again in Christ

The liturgy would have no reality, indeed we should not be celebrating Mass at all (either priests or people), if we did not participate in Christ in his death to "the world" and his life of glory. If we stop short at the gestures and hymns of a liturgy that is no more than a sign, then we are not exercising our Christian priesthood, we are not accomplishing in our own persons the

---

[3] "Sacrificium illud offerimus de quo martyrium sumpsit omne principium": "We offer up that sacrifice from which all martyrdom derives its meaning" (Secret for Thursday after the Third Sunday of Lent).

sacrifice of Christ—for our salvation demands a real participation in the redeeming act.

Christ is a priest and an offerer of sacrifices by the death in which he is glorified. He did not celebrate a worship of sacramental signs; he did not offer a sacrifice external to himself. His priesthood brought with it no apparatus of ritual, no appearance of priesthood, no sacred gestures. Our Lord pontificated without altar, incense or candles. He did not bear a silk cross embroidered on a chasuble, but a wooden cross on which he was crucified. He intoned no ritual hymns; he said no liturgical prayers but the psalm phrases that expressed the intensity of his feelings, his longing for God and his help, and his complete abandonment to his Father: "I thirst" (John 19.28; Ps. 69(68). 22); "My God, my God, why hast thou forsaken me?" (Mark 15.34; Ps. 22(21). 2); "Father, into thy hands I commend my spirit" (Luke 23.46; Ps. 31(30). 6).

In Christ's sacrifice everything was reality—the gift of self, the immolation and the consecration. Everything was personal to Christ, inalienable and inseparable from him. His sacrifice was carried out in his own person, in his death to himself whereby he went to the Father. This reality of Christ's priesthood, the personal nature of his sacrifice, is another key theme of the Epistle to the Hebrews: ". . . neither by the blood of goats or of calves, but by his own blood, entered once into the holies" (Heb. 9.12). His sacrifice was nothing but the bloody, anguished gift of his own being, his own passage from the world to the Father. The veil through which he entered the Holy of Holies, the sanctuary of God, was not the thick canvas that the Jewish high priest lifted aside, but the destruction of his flesh, by which he opened a path to God (Heb. 10.20). This was the worship in spirit and in truth, the sacrifice of self in the charity of God.

Realizing this can hardly make us think the sacramental cult less important—Christ himself commanded, "Do this in commemoration of me": continue to celebrate this mysterious rite! But it can preserve it from any suggestion of routine, from any deviation from reality and truth. It removes the danger of any forgetting of essentials, of any return to a liturgy of shadows and figures. Christ died to abolish all merely external worship. When he died on the Cross, the veil of the Temple was rent; with Christ's death the Temple of this world's worship crumbled, never to be rebuilt. The only worship pleasing to God thenceforth was a personal worship, the worship personal to Christ. The Church has never known any priesthood apart from the priesthood inherent in the person of Christ; she has never admitted of any sacrifice but Calvary.[4]

If the only Christian sacrifice is the death whereby Christ gave himself over to the glory of the Father, a death inseparably bound up with his own person—for Christ's death was to himself alone —who then can celebrate the Christian sacrifice? No one but Christ. No one, unless he be integrated into Christ and his sacrificial act, unless there be realized in him, by the mysterious power of God, the Lord's own pasch. To be real and of value to us, our liturgy demands that we be fitted into Christ, into his redeeming act. We should be no longer exercising the Christian priesthood, were we content to offer a sacrifice exterior to ourselves, a host held simply in our hands. How could we offer Christ's sacrifice if we merely celebrated his death with hymns of mourning and his triumph with hymns of victory? Since Christ's sacrifice consists in Christ's dying and being glorified in God, we can offer it only by dying and rising in Christ.

One cannot therefore be a genuine celebrant of the Eucharist without a communion in Christ and a personal involvement in his redeeming mystery. Apart from that, the lay Christian can certainly perform the gestures of the Liturgy; the priest can even be the instrument whereby Christ makes himself present to his Church and offers himself in her. But if they are not personally associated in the redemptive act, in the love of Christ for his God, in his death to the world and in the grace of his resurrection, then the Mass

[4] The first Christians used to say they had no temple or altar (Minucius Felix, *Octavius*, ch. 32,1; Tertullian, *De. Spect.*, ch. 13). They avoided using priestly words, since Christ had assumed all priesthood into himself. The leader of the liturgy was given a name of profane origin (*presbyteros, episcopos, antistes, praepositus,* etc.).

will not be their sacrifice. They will be merely ministers of the sign, of what is imperfect and earthly in Christian worship; they will be like the priests of the Old Law, who offered a victim external to themselves. They will not be priests in spirit and in truth, not priests of real and heavenly worship. They will not be offering the Christian sacrifice.

Such is the grandeur and magnificence of the Christian Liturgy: it can only be celebrated by those who celebrate it in Christ, those for whom their Saviour's pasch becomes a personal reality. For since that time there has been but one Liturgy, containing the consummation of the world—the redeeming sacrifice of Christ.

All Christian life is a celebrating of the mystery of redemption

Thus the eucharistic celebration is inseparable from our lives. The liturgy of the sacraments is not an end in itself, but is ordered to the Church, and intended to make her become wholly Christ in his redeeming act. It is not the celebration of the sacraments which is the high point of the Church's activity; the Church is not primarily a community of worship—unless by worship one means that worship in spirit and truth which is a living participation in Christ's pasch—but a community of life and death in Christ.

That participation extends beyond the moment when the sacraments happen. St. Paul did not speak of dying and rising with Christ only in baptism, but in his whole life: "I am crucified with Christ; I live now, not I, but Christ liveth in me" (Gal. 2.19). It is not just in the short time it takes to celebrate the Eucharist that the Church must be the Mass, the redeeming Christ present in the world, but throughout history till the parousia, for her own salvation and that of the world. Christ's liturgy on earth, solemn and unceasing, is none other than the very life of the Church.

The Church celebrates Christ's sacrifice even outside her liturgical action; she celebrates it in her faithful who die to themselves through obedience, with Christ on the Cross; in those who struggle to gain heavenly love, who raise themselves out of this world towards purity and poverty of heart, with Christ who went to the Father; in all her faithful who work and suffer, who love God and neighbour, who give themselves for the salvation of others. In all of them the Church is the redeeming sacrifice, the Mass celebrated in spirit and in truth.

When a Christian, priest or layman, dies in faith and love, he is exercising his Christian priesthood for the last time, saying his last Mass; he is playing his part, for the last time, in redeeming the world, and entering the fullness of Christ's death, the totality of his glory. That last Mass will, by God's grace, be the holiest and most real of all. Not that our death can be more precious than the death of Christ we celebrate in the Eucharist, but because it is our most total sharing in it. Our liturgical celebrations, if they are to be real, must resemble that moment when we shall say, with Christ who accepts, adores and loves, "Father, into thy hands I commend my spirit."

The Mass is said in order that the whole Church and the whole of our life may become a Mass, may become Christ's sacrifice always present on earth. St. Francis of Sales resolved that he would spend the whole day preparing to say Mass, so that whenever anyone asked what he was doing, he might always answer, "I am preparing for Mass."[5] We also could resolve to make our whole lives a participation in the divine mystery of the Redemption, so that when anyone puts the question to us, we can always answer, "I am saying Mass."

[5] F. Trochu, *St. François de Sales,* Lyons, 1941, vol. I, p. 272.

5

A Second Baptism

The Curé of Ars began one of his sermons by declaring: "To talk to you about confession is to talk about all that is most precious in religion."[1] Such a statement might today seem exaggerated. With our wonderful richness of community worship, and accustomed as we are to God's generosity in seeming to ask no more of us than to open our mouths with joy and longing faith before he gives us the body of Christ, we today find it hard to place such value upon a sacrament shorn of all ritual splendour, whose reception seems simply an ascesis of individual purification. Yet the sacrament of penance reveals a majesty and a tenderness which are quite enough to explain the saint's words. Our Lord instituted it on the evening of his resurrection day, when he appeared in the fullness of his mystery, to reunite all men in the communion of Easter. If one is to speak of confession in fact, one must indeed speak about all that is most precious in religion.

God's action in his Christ presents two facets to the world: one of justice, the other of salvation. In Christ, God has come to save and to judge the world. A true sacrament of the redemptive mystery, penance brings God's action both as dispensing justice and as saving us into the midst of men. And the glory of this sacrament is that in it man finds that both actions are one, that

[1] *Sermons du Vén. Serviteur de Dieu, J.-M.-B. Vianney*, vol. II, p. 440, Lyons, 1882.

the God of justice and salvation has but a single face, the face
of redeeming love. Man, called before this tribunal, realizes that
God is bringing him into the banquet room where he can communicate with Christ in his death and his divine resurrection.

I. *A SACRAMENT OF REDEEMING JUSTICE*

Christ has come into the world for judgement. Indeed nothing
is expressed more forcefully in Scripture than this divine will to
justice. The gospel message is the announcement of a judgement,
from its beginning when Christ separates those who are placed
from those to whom he cries "Woe!", to the final discourse where
he sets all men on one or other side of the judge. The hour will
strike when God's justice is imposed upon the world in its fullness,
the hour of that triumphant death which Christ describes by
saying: "Henceforth you shall see the Son of man coming in the
clouds of heaven" (Matt. 26.64), and "Now is the judgement of
the world" (John 12.31). It is an hour whose final effect will take
place on the Last Day.

When the hour had struck, and Christ was seated at the right
hand of God upon the clouds of heaven, when judgement, the
separation of life and death, had begun, Christ appeared to the
Apostles and said: "Receive ye the Holy Ghost. Whose sins you
shall forgive, they are forgiven them" (John 20.22-3). The justice
which God exercises in Christ the Redeemer is a justice of justification. The sentence he pronounces is a gift of his own justice; he
judges by the fire of the Spirit which is a fire of divine charity:
"Receive ye the Holy Ghost," the Spirit who "is himself the
remission of all sins."[2] Whoever accepts the judgement of God
will be free of condemnation however great a sinner he may be;
he is judged by the fact that he "is passed from death to life"
(John 5.24).

Such is the sacrament of penance. The great assizes of the last

[2] Postcommunion for the Tuesday after Pentecost.

judgement began when Christ rose from the dead: "Henceforth you shall see the Son of Man coming on the clouds of heaven." When we kneel to confess our sins we are confronting the justice of him who is coming to judge the living and the dead.

But how paradoxical is the justice of penance, upsetting all our ideas, contradicting every possible analogy from human justice! Whereas our justice is carried out, ideally, by proclaiming innocence or punishing guilt, everyone who comes before the tribunal of God is a "debtor." So noble, so utterly different from this, is God's justice, so unbounded his own personal justice, that it makes the sinners who have recourse to it just too. The sacrament of penance proclaims the transcendence of God's justice.

God's justice is overflowing, for it is simply a love that gives itself. It is a love that gives itself, for it is none other than the Spirit of God, the infinite holiness, by which God is both the Just One and the Judge, by which he is love. The light this sacrament casts upon God should affect us profoundly. Divine justice is shown by it as being a justice of salvation which is carried out by giving itself in love. That justice gives itself to man, not because of his merits, but because he has forfeited all claim to it, and hopes to receive it from a God whose justice is greater than the heart or the sin of man.

The most perfect illustration of this redeeming justice is the parable of the Prodigal Son. When the father recognized the prodigal in his rags coming in the distance, his youngest, his Benjamin, his heart was touched, he ran to him, saying nothing, but only rushing to embrace his son. Before coming back from the faroff country, the son had said to himself: "How many hired servants in my father's house abound with bread, and I here perish with hunger? I will arise, and will go to my father, and say to him: Father, I have sinned against heaven and before thee: I am not worthy to be called thy son: make me as one of thy hired servants."

Now, amid the outpourings of his father's affection, he recites the words he has rehearsed: "Father, I have sinned against heaven, and before thee: I am not worthy to be called thy son," but he dares not add, "Make me as one of thy hired servants." He realizes that to speak of hired servants in face of his father's kisses and tears would be a further affront to his paternal love. "Bring forth quickly the first robe, and put it on him, and put a ring on his hand, and shoes on his feet: and bring hither the fatted calf, and kill it, and let us eat and make merry: because this my son was dead, and is come to life again."

So it is with the sacrament of the penance of sinners. The joy, the haste to give back to the prodigal his privileges of sonship, the banquet which would never have been prepared had the son not been a prodigal—all this is the sacrament of penance. That is how God's love works: he prepares a banquet for the prodigal son, just because he is a prodigal, as soon as he returns home. In God love and justice are not opposed; the one is contained in the other. He proves his love by giving his justice; he carries out his justice by giving his love. For the Spirit he gives is both justice and love.

Catholics know well that they are near to God's heart because they are sinners seeking salvation. Therefore they say, "Bless me Father, for I have sinned." They say this quite straightforwardly, with no sense that there is anything strange about their logic. That *"for* I have sinned" is wonderful. "Be kind to me, *because* I have been such a bad son. Give me your blessing, *because* I have offended you." The seal of divinity is on this sacrament. The justice of God is shown in it as something quite different from the justice of men: it is a justice of redemption, a gift given to man because he is a sinner, on the sole condition that he accept it.

So it was with Christ, to whom the life of justice, the life of resurrection, was given, because he made himself sin for us (2 Cor. 5.21). He took the form of life of sinful humanity (Rom. 8.3); in sinful flesh, he was far away from the Father, but in his death he submitted to the justice of God, and the man returned to his Father. God received him in justice, embraced him in his Holy Spirit, and "he was justified in the Spirit" (I Tim. 3.16). The new

life entered mankind through the wound of sin, and is forever a
life of resurrection from the dead, a justification.

Every confession is a miraculous event, filled with paradoxical
splendour. Man presents himself before God who comes in Christ
to judge men at the end of time. And the fire of judgement which
God makes him pass through is none other than "the redemption
that is in Christ Jesus."

II. PENANCE, A PARTICIPATION IN
THE REDEMPTION

The judgement of justification is pronounced for men in their
communion in the death and resurrection of Christ; it is there, in
Christ who dies and rises again, that God executes the great
judgement of the messianic era. "Now is the judgement of the
world," said Our Lord. The world of sin is condemned in him,
and in him a new creation is set up in justice. God says, "Ego te
absolvo" to the sinner because he sees him kneeling in Christ and
in the mystery of the Redemption. There is no forgiveness, no
justification, except in Christ and in his redemption; the mercy of
God is exercised nowhere else: ". . . through whom we have
redemption . . . the remission of sins" (Col. 1.14; Eph. 1.7).

Communion in Christ's death

"God hath condemned sin in the flesh" of the dying Christ
(Rom. 8.3); he destroyed it when, by dying, Christ left sinful
flesh to enter into justice. To have his sins blotted out, every man
must communicate in the immolation of that body. He must take
part in the same death, that there may flow over him "the precious
blood of the Lamb unspotted and undefiled" (I Pet. 1.19), the
blood of the Lamb "who taketh away the sins of the world" (John
1.29). Christians are purified by the sprinkling of blood, according
to St. Peter (I Pet. 1.2); they come and dip their robes in the

purple of the Lamb's blood to take them out dazzlingly white
(Apoc. 7.14). To enter the sanctuary of God, they take "the new
and living way" (Heb. 10.20) which leads through the torn veil
of Christ's immolated body. They unite themselves to Christ in the
death in which he offered himself to the Father. These texts are
tremendous, and quite clear. They do not say that the remission of
sin is gained in virtue of the merit acquired in the past by that
death—one must not water down the reality of a single word of
Scripture on the ground of reason being unable to cope with it;
they say that it is gained in a communion in that immolation.[3]

The Christian's whole existence is rooted in Christ and in his
death. Because of this, it is Christian, "holy." St. Paul knows
himself to be in a continual communion of immolation with Our
Lord: "With Christ I am nailed to the cross" (Gal. 2.19); he is
aware that that is his point of contact with Christ, that the unceasing encounter between Christ and the Church takes place in that
same death lived by them both. But there are special moments in
the Christian life when that union becomes intensified: the sacraments. What is said of baptism: "It is in Christ that you are
baptized, in his death" (Rom. 6.3), can also be said of penance.
It re-creates or reinforces our contact with our Saviour, in his
immolation.

The first virtue the Christian must have if he wants his sins
forgiven is faith in the death of Christ to which he unites himself,
just as this is the first virtue for baptism. If Christ's body is to be
food in the Eucharist, it must be eaten, and it is faith that comes
to it and eats (John 6). If Christ's blood is to purify man from
sin, he must first have the faith and the desire for salvation to go
down to the "pool of Probatica," filled with the blood of the Lamb.
Whenever the sacrament of penance is found to fail in effective-
ness, the first failure has been one of faith.

---

[3] As well as assuring us of the absolute reality of the sacraments, these
texts also make clear the reality of sin which can be blotted out only in
the immolation of Christ.

The Fathers often compared penance to baptism, in which man is immersed in Christ's death for the remission of his sins. But this renewed sacramental immersion is not the effect of a symbolic rite, but of man's associating himself by his own actions with Christ's immolation. That is why this second baptism is painful, a *baptismus laboriosus,* as it used to be called. "Because man cannot conform himself to Christ's death by the sacrament of baptism a second time, those who sin after baptism must become like Christ in his passion by virtue of imposing a penance or a suffering upon themselves."[4]

Baptism has placed a redeeming grace at the roots of our being, like a profound potentiality destined to grow till it reaches the surface, the visible man and the things he does in his life. The rite of baptism cannot be performed again when the Christian sins. His sin consists in the fact that his response to that profound grace of baptism has not extended to "his earthly members." His sins will not be forgiven by the effect of a rite, but by virtue of making himself once again become faithful to the demands of his baptism, by a participation in the redemptive death of Christ which he has once rejected, but now, penitent, imposes on himself for the future. This second baptism is painful. It immerses man once again in that daily dying which was demanded by the first baptism. Sinful man must once again practise the daily virtues of mortification, humility, asceticism, forgiving injuries; he must turn his whole being towards God; and, in penance, it is these actions which take on a sacramental power to re-establish and develop the holiness conferred at baptism. Penance is the Christian life being lived again and lived more intensely; it is Christian effort made a sacrament.

The sacrament of penance contains the proof of a tremendous truth. Grace cannot be gained in virtue of our own activity—being the justice of God, it can only be gained by God's freely giving it; yet it is only received in the framework of the effort man makes to place himself at the disposal of that justice. It is a gift, but its

[4] St. Thomas, *Summa,* pt. 3 q. 49, art. 3 ad 2m.

reception involves intense activity—the sinful man dying to self, and wholeheartedly consenting to God's holiness.

If they are once again to realize the value of their penitential practices, Christians must come to see the need and the sacramental meaning of their own acts in confession. We sometimes describe our examination of conscience and contrition as preparatory acts, yet they are sacramental acts which bring man into the passover of death and resurrection.

The sinner begins by subjecting his life to an examination; he discovers that he is a sinner and admits his guilt. He has begun to enter the redeeming mystery: he unites himself to his Saviour on the Cross, who accepted to be what he was—a man involved in the existence of sinful humanity and subject to the punishment of sin. Then he repents. In the distant country to which his sin had exiled him, the Prodigal Son in the parable said to himself, "I will arise and will go to my father." When the Christian sees himself, surrounded by his sins as the son was surrounded by the animals he tended, he says in his heart, "I will arise and will go to my father." For that is what contrition is—man turning away from himself and returning; he leaves the distant country, evil, which holds him away from God, and goes towards his Father. This contrition unites him to the mystery of the true Son who returned to his Father from a far country. The mystery of redemption was for Christ simply his return to the Father from the far country where sinful men lived. "When his hour was come that he should pass out of this world to the Father" (John 13.1), Our Lord said, "Arise, let us go hence" (14.31). So it is Christ's words they use, as they set out on the road with him, and walk in him who is the way—these prodigal children who rise up and say, "I will arise and will go to my Father."

Then they fall on their knees, and cry, "Father, I have sinned against thee, I am no more worthy to be called thy son." They say it in Christ on the Cross; by admitting it they are crucified with him. For Christ came in our "body of sin" and on the cross recognized the distance separating him from his Father: "My God, my God, why hast thou forsaken me?" His death was the result, marking him in the eyes of God and the world as him who "made himself sin for us." Then the Christian who submits to an outward suffering, a "penance," which gives him the assurance that with Christ with whom this suffering associates him, he will enter into glory: "This is a faithful saying: for if we be dead with him, we shall live also with him" (2 Tim. 2.11).

The effect of the sacrament depends on the worth of these actions. They are what effect our union with Christ in his death: "Everyone receives forgiveness of his sins in so far as he unites himself to Christ who died for our sins."[5]

How else could the Christian find forgiveness for sin except by a personal participation in the redeeming mystery? For the forgiveness of sin gained on the Cross was not simply a juridical result of Christ's death, but a reality personal to Christ. This forgiveness merited on the Cross was simply Christ's own glorification won in his "death to sin" (Rom. 6.10). To win this forgiveness is to be raised up with Christ. And how could God raise us in Christ, simultaneously with him, unless we are involved in his death?

Even baptism with water would have no effect if man did not associate himself personally with the mystery of Christ. "You are washed" says St. Paul (1 Cor. 6.11), underlining the part man plays by immersing himself, through faith and longing for salvation, in the water of baptism. In the second baptism, there is no "laver of water" (Eph. 5.26) prepared for man. It is the penitent's own actions that immerse him in Chirst the Redeemer.[6] The waters of this baptism are the recognition of our wretchedness as sinners, contrition, confession, and penance; by them do we immerse ourselves in Christ's death. Why does confession not succeed in bringing more people back to the purity of their "Easter

[5] *Summa* pt. 3, qu. 86, art. 4 ad 3m.
[6] *Summa Contra Gentiles,* bk. 4, ch. 72; "Everyone receives the effects of the remission of sins according as he unites himself to Christ in his Passion . . . Now [in penance] we unite ourselves to Christ by our own activity."

morning," in giving them back the full brightness of their baptismal youth? Christ's death has always had the same power of raising from the dead; but it is in virtue of our own actions that this sacrament associates us with Christ in his death, and if we are to rise with him in glory, we must bury ourselves in death to self with the same force with which Christ went to his Father.

Communion in Christ's resurrection

In the sacrament of penance we find again the paradox common to baptism, the Eucharist and all Christian life: we must die with Christ in order to rise with him, and yet it is only in our union with Christ in glory that we participate in his death.[7] The Apocalypse pictures the faithful dipping their clothes in the blood of the Lamb, yet that Lamb is standing in glory (Apoc. 5.6). According to the Epistle to the Hebrews, we will enter the holiness of God by the way marked out in his immolated body, a way of death which is, at the same time, "new and living" (Heb. 10.20). The principle of all sanctification is the Christ of Easter, "raised up for our justification" (Rom. 4.25). In him we find death to sin, because in him we are raised up to life. Thus Christ himself is "dead to sin" and the flesh, by the glory he has entered.

We are forgiven in grace, in the glory of God revealed in the man Jesus. The remission of sins is an objective reality; it is not simply a declaration made by God, but an action performed by God—the action that raises Christ and in him raises us to the same life. It is none other than the Holy Spirit, the holiness and glory of God, taking possession of the man Jesus, and effacing in him "the likeness of sin" (Rom. 8.3) in order that, for us, he may henceforward be the justice and holiness of God (1 Cor. 1.30). Forgiveness is a gift, the gift of the Holy Ghost. The penitent comes to Christ in his crucifixion and his glory; and from the stream flowing from his opened side, he drinks the new waters of life, the rivers of the Spirit "who is the remission of sins." The

[7] Cf. *The Resurrection*, pp. 224–5.

Lamb of God, immolated at the Pasch, "taketh away the sins of the world" in the holocaust which consumes him, in the glory of the Holy Spirit.

That is how God's justice is accomplished: God "justifies" (1 Tim. 3.16), God "sanctifies" (John 17.19), God glorifies his Son who gives himself to him in death, and whoever, with that Son, returns to the Father. The glory, the Spirit of holiness, the justice of God and the forgiveness of sins are all one. The justice of God triumphs in the resurrection of men.

That is why penance is like a baptism; man, who has gone afar off, is brought back by it to the waters of his birth, for the Holy Spirit is always, not merely at the first baptism, a water of divine generation (John 3.5; Tit. 3.5), the divine womb from which the children of God are born. The Christian once more finds the joy of his baptism, the joy of being born, and opening his eyes, and loving the Father with a child's love.

Once more, let us remember that the prime virtue of the Christian who seeks forgiveness of sin is faith. He must believe in the Spirit who flows for him in the redeeming Christ: "If any man thirst let him come to me, and let him that believeth in me drink" (John 7.37).

By thus going back to the origins of his life, by becoming once more a child in the womb of God, the Christian comes to the source of his power. The grace of resurrection, which is the Spirit, does not merely wipe out sin, but combats it, for the Spirit is not only holiness but power too; he is the personal expression of the infinite might of God, both "the Holy Ghost . . . and the power of the Most High" (Luke 1.35). He creates in holiness, and gives the strength to remain and grow in it. Penance is not merely the giving of pardon, but a sacrament of Christian life; it provides the arms for our struggle against "the spiritual powers," for the great Messianic temptation we are engaged in. It is the help given in answer to the Church's plea: "Lead us not into temptation, but deliver us from evil." It is not meant simply for the forgiveness

of grave sins; it is a special means of perseverance and progress
in charity.

Every grace of the Spirit is given in the body of Christ. If by
penance man finds once again the primeval waters of salvation,
it is because he is making contact there with the body of Christ
(John 7.9). The feast prepared for the prodigal son is the paschal
feast of the body of Christ; the robe and sandals and ring are
Christ, his saviour, being given back to the sinner. That is why
God sends the sinner to the Church when he seeks salvation, for
the Church is the body of Christ visible on earth.

By no other sacrament, perhaps, is it made so abundantly clear
that the Church is the body of the Saviour, dead and risen again,
in whom alone is forgiveness of sins. In the early Church, penance
was seen as a reconciliation with the community of the Church,
and for that reason with God. The first aspect was so stressed that
historians have thought — wrongly — that the second was not
included in the early theology of penance. St. Augustine saw a
living communion with the Church as the thing that brought
forgiveness, the instrument of grace. The remission of sins is in
the body of the dead and risen Christ, and that body is accessible
to us in the Church which is identified with it.

The Christian's penance is ineffective except in relation to the
Church. Having become invisible to sinful men by that very Easter
glory which consecrates the redemptive completeness of the incarnation, Christ extends his incarnation in the world by way of the
Church. "As the Father hath sent me, I also send you" (John
20.21), he said, after he had risen. "Him whom the Father hath
sanctified" in his Spirit "and sent into the world" (John 10.36)
dwells among us in the form of the Church in the fullness of the
Spirit.

By his first baptism, man is united to Christ's body in mystery,
by virtue of a rite. The baptism of penance takes place without
any such rite, in the reality of the actions of the Christian life, and
it brings us face to face with the body of Christ as it may be found

on earth apart from rites, yet in the reality proper to it, in the Church.

Despite its individualistic appearance, penance is a sacrament of the Church, administered in the community and for the sake of the community. Sin tends to make the Church fall to pieces; it separates Catholics from the Body and the Spirit, from the centre at which all communion takes place, and isolates them. But penance brings them back into unity, and they find themselves forgiven by the very fact that they are brought back.

No paschal sacrament can be anything but a sacrament of communion, for the mystery of the Pasch is essentially a mystery of communion.[8] Every element in penance bears the imprint of the Church's charity: in it God is giving his Spirit of charity. He may be a judge, but he judges in the fashion of a redeeming God, exercising justice in Christ by justifying; if he condemns, it is only by the justice he wants to bestow which some reject.[9]

All this helps us to realize the splendour of this sacrament in which the justice of the Last Day is already being carried out; to realize the feast of death and resurrection in which we join by penance. It shows us with what trust we must receive this sacrament, with what longing of love, for God exercises his justice by giving charity, and we expiate our sin by the welcome we give it. And, finally, it is a reminder not to neglect this means of salvation, but to make regular use of this power of the Spirit placed at our disposal, without which we are weaker than the Evil that tempts us.

Was the Curé of Ars exaggerating? Surely, to speak of confession *is* to speak of all that is most precious in religion. We cannot think about penance without being drawn into speaking of the central mystery, without having to think of Christ and his Pasch. Confession is always paschal. Easter is the source of our Christian life, and is also its distant and difficult goal which we shall attain on the Last Day, when we are wholly baptized in the

---

[8] See *The Resurrection*, pp. 72–7.

[9] The expression "to bind and loose" expresses the completeness of the Church's power in forgiving sins.

mystery of redemption. The sacrament of penance is an assistance granted to the weakness of Christians: it helps us to return unceasingly to the source of our life, in order that we may be certain of attaining it on the last day.

PART III
CHRISTIAN VIRTUES

6

Believing in Christ the Redeemer

Faith is at the beginning of the Christian life. "He that cometh to God must first believe that he is" (Heb. 11.6). As he enters the Church, on its threshold, the catechumen is asked the question: "Dost thou believe in God? Dost thou believe in Jesus Christ?" Faith is the virtue of the threshold, the gate of the Kingdom.

The doctrine of faith, then, is part of "the word of the beginning" taught to Christian neophytes (Heb. 6.1). It almost seems as if the author of the Epistle to the Hebrews wants to reserve it to those still fed only on milk, "unskilled in the word of perfection" (Heb. 5.13). But because it is the gate, faith is necessary even to those who have penetrated to the heart of the Christian life. For right to the very end of his life on earth, the Christian is still in some ways on the threshold; though he is in God's house, it is still through that gate of faith that he finds himself there. Until he dies, faith will be the beginning of his life, its permanent foundation. Even those who have reached the summit of Christian life know that it is on the base of faith that the ladder rests. The most sublime contemplation, as well as the humbler virtues, is developed in faith. And the apostle's effort is also rooted in faith: "We believe for which cause we speak also" (2 Cor. 4.13).

And thus, though the Epistle to the Hebrews starts by setting "the doctrine of faith" among the first elements of our teaching, when it comes to the end of its exposition for "the perfect," it still devotes three chapters to exhorting them to faith. For faith is the virtue that continually initiates us into life in Christ; it is always the foundation and the start of that life, a living base which must be unceasingly nourished and consolidated.

It is a foundation that is too frail in us all. Who can pride himself on possessing a total faith? To prove how weak our faith is, smaller than "the least of all the seeds" in the garden (Matt. 13.32), we need only a single gospel text: "If you have faith as a grain of mustard-seed, you shall say to this mountain: *Remove from hence hither,* and it shall remove . . ." (Matt. 17.19).

Our faith is slight and weak, and constantly in danger in our souls. We are forever in danger from the great temptation of the end of the world in which man's lot is determined, from which we pray the Lord to deliver us—the temptation to incredulity, or failing faith: "The Son of Man, when he cometh, shall he find, think you, faith on earth?" (Luke 18.8).

We must work, then, unceasingly to strengthen the faith in our hearts. But what exactly is faith?

I. *CHRIST, THE OBJECT OF FAITH*

The prime object of our faith is the person of Christ, and the person of God who reveals himself in Christ

The essential, basic reality of faith is this: man is borne towards another, towards God, who, revealing himself in Christ, gives salvation. What the believer affirms, the object towards which he makes his "leap of faith" is not merely a truth of reason, or even a series of truths. The Apostles were not teaching doctrines, propagating religious ideas. They were the heralds, the witnesses of a person. Their preaching was proclamation rather than teaching: "What we preach is Jesus Christ our Lord" (2 Cor. 4.5). They were giving witness of Jesus Christ to a people which did not as yet believe; they were proclaiming the Lord Jesus.

The men who accepted that word were not simply giving their assent to a doctrine. They were attaching themselves to a person. There were believers then who did not know most of our finer points of dogma—which, after all, took centuries to formulate—who could not have answered most of the questions in our catechism. Yet they were true believers, who could shed their blood for what they believed. When it was a question of getting them to deny their faith, what they were asked to renounce was Christ. He was the object of that faith.

It could not be otherwise, since the Word spoken by God in the world, which the Apostles proclaimed, and in which they asked men to believe, was a person, the word of God which men must "receive" (John 1.11).

The faith demanded by Christ is almost His faith in a person: "Have the faith of God" (Mark 11.22). "Dost thou believe in the Son of man?" (John 9.35). He told Martha of Bethany, "I am the resurrection and the life: he that believeth in me, although he be dead, shall live. Believest thou this?" (John 11.25-6). In the text faith has a double object—first a person, the person of Christ, "he that believeth in me": then a statement: ". . . though he be dead [the believer] he shall live. Believest thou this?" Here faith bears upon a person and upon a truth, but the second is closely dependent on the first: the believers in Christ, who is the Resurrection and the life. The object to which faith attaches, then, is more sublime than any truth of reason, for it is the person of Christ, subsistent Truth, revealed to the world.

There are various ways of formulating the act of faith. But all characterise it as an adherence to the person of Christ. Whereas the Jews, in their unbelief, refuse to receive Christ (John 1.11; 5.43), the believer, by his faith, welcomes the Logos of God (John 1.12). Chapter 6 of St. John even goes so far as to compare faith with receiving the Eucharist: by both we receive the bread of heaven, which is Christ.

In every act of faith, even a purely human one, what comes first is always the person to whom we are giving our faith, according to St. Thomas; the truths we accept are secondary to that first object.[1] In Christian faith, Christ is even more fully the prime object, because he contains in himself all the truths he reveals. One may say that he is not merely the prime, but the total object of faith.

Such, then, is the faith of the Church: she believes in her saviour. As a bride, she believes whatever the Bridegroom tells her, but above all she believes in him; she has faith in him, gives her faith to him, to him the Son of God, the fullness of all truth, as also of all goodness, beauty, power and fidelity.

To strengthen our faith, it is helpful to declare that we believe in this truth or that. But it is when we declare our faith in Christ, when we say, "I believe in you," that our faith is leaping up to its prize object, the living person of Christ, compared with whom all other truths are secondary (though not therefore inessential).

When the Christian starts to pray, he wants to give his mind to God, he tries to "make an act of the presence of God." But he should not be content simply with a conviction that God is present. The believer cements his contact with God in prayer by saying, "I believe in thee." For, in itself, thinking about God's presence need not mean thinking with faith, but could still be in the realm of philosophy. The object of Christian faith is the person of God— not merely his presence—and the person of Christ. The effect of recollection brought about by thinking of God's presence might never attain the contact with him involved in the act of faith. For faith has the power of making us "go to Christ," of directing all our faculties towards Our Lord[2] and holding them there.

When Christian truth is being taught, it is above all on the person of God, the person of Christ, that people's minds must be fixed. If the purpose of such teaching is to move people to be joined to him in faith, then it is above all the chief objects of faith which must be presented in it.

[1] *Summa* pt. 2 of pt. 2, qu. II, art. I.
[2] See the second part of this chapter.

The object of faith: the person of Christ the Redeemer

The object of Christian faith is not the person of God in his serene majesty, a motionless God of static perfection; nor is it Christ simply as possessing both a divine and a human nature. Faith bears upon God acting in the world, intervening in history, on God who, having created the world, leads it to the salvation of eternal life (Heb. 11.6). It bears upon the Christ "who is coming," that is, in whom God intervenes in the world for its eternal salvation.

In the Fourth Gospel, Christ declares that he is transcendent, in a phrase reminiscent of Yahweh's supreme title: "I Am" (John 8.58). But there is generally added to this phrase some statement that defines Christ's transcendence as essentially redemptive: "I Am the bread of life," "I Am the light of the world," "I Am the good shepherd," "I Am the true vine." "He who is" is at the same time essentially "he who is to come"; he will only be revealed as "he who is" in the act of redeeming us: "When you shall have lifted up the Son of man, then shall you know that I Am he" (John 8.28).

"I Am the resurrection and the life. He that believeth in me, although he be dead, shall live" (John 11.25). Christ demands faith because he is the Resurrection, because he comes into this world to save it. "Believest thou this?" he asks Martha. And her reply is: "Yea, Lord, I have believed that thou art the Son of the living God who art come into this world" (John 11.27).

Peter believed that his salvation was in Christ, and gave him his faith: "Will you also go away?" And Simon Peter replied, "Lord, to whom shall we go? Thou hast the words of eternal life. And we have believed and have known, that thou art the holy one of God" (John 6.69-70).

Faith leads to salvation by its object. It is directed to God who saves us in Christ, and receives Christ, in whom salvation comes: that is why "he that believeth shall be saved" (Mark 16.16).

But what in fact is God's great intervention in history, the bursting of God's life into the world of sin, the divine action whereby sinful man is forgiven? According to St. Paul, it is simply the action of raising up which God performed in the man Jesus, that defying action accomplished in Christ's human being, which sanctified him in the life-giving holiness of God, in order that all men might be sanctified in him: "He rose again for our justification" (Rom. 4.25).

This, then, is God's great intervention of salvation: in the man Jesus the eternal life of God has broken through into the world. And Christ's "coming" into the world—is what Christ meant when he said, "When the Son of Man shall come," or "I go away and I come," or, again, "Hereafter you shall see the Son of Man coming in the clouds." Christ's great coming is the coming of Easter, when he comes upon the clouds of heaven, seated at the right hand of Power, to judge and save the world. All power of saving is given him in his paschal glory, all the eschatological fullness of the new world, in order that it may unfold for mankind. "In him it hath well pleased the Father that all fullness should dwell." The kingdom of God broke through in him, for us.

This is the object of our faith: we believe in God who raises Christ, in the risen Christ in the fullness of the power of salvation. The Jews had faith according to the Mosaic creed, yet Paul ranges them with the infidel (2 Cor. 4.4): they did not believe in God as raising Christ. This is what St. Peter was proclaiming, what he was calling upon the Jews to believe: "This same, whom you by the hands of wicked men have crucified and slain, God hath raised up" (Acts 2.23-4). "This Jesus hath God raised again, whereof all we are witnesses" (Acts 2.32). "Let all the house of Israel know most certainly, that God hath made both Lord, and Christ, this same Jesus, whom you have crucified" (2.36).

Moses had "lifted up" the brazen serpent in the desert, as a sign of salvation among the Hebrews. Similarly the Son of man must be lifted up by the Cross into the glory of God, to be the everlasting cause of salvation for all who gaze upon him in faith: "So must the Son of Man be lifted up, that whosoever believeth in him may have life everlasting" (John 3.14-15). Raised up in glory on the hilltop, his pierced heart pouring out the rivers of the Spirit along with the blood of sacrifice, Christ offers himself to the faith of everyone who seeks salvation: "They shall look on him whom they pierced" (John 19.37). Christ in the glory of his sacrifice is the object of man's faith.

Thus the Christian s faith may be defined as "Faith in the operation of God who hath raised him up from the dead" (Col. 2.12). For him God is from now on always the God-who-raises-Christ-from-the-dead. He is essentially the "God of Jesus Christ," the "Father of Jesus Christ" (Rom. 15.6; 2 Cor. 1.3) who says, "Thou art my Son, this day have I begotten thee," because he has raised him from the dead (Acts 1.33). It is there, in the Resurrection, that God reveals himself fully as the Father who engenders our Lord Jesus Christ. So central is the Resurrection to our Christian faith that "if Christ be not risen again . . . then our faith is vain," empty of all content (1 Cor. 15.14).

Abraham's faith is the image of ours, because the patriarch believed that from the dead womb of Sara, as from a tomb, God would raise a vast people. But our faith is loftier still, for we believe that God raised to life his Christ who had been crucified, and in him the whole world.

The earliest creed taught by the Apostles declared that Christ had died and risen (1 Cor. 15.1-4), that he was "delivered up for our sins, and rose again for our justification" (Rom. 4.25). That creed was summed up in the phrase used by the martyrs when asked to worship Caesar: "Jesus is the Lord!" The Holy Spirit himself put the words in their mouth (1 Cor. 12.3). God has lifted up his Christ to the very summit of creation, and henceforth every knee shall bow and every creature proclaim "Jesus is the Lord!" (Phil. 2.11). That *is* our faith.[3]

[3] Faith in all other truths is born out of faith in Christ's resurrection. So it is with faith in the divinity of Christ, in God's fatherhood of Christ, in the spirit, in the church. All of the New Testament was written in the light of the Resurrection.

The Christian—if he has faith—believes that the world of death and sin has been invaded by the tremendous power of the Resurrection, before which the Apostle stands dumbfounded (Eph. 1.19-23), and which will overwhelm and transform the world. He believes that the destruction of sin has already taken place in Christ, that death is vanquished, that our humanity is glorified and divinized; that all our world, whose present form seems so important to us, is already judged in Christ and condemned—"Now is the judgement of the world" (John 12.31)—and that any value it may have for eternity must depend on its being remade in the charity of Christ.

All God's sanctifying power is contained in Christ's resurrection; all that creative action of God which will one day raise up our bodies too, and re-create the world in holiness, is wholly concentrated in the resurrection of Christ which *is* "the resurrection of the dead" (Rom. 1.4). The resurrection of Christ is total outpouring of the Holy Ghost, the exercising in Christ's body of his power to create, sanctify and judge. The eschatological creation of the world is actually present in the risen Christ.

I believe, then, that Christ has become Lord, the world's ruler to save and judge it: "He hath given him a name which is above all names . . ." (Phil. 2.9); "He was constituted Son of God in power . . . by the resurrection from the dead" (Rom. 1.4). I believe that he is the principle by which the world will be revolutionized, in whom is life everlasting, the life of love, eternal youth. I believe that he is already the Christ of the last parousia who is "coming upon the clouds of heaven, sitting on the right hand of the Power" (Matt. 26.64) to "judge the living and the dead" (1 Pet. 4.5), and that his judgement-seat, for damnation and salvation, is established amid mankind. When, in the Eucharist, I receive the body of my saviour, that is what enters within me, the mustard seed received in faith which bit by bit transforms my wretchedness.

The object of faith is essentially the Redemption: man believes in the God who effects salvation in Christ. That is why no one can be brought to the Christian faith without wanting it, and without humility. It is not enough to know the truths of doctrine and admire their structure; one must, recognizing one's essential poverty, want the salvation that comes from God.[4] Having come to believe, man must preserve in himself that desire which opens his heart to the object of faith, or he will succumb to the temptation to unbelief by which believers are always besieged.

Faith is indissolubly linked with hope; it can never exist apart from it. For the object of faith is God who raises the world in Christ; and this object of faith is at the same time our motive for hope. One cannot have faith without having hope too. That is why faith is a dynamic virtue. It attempts all things, doubts nothing. To believe in Christ's resurrection is to believe that henceforth nothing is impossible, that God's power is at our disposal for our salvation and the salvation of the world.

"It is easier for a camel to pass through the eye of a needle, than for a rich man to enter into the kingdom of God" (Matt. 19.24). "Who then can enter the kingdom of heaven?" wonder the Apostles. It is easier for a camel . . . than for me to sanctify myself for eternal life. How then am I to find salvation? "With God all things are possible," whether to make a rich man enter the kingdom, to raise Christ's mortal body to eternal life, or to transform my wretchedness into the holiness of God.

"With God all things are possible." Therefore "all things are possible to him that believeth" (Mark 9.22). For God's power bursts forth in the risen Christ, and in the believer who is joined to him (Eph. 1.19 ff). The apostle will be deterred by nothing, for "the Gospel is the power of God" (Rom. 1.16), the irresistible force of God who raises up Christ, and in Christ the whole world.

[4] St. Thomas teaches that the origin of the act of faith is love—not yet an act of charity, but a desire for the good things promised, a seeking after salvation (*De Veritate*, 14,2 ad 10).

II. *THE ACT OF FAITH*

Faith as a personal attachment

Since it is the person of Christ that is the object of faith—Christ who is not merely the revealer of truth, but Truth itself—faith cannot consist simply in an assent of the intellect. If truth is a person, then faith in that truth involves a personal move; it is a welcome given to the person of Christ, a uniting and a submission. There are certain special phrases for this in Scripture which define faith as a being joined to Christ. In the expression *credere in Christum,* the preposition *in* indicates movement and adherence. St. Augustine comments: Scripture says "that you may believe in him and not that you may believe him. One can believe him without believing in him . . . We believe Paul, but we do not believe in him; we believe Peter, but we do not believe in him."[5] But we believe in Jesus Christ. Faith is a dynamic perception, moving towards Christ and attaching itself to him.

This idea of a movement bearing the believer towards Christ is confirmed in these texts in which the phrase "to believe in Christ" is synonymous with "to go to Christ." With Our Lord, the believer is "he who comes to me." "If any man thirst let him come to me, and let him that believeth in me drink" (John 7.37). The two phrases are strictly parallel—the "coming to me" is synonymous with the "believing in me." By giving his faith, man comes, so near that he can drink from the water that flows from his saviour's side: "Let him that believeth in me drink. From his belly [Christ's], as the Scripture saith, there shall flow rivers of living water."

After he had promised the Eucharist, Christ lamented the failure of Judas and others to accept it. They had followed him and appeared to be his disciples, yet they had never come to him:

[5] *Tract. in Joh.,* VII, 14–18. *PL,* 35 (1631).

"There are some of you that believe not . . . Therefore did I say to you that no man can come to me, unless it be given him by my Father" (John 6:65-6).

When Christ is a spring of water, faith comes and drinks; when he is bread come down from heaven, faith comes and eats: "I am the bread of life: he that cometh to me shall not hunger: and he that believeth in me shall never thirst" (John 6.35). Here again "believing in me" is synonymous with "coming to me." But this time the believer does not merely put his mouth to the wound in Christ's side from which the living water flows, but actually eats the bread that is Christ. Christ is the bread of heavenly life which the Father has given to appease man's hunger, and man eats it by faith. That is why the Eucharist and faith come in the same chapter of St. John. Christ is the bread come down from heaven, we eat him by faith, and when that bread from heaven is offered in the form of the eucharistic bread, the faith that eats him is expressed by an actual physical eating. Eating, indeed, is a perfect image of faith welcoming and absorbing, and faith is expressed in reality by the eating of the Eucharist.

Believing, then, is accepting and "receiving Christ," as the communicant accepts and receives the bread of heaven in the Eucharist. Unbelievers are they who have not received him: "And his own received him not" (John 1.11). Our Lord made the reproach, "And you receive me not" (John 5.43), while "as many as received him, he gave them power to be made the sons of God, to them that believe in his name" (John 1.12). Man's heart, like the good ground of the parable, receives the Word sown in it, which is Christ himself.

"He who comes to me" Our Lord said, speaking of the believer. Man is drawn (John 6.44) and, by his faith, "comes" and attaches himself to Christ, becomes his disciple. Several of those who followed Our Lord were disciples in name only, like Judas, who never had faith (John 6.65-6). At the decisive moment, they deserted him, some at Capharnaum, one not till the Upper Room. "Will you also go away?" Our Lord asked the others. "To whom

shall we go?" was the answer of faith; "Thou hast the words of
eternal life. And we have believed . . ." (John 6.68-70). When
he had attained his redeeming fullness, in the Death and Resurrection, and become totally the object of faith, Christ commanded
his Apostles to make all mankind his disciples: "Go into all the
world. Make disciples of all nations" (Matt. 28.19).

The believer is joined to Christ whom he accepts and follows:
faith, then, is a total submission to Christ. Thus St. Paul often
speaks of "obedience to the faith" (Rom. 1.5; 16.26), of "obedience to the gospel" (2 Thess. 1.8). Conversion to the Faith is a
submission to the Lord Jesus: "The word of the Lord increased
. . . a great multitude also of priests obeyed the faith" (Acts 6.7).
The Christian faith proclaims that "Jesus Christ is Lord" (Phil.
2.11), and when we profess that faith, Christ becomes "our Lord
Jesus Christ," to whom we submit ourselves in deed; the Church
becomes the Bride, subject to her head and Lord: she weds the
Lord in faith.

Thus faith is the virtue that belongs to life in this world, to the
time of conquest, when the Kingdom is being established, and
mankind saved. It opens man's heart so that the Lord may enter
and dwell there. Charity follows close upon its heels: faith is the
welcome, the door of the Kingdom, whereas charity is possession,
the Kingdom. We need faith as long as our possession is not complete, in other words, till death.

Faith and eucharistic communion

The Eucharist is supremely "the sacrament of faith." To believe
is to go, to receive, to adhere to Christ, and all of this takes place
in eucharistic communion. Communion is the act of faith made
visible, the paradigm of Christian faith, faith carried out sacramentally. That is why we cannot distinguish what Our Lord says
of faith from what he says of the Eucharist, since the same phrases
are used for both. In one place it is the substantial word, come
down from heaven and nourishing men, which he offers to satisfy

our hunger: "I am the bread of life: he that cometh to me shall not hunger: and he that believeth in me shall never thirst" (John 6.35). In another it is the eucharistic bread which we are invited to eat: "I am the living bread which came down from heaven. If any man eat of this bread, he shall live forever; and the bread that I will give is my flesh for the life of the world" (John 6.51).

Johannine theology would certainly give a eucharistic sense also to that other statement about faith: "If any man thirst, let him come to me, and let him that believeth in me drink: from his belly [Christ's] there will flow rivers of living water" (John 7.37). He who believes and he who receives the Eucharist are one and the same; he comes to Christ and adheres to Christ by one and the same movement; he eats the bread, and drinks of the spring flowing from Christ's side. Here we find, applied to faith, a law which is true of all Christian life: the celebration of the Eucharist is the complete illustration, the visible realization of the mystery of the Church. When, therefore, the Church calls upon her children at Easter, to make their official profession of faith, she demands that they receive Communion. Sunday Mass is also a profession of faith, and every Sunday brings its census of believers, of those who come to Christ.

Faith and charity

The act of faith is not just a once-and-for-all acceptance of ideas we are presented with, of the outlook of a given way of life. Faith as an act is something we do; like other virtues, it is a dynamic *habitus,* a movement towards Christ, which must be unceasingly kept up and strengthened. Faith, far from meaning rest in the truth we have found, is a perpetual conquest. We cannot believe once and have done with it, because believing is going to Christ, and till we die, we shall never have wholly reached him. That is also why, on earth, we do not love once and for all, because we must still believe, still go to him when we love. We must be constantly loving afresh if we are to love at all and we must believe at every moment with the freshness and vigour of our first faith.

The Christian's act of faith is no mere assent of the mind. The scholastic definition of faith is certainly perfectly true: *"Assensus mentis veritati revelatae, sub influxu voluntatis, proper auctoritatem Dei revelantis"*—"The assent of the mind to revealed truth, moved by the will, on account of the authority of God revealing." But by that will man is wholly caught up, his mind and heart and entire self, and borne to Christ his Saviour. That movement is of the essence of supernatural and saving faith. "The devils also believe" (James 2.19), they assent to all the truths of revelation, for they know that God cannot deceive. But theirs is not Christian, supernatural, saving faith. Christian faith goes to Christ and clings to him, while the devils can only cry, "What have we to do with thee Jesus, Son of God?" (Matt. 8.29), go away from us!

It can happen that someone without Christian faith accepts by natural faith the Christian truths which are taught in the society he lives in: heaven, hell, the Eucharist. He does not believe in God, nor in his Christ; he admits their existence, but he has, perhaps, only hatred for them. Faith is not something purely intellectual, but belongs to the moral and supernatural order. It is a movement towards God who saves, and presupposes a wish to be saved, a starting-point of humanity, and some flicker of charity towards God and his Christ.[6] Even those who are equally well-instructed in religious matters may go different ways where Christ is concerned, may accept or reject him. St. John's Gospel, with its great stress on the personal nature of faith, is also the most insistent on the necessary dispositions. You must be a child of the light before you can come to the light (John 3.21), must in some sense belong to the Kingdom if you are to enter it: "He that is of God heareth the words of God. Therefore you hear them not

---

[6] St. Thomas, *loc. cit.*: "Inchoatio etiam fidei est in affectione, in quantum voluntus determinat intellectum ad assentiendum his quae sunt fidei." ("The beginning of faith is from the appetitive part of man, in so far as it is the will which determines the mind to assent to the things we believe.")

because you are not of God" (John 8.47). "You have not the love of God in you . . . How can you believe? . . . The glory which is from God alone you do not seek" (John 5.42-4; 6.44).

If love is needed before we can come to faith at all, then there can be no better way to preserve and strengthen faith than love. Love is the best of all dispositions for faith. Faith involves a movement towards God of everything in us which is not yet fixed upon him; it brings about a union; and that union can only be effectively made strong and unshakable by the weight of charity which pulls us towards God, attaches us to God and makes us live by God. The Christian, though still moving because he is still in this world, has cast his anchor into the sea of eternity because of the element of eternity, the charity, that is in him. What makes a man already in the Kingdom is also what holds open the door of faith by which he continues to enter it—till the day when the open door is not needed, when his charity is total, when the Christian dwells wholly within the house. The Church cannot count on the faith of those Christians who habitually live outside charity, in sin. In a world where faith is assailed by everything in the life around us, only the man whose faith is anchored in charity can persevere.

The first object of anyone teaching Christian doctrine (though it is not always necessary to say so in so many words) is to lead his hearers to the love of Christ, to make them give themselves to the Lord. Instruction must not be simply a course, a clear setting out of truths. The end of Christian revelation and of all Christian teaching is to unite men to the person of Christ. Assent to a collection of truths is "secondary"[7]; those truths are revealed by God, and taught by the Church with the realization of that end in view—in other words to unite men to Christ, their salvation.

However, in declaring that the teaching of Christian doctrine has this first end which is more important than the teaching itself, we must beware of succumbing to the grave temptation of neglecting that teaching, of giving too little value to exact knowledge.

[7] St. Thomas, *Summa*, pt. 2 of pt. 2 qu. ɪɪ, art. ɪ.

The truths are a necessary means of coming to the Truth, and if we neglect the means we cannot attain the end. Teaching must always be directed towards giving disciples to Christ, and is therefore a work of apostolic charity.

Faith as a participation in the Easter mystery

Since the prime object of faith is a person, the person of God in Christ, the act of faith cannot merely be an assent of the mind; it is a contact of two persons, the beginning at least of a gift of oneself. But it is more: the object of faith is not a person in his unchanging reality, but God raising Christ and Christ who, in dying to self, to the world and to sin, is raised into the life-giving, eternal omnipotent holiness of God—Christ in the mystery of Easter. The act of faith by which man unites himself to that Christ is a communion in the Easter mystery, in the means whereby we are saved: "If thou . . . believe in thy heart that God hath raised him up from the dead, thou shalt be saved" (Rom. 10.9).

Many of the phrases that define faith as union with Christ suggest that it introduces us into the Easter mystery. Believing means following Christ, being a disciple and therefore walking with him, sharing in his fate. And Christ's fate, the essential path he walks, is the Death and Resurrection: "If any man will come after me, let him deny himself, and take up his cross . . ." (Matt. 16.24). When the discourse on the bread of heaven, in John 6, is developed eucharistically, this bread offered to our faith is the body given for the life of the world and glorified in the Spirit (John 6.51,62 ff). How can one eat of that sacrificed body without being drawn into the sacrifice?

Faith is not simply a necessary condition for participating in the mystery of salvation; it is by faith itself that man follows Christ, that he eats the bread of sacrifice: it is in the act of faith that he dies to self and to the world of sin, that he is vivified in God: faith *is* participation in the mystery of salvation.

Faith as participation in Christ's death

To believe this—to believe that God has raised up Christ for our salvation—is a real death to self and to the world of sin. The believer is refusing to find in himself his salvation, the grounds for his certainty—not merely the certainty about what he thinks, but about what he is; at God's word, he comes out of himself, his self-sufficiency, and his poverty, to seek his true self, and believes that he finds it by coming to God in Christ. So Christ accepted to live no more in himself, but to come out of himself to receive life from his Father.

"Fleshly" man, as Scripture calls him, isolates himself in an autonomy of poverty in the pride of self-sufficiency. The believer goes to God and seeks the salvation revealed in the risen life of Christ, "he dies to the flesh," he has gone out of himself, left behind his earthly mode of being, his earlier fashion of living and thinking; he rises above himself in God-who-saves. He acclaims as an eternal triumph what must be, for fleshly man, fundamental failure: death. With the eyes of the flesh, man sees Christ hanging on a cross, dying there; but the believer sees in that death the irrepressible bursting forth of the life of God. For him the failure is triumph, life is in death, salvation lies in condemnation. He undergoes a complete reversal of himself, dies to what he was at first, to his own ways of thinking, and begins to live outside and above himself.

Believing then, is also dying to "this world," leaving it to enter another world, that of the resurrection of the dead. For faith in the Resurrection assumes that the world of sin is *already* condemned, that it is *already* in its death throes—"the world is crucified for me" (Gal. 6.14), "the form of this world passeth away" (1 Cor. 7.31)—that its values and judgements are only provisional, that the true value, the true ideal, is different from that of this world. For by raising Christ from the dead, God has created the true world, the eternal world, and the other has become simply the veil that will one day be drawn away.

Thus the believer leaves behind the whole system of life and thought that rests only on the tangible, visible certainties, to take up another system of life and thought resting upon the risen Christ. He relinquishes the support he finds in himself and in the world, lets go of what he has in his hand, of the firm ground beneath his feet, abandons the certainties of this life, to believe in a world he cannot see, in a triumph of Christ that he cannot prove, to lean his whole weight on what is by nature non-existent, but which, because he has heard God's word in his heart, he believes does exist.

The believer risks all to win all. St. Paul left behind the justice of the Law, that tangible, governable justice, "his own justice," upon which he could depend, all that was by nature gain, good, solid capital, in order to win Christ and a justice not the work of his own hands, but possessed in faith. He felt that this faith tore him away from himself and made him participate in his saviour's death: "That I may know the fellowship of his sufferings, being made comformable to his death" (Phil. 3.7-10). This involves a total giving of self to God, the supreme gift. The believer risks all he is sure of, even life itself, believing that God himself will be his life, in Christ raised from the dead.

There are some among the faithful who do not marry, who do not seek this world's approval or its wealth, because they believe that happiness and honour and fortune lie elsewhere. There are Christians who even give their life, the life they have, for another which they have never seen but which, on God's word, they believe they can find in Christ. Martyrdom is the supreme act of faith, the visible and essential expression of the risk it involves.

Because it is a total giving, God purifies the faith of his saints. He wants to lead them to believe in his word even when everything in this world seems to witness against it, to believe in spite of and in the face of everything, in desolation, in disgust, in the visible certainty of Christ's failure. When "the world" triumphs, when the

Church seems defeated, God brings his saints to the attainment of the total giving of themselves in pure faith. "Blessed are they who have not seen but have believed," said Our Lord to Thomas. "Faith is the conviction of things that appear not" (Heb. 11.1).

Since it is a dying to self, a total risk, a leap into the unknown on the word of God, faith does not admit of any seeking for palpable certainty: "Do not touch me," said Our Lord to Mary Magdalen, whose expressions of affection he had always allowed before, "for I am not yet ascended to my Father." Henceforth Christ belongs to another world, and can only be embraced in faith. To those who kept seeking sensible signs, who thought they needed to see a sign, Our Lord declared, "This unbelieving generation seeketh a sign" (Luke 11.29).

For Abraham, our model, faith consisted in believing in a promise of posterity: "Neither did he consider his own body, now dead, whereas he was almost an hundred years old, nor the dead womb of Sara" (Rom. 4.19). With Zachary, faith would have consisted in believing the angel's word in spite of all the appearances. For our Lady, faith consisted in believing that by God's word, her virginity was made fruitful: "Blessed art thou that hast believed those things that were spoken to thee!" cried Elizabeth. And she replied, "Behold, all generations shall call me blessed" (Luke 1.45-48). Mary's blessedness lay in her faith. For the Christian, faith is believing that in the man Jesus, who was seen by all to have died and to be dead, God makes everlasting life spring up for the world.

"Ye of little faith," Christ called his apostles. In that terrifying storm, with their boat almost overturned, and death a certainty, they should have believed that salvation was with them, in this man who lay asleep. Having "little faith" was also the reproach made to Simon Peter: "Why hast thou doubted?" As the wind and waves tore against him, he should have rejected everything his senses told him, and believed, at Christ's word, that he could walk on the sea.

Faith as participation in Christ's resurrection

Yet, for one brief moment, St. Peter did embody in the storm the magnificent, serene image of the believer who can walk on the water. At God's word, he left his boat with its security, and risked all by setting out to walk on the water. He left the sphere of this world, and trusted himself to the forces of the Kingdom; delivered to death, he became a son of the resurrection of the dead in the power of the Holy Ghost. "Buried with him, in whom also we are risen again by the faith of the operation of God, who hath raised him up from the dead" (Col. 2.12).

The believer has attached himself recklessly to Christ, and has entered into communion with this man whose existence is a mystery of death and of entry into the life of God. His own existence is from now on rooted in that of the Christ placed at the centre of his personality—"May Christ dwell by faith in your hearts" (Eph. 3.17)—who communicates to him his own power of eternal life. In Johannine terms, the believer "comes" by faith, drinks from Christ's side the flowing waters of the Spirit of resurrection (John 7.39); he eats Christ's body, drinks from the eternal spring (John 6.35), and possesses eternal life (John 6.40)[8].

Thus, by communicating in Christ through faith, the believer is charged with the dynamism of the Resurrection, with that immense power of the Last Day which will raise up the whole of mankind: "The exceeding greatness of . . . his power which he wrought in Christ [is exercised] towards us who believe" (Eph. 1.19).

That is why faith works miracles. Christ is risen, all power is given him in the eschatological kingdom, and he grants to those that believe in him to do greater things even than those he himself did on earth.

[8] "He that believeth in me, he said, comes to me, and he that cometh to me, possesseth me. What does it mean to possess him? It is to possess eternal life." (St. Augustine, *Tract. in Joh.*, XXVI, 10; PL 35 [1610].)

Even during Christ's life on earth, faith in the kingdom of God raised men above the earthly state and made them do signs, wonders and marvels. Peter walked on the water in so far as he had faith. "Daughter, thy faith hath made thee whole," Our Lord said to the woman with the issue of blood (Mark 5.34). "He could not do any miracles there . . . because of their unbelief" (Mark 6.5-6). When the Apostles asked him why they had not been able to drive out a devil, they were told: "Because of your unbelief. For, amen, I say to you, if you have faith as a grain of mustard seed, you shall say to this mountain: Remove from hence hither, and it shall remove; and nothing shall be impossible to you" (Matt. 17.19).

Faith which is of no value to the eyes of the flesh, a mere mustard seed, smallest of all the seeds of the garden, has no limit to its power, for it is the power of God who creates the new world. It works the miracle of transforming our life, a thing so small that of itself it would be lost in the emptiness of all things, and fills it with the holiness of God. A tiny seed, and at the same time a tree in which all the birds of the air can nest.

Because he believes in the action of God raising Christ, the believer takes hold of that power of the new world, he believes, and he speaks: "I believed, for which cause have I spoken" (Ps. 115.10; 2 Cor. 4.13). The apostle works, never doubting, never stopped by failures, because he can see Christ's cross, where success is.

Thus faith brings salvation: by the object to which it clings, in which it communicates, which is Christ in the salvation of his death and resurrection. "He that believeth shall be saved" (Mark 16.16). From this death and resurrection that go with faith, the believer is brought to realize the oneness of his being in faith, is obliged to engage himself totally in what may well be called the crucible of Christ's death and resurrection. During his life on earth, he remains weighed down by a remnant of his former self, a piece of the "old man" not yet rejuvenated by grace, of the "outward man" which still conceals the "inward man." The believer must make himself one by his own efforts, by impressing a single movement upon his divided being, in order that he may be a Christian through the salvation already achieved, and through his movement towards total salvation. Faith is doomed in anyone who does not want to carry that death and that life into "his outward members," whose heart is divided between "the flesh" and the Spirit. Faith, which is the beginning of dying and of risen life, and a movement towards the fullness of that death and that life, can only be grievously harmed by any turning back to "the flesh," until eventually the wound becomes mortal, and man re-makes his unity—if unity is then the word for it—in the fact of belonging to "the flesh." Every sin to which we assent is a threat to faith.

Welcome to the question: if salvation is gained by faith, what room is there for the power of a sacrament? Salvation lies in faith, and yet Scripture also attributes the fullest efficacy to baptism. Each of them effects salvation perfectly: does not one, then, exclude the other? While recognizing that both are fully efficacious, Scripture does not separate them. Though faith effects salvation wholly, it does not effect it alone. Faith and sacrament effect salvation wholly, each in its own way. The exemplar sacrament, the Eucharist, helps us to understand this difference of opinion. The Sacrament is an objective means, placing the grace of the Kingdom, the redeeming Christ, at man's disposal. But it remains for faith to welcome it, to eat the bread of heaven, to assimilate Christ and his mystery of salvation.

There is no substitute for faith in the work of our salvation. The Sacrament works by its own power, *ex opere operato,* yet remains without effect in us in the absence of faith. For though the power to nourish us is in the bread of the Sacrament, it is faith that eats, digests, and assimilates it.

For sacraments to be efficacious, then, faith is not merely a necessary condition, its power coming together with that of the sacrament. The mystery of salvation works of itself and man works by receiving it. "They that are Christ's, have crucified their flesh" (Gal. 5.24), says St. Paul, underlining man's part in the death whereby he is saved. "You are washed" (I Cor. 6.11), he says also: for though the Spirit of sanctification is given by washing with water, it is still man who enters that water by faith. Therefore he attributes justification to faith as well as to baptism: "Buried with him in baptism, in whom also you are risen again by faith . . ." (Col. 2.12).

Salvation is always offered in its fullness. It is not always accepted. That the holiness of many Christians does not increase, despite frequent reception of the sacraments, is due to a failure of faith, the faith that attaches itself firmly to the salvation of Christ's death and resurrection.

III. *CHRIST, THE SOURCE OF FAITH*

There is a text that is famous for the difficulty involved in interpreting it: "He rose again for our justification" (Rom. 4.25). This text has often been seen as the conclusion of a chain of reasoning. The Resurrection, it is said, is a proof; it proves Christ's divinity, and God's acceptance of the sacrifice of the Cross; it is the great miracle which, by providing a motive of credibility, makes faith possible. And faith is the principle of our justification. Thus "he rose again for our justification." This would make the Resurrection only indirectly the cause of our justification, by means of the faith for which it supplies an adequate proof, a rational basis. But this is far from St. Paul's line of thought. According to him, God's action in raising Christ is justifying and sanctifying in itself, and directed not only to Christ alone, but to the justification of all mankind, to raising them together with Christ into the life-giving holiness of the Holy Spirit. Once, Christ was "made sin for us" (2 Cor. 5.21), now, by the Spirit of the Resurrection, he "is made justice of God" (I Cor. 1.30), and we are made so with him. God's action in raising Christ is not merely the great miracle, the motive of credibility, but the great grace of redemption, of universal justification.

It remains true that in us the principle of justification is faith, that faith is at the origin of our new life. While it is true that we are justified by God's action in glorifying Christ, it is by that same action that we are made believers. But the Resurrection is not simply a marvellous intervention by God intended to authenticate our faith; it is the universal grace of salvation which makes us God's believers. The grace of faith is contained in the redeeming glory of God which shines out in Christ.

The cause of our faith

In his glorification, Christ has become the principle of all the economy of salvation, for God has made all the fullness of the divine life dwell in him.

Christ in glory, the fullness of salvation

Stoic philosophy used the word "pleroma" to describe the universe filled with the power of divine life. St. Paul tells us that God has made the whole pleroma dwell in the man Jesus, raising him up from the dead. All fullness of being and of creative and sanctifying power is concentrated in Christ, in this man who is Son of God, who has, in his resurrection, attained the perfection of his filial being: "In him it hath well pleased the Father that all fullness should dwell" (Col. 1.19). In Christ, the Lord, is summed up the fullness of God's power, the eschatological force of the world to come, the whole life-giving holiness of the God who creates that world. "The Lord is the Spirit," says St. Paul again (2 Cor. 3.17), and in that spirit, the rich and complex pattern of his thought sees the holiness of the Holy Spirit, and the fullness of being and life-giving power personified by him.

The Synoptics had, more simply, presented Our Lord as the personification of the Kingdom of Heaven. The Kingdom which comes at the end of time, in which dwells the sanctifying glory, the redeeming power of God; for them, this Kingdom is concentrated wholly in Christ who comes upon the clouds of heaven.

Christ in glory, the source of salvation, and first of faith

That Kingdom which is coming at the end is the source of the whole economy of salvation, of all the realities that lead to it.

To St. Paul, Christ is "the principle" (Col. 1.18); this means that he is the leader, but also that he is the cause and origin. In this same verse, he is called "the first-born from the dead"; this indicates not merely that he opens the era of the Resurrection and walks at the head of all who are raised from the dead, but further that he is the "prince of life" (Acts 3.15), that the resurrection of all the dead is in him. God has willed it so "that in all things [Christ] may hold the primacy," primacy of perfection and of dignity, and, even more important, of causality, "because in him, it hath well pleased the Father, that all fullness should dwell" (Col. 1.18-19).

That is why the imperfect realities that came before, from the creation of the world, and the whole of the economy of preparation for that final Kingdom, are no more than a participation at a lower level, a kind of emanation, an overflow in reverse, of the fullness that is in Christ. We may say that the earlier realities were created by the final reality of which they are a kind of projection in advance in history, that the final Kingdom is the first cause, because it contains the fullness of time and of all things, that Christ is the Alpha just because he is the Omega, because he is the pleroma in which all reality is concentrated.

Thus this creation is based on its highest point which is still to come, Christ in glory; from the beginning it is held in existence by its future "head of the corner": Christ, first born of all creatures. "In whom we have redemption through his blood, the remission of sins; who is the image of the invisible God, the first-born of all creation, for in him were all things created in heaven and on earth" (Col. 1.14-16).

The Old Testament existed because of its fullness—the New, the Redeemer in glory. The history and the realities of the Old Testament were things of shadow which heralded the body casting that shadow: "All these things were a shadow of things to come. But the body [which cast that shadow] is of Christ" (Col. 2.17). St. Paul can therefore say that the rock in the desert was already Christ. Our Lord could use the same word—"temple"—for the sanctuary in Jerusalem and his own glorified body (John 2.19). In each case there are two analogous realities, with the first dependent on the second. The Old Testament, the "pedagogue" that led to Christ, received from Christ the power to go to him and to lead men to him.

A fortiori, then, are the realities of the New Testament, whose purpose is to take us to the Kingdom, simply an earthly presence of Christ in glory and of that eschatological Kingdom: "Henceforth you shall see the Son of Man coming upon the clouds . . ." from now on "he comes," not by casting his shadow upon us, but in person. By his resurrection, Christ comes into the world more than he did while living his earthly life: "I go away, and I come unto you" (John 14.28). He shows himself more than he did then: "Again a little while and you shall see me" (John 16.16). They had seen him only with their bodily eyes, and he had been present only in a bodily way. Present now to the world in all the concentration of a divine presence, he is, though absent to our senses, closer to men and more visible than ever: "Our God Jesus Christ, being in his Father, makes himself better seen."[9]

The Christian reality, all the grace of the New Testament, is simply the presence, though still in a veiled manner, of the Christ of Easter and his power of resurrection. Thus the Church, which is the body of Christ in glory, is the eschatological kingdom of God in its (as yet) earthly realization. Thus the Apostles, who are a presence of Christ in glory acting upon the world, are a life-giving emanation from him, "the good odour of Christ" (2 Cor. 2.15). Thus the sacraments are points of contact between the Kingdom and the world, are indeed that Kingdom really made present— especially the exemplar sacrament, the Eucharist—in order that men may touch it. Thus, too, the invisible graces—of justice, of

[9] St. Ignatius of Antioch, *Rom.,* iii, 3.

faith, hope and charity. They are lights coming from the Light, a shining forth of the mystery of redemption, an extension to us of the power of God raising up Christ. Thus, finally, the visible graces —charisms, prophecies, miracles in the physical order and the moral, such as the holiness of the Church, and her stability and unity. They are simply the effects of the power of Christ's resurrection, signs that the eschatological kingdom, though hidden, is present. The law of the risen life, divine charity, is already made manifest in the world; the Last Time is already opening out as the years go by, that era of the children of the Resurrection, who love with a new love. Miraculous forces are already woven into the pattern of the world, superior to this world's laws, and bearing witness to the liberty of the Spirit who creates and to the power of the world to come. These are the forces of the Last Times, latent in the Church which is, in embryo, the body of Christ in glory, the eschatological kingdom of God.

Christian realities, invisible graces, outward signs, all the things that draw man to faith are not separate from the object of faith itself, but are permanent or passing manifestations of the Kingdom, the object of faith, which is present to the world in the Church; they are the glory of Christ shining through into history. Miracles of holiness, physical miracles which astound, miracles of the grace that calls to our hearts—all are rays of the one and only glorification of Christ, refracted in the prism of the Church and her history, soliciting our faith. Faith is the effect in man's heart of the glory of God in Christ.

The object of faith is also its cause

The object of faith, Christ in his glorification, is at the same time the cause of it, both the miracle we believe and the miracle that solicits our faith, the goal towards which faith runs and its centre. Christ, lifted up like the serpent in the desert, on his cross and in his glory, saves all men who look towards him in faith (John 3.4), and it is he who draws them to him (John 12.32). In the act of

faith as in the whole of sacred history, Christ in glory is the Alpha
and Omega, the beginning and the end.

Since the object of saving faith is the God who raises up Christ
for our justification (Rom. 4.25) and Christ in his saving glory, the
object of faith must necessarily be also its cause. God saves, justifies
and glorifies men by the same action with which he raises Christ—
they are "raised with" him; in that same action he arouses faith in
them, the necessary first step in their justification.

It was in the Holy Spirit that God "justified," raised up his Son.
The Spirit is the gift of justice in whom "we rise with" him. That
is why the Spirit is also the grace of faith by which we profess in our
hearts and proclaim with our tongues the lordship of the risen
Christ (Rom. 10.8-10): "No man can say, the Lord is Jesus, but by
the Holy Ghost" (1 Cor. 12.3).

We believe the mystery of salvation, and that very mystery is
what turns us into believers. To believe is to open one's heart to the
mystery of salvation, and it is by this mystery that man's heart is
opened: "The Lord opened her heart" (Acts 16.14)—"Behold, I
stand at the gate and knock" (Apoc. 3.20).

An abstract truth may be an object of faith, but it could never
be the cause of that faith.[10] But if the truth is a person, if faith is a
personal action, a gift of self, then that truth could not even be an
object of faith without also being its cause: we give our faith to
God who reveals himself in Christ, and who, revealing himself in
Christ, "draws" (John 6.44) us to Christ and inclines us to give him
our faith: just as the sun, which we see with our eyes, is what makes
it possible for us to see at all.

Unlike what happens with human faith, Christian faith has an
immediacy of knowledge, a grasp of the object believed: truth
makes itself known to the believer, is itself taken hold of—the first
truth which is the very person of Christ.[11] That is why Christ is the
object of faith only in his glory, in the revelation of his mystery,

---

[10] If we believe upon a man's word a truth which is not in itself evident,
the cause of our faith in that truth is not the truth itself, but the authority of
the man who tells us of it.

[11] This revelation of Christ, however, remains veiled.

when men can gaze in him at the light of redemption, can hear the word of salvation, can recognize the Son. "He manifested his glory and his disciples believed in him" (John 2.11). So on the eve of his passion, he prayed the Father to let the glory of the Son shine through his Christ, so that all men might believe in him (John 17.1-5). The Father heard this prayer, and by glorifying his Son, invited men to believe.

Our Lord had foretold a sign—there would be but the one—that would establish the Christian faith in the world: that sign was to be the very object of faith, Christ risen from the dead: "As Jonas was a sign to the Ninivites, so shall the Son of Man also be to this generation" (Luke 11.30). He had proposed the same sign to the priests when they asked him, "What sign dost thou show unto us?" and he replied, "Destroy this temple, and in three days I will raise it up" (John 2.18-19). Christ's resurrection is the foundation of all faith, a miracle to authenticate it and a grace to draw us towards it.

Faith involves an encounter with Christ in glory

No one can believe without having seen that magnetic sign, without having met, somewhere along the road to Damascus, Christ risen from the dead. The ways of conversion are numberless, for there is no end to the possible meeting-places, the places where the risen Christ can appear. The Kingdom is, from now on, at the centre of the world, and can show itself on any part of its surface: in the Church, in her faithful, her preaching, her sacraments and other signs. But in the last analysis, if man is to come to faith, Christ must personally offer himself to him, must appear to him in the upper room of his own heart. Only then could Thomas cry: "My Lord and my God!" Only then could the people of Sichar, drawn by what the Samaritan woman had told them, say to her, "We now believe, not for thy saying: for we ourselves have heard him, and knew that this indeed is the Saviour of the world" (John 4.4-42). The Word itself—which is a person—speaks to man to win his faith.

This encounter with Christ inspires love, and that beginning of love helps to arouse faith. "No man can come to me [in other words, believe in me], except the Father draw him" (John 6.44)— but by what chains does the Father draw men to Christ? There are chains of the heart, St. Augustine tells us, holy delights of the heart by which man is drawn along. God draws us by these. "Man delights in truth, delights in happiness, delights in justice, delights in everlasting life—and Christ is all these."[12] The Father begets his Son to the world in the Incarnation, begets him to the world in majesty by raising him, and begets him for us also by raising him. And that is how he draws men to Christ: he begets his Son in whom he is well pleased (Luke 3.22) for them. All Christian life begins where it ends: in charity.[13] If there were no element of charity in faith, how could faith lead to charity?

To believe, one must accept the grace of Christ's resurrection

One cannot then attain faith without letting oneself be opened by this grace, without welcoming this divine grace which raised up Christ for the salvation of the world. The same miracle will rouse faith in some and leave the incredulity of others untouched. One must have an open heart, a heart in a state of prayer, a state of longing and humility. For prayer is the breach in man's self-sufficiency, the opening for God's grace of resurrection. If anyone is to be brought to faith, he must be made to pray. He must pray to be preserved in faith. Faith cannot die in a man who prays. But where prayer fades out, faith is stifled; and if faith grows weaker in an individual or a nation, it means that the level of prayer has gone down.

Needless to say, this grace of prayer is itself an effect of God's

[12] *Tract. in Joh.*, 26,4; *PL*,35(1608).
[13] "Fides, quae est donum gratiae, inclinat hominem ad credendum secundum aliquem affectum boni, etiamsi sit infirmis"—"Faith, which is the gift of grace, even if not yet transformed by charity, moves a man to believe by giving him some inclination towards good" (*Summa*, pt. 2 of pt. 2, 5.2, ad 2).

action in raising Christ, an effect of that action which creates the new world and which we are called on to accept. But this grace is given to all, for God raised up Christ for all. It is up to man to follow the call of prayer, which is the first call of faith.

Living within the Kingdom of the Resurrection

Since faith is an effect of the mystery of the Kingdom, of God's holiness and power of resurrection which have blazed forth in the man Jesus, it will be the stronger and more living in us as we live more inside the Kingdom, more wholly subject to that power of justification.

To believe firmly we must love; we must love Christ and live by him if we are to believe in him fully. If you live in Christ, faith becomes a necessity; it is like sap rising in your mind and heart; it produces its natural result which springs from the root of all faith and justice—the risen Christ, become the root of the Christian life.

In St. Polycarp's letter to the Philippians, we find this curious statement: "Faith is the mother of us all; it is followed by hope and preceded by love of God."[14] This text may mean nothing more than that charity has a primacy of dignity. But it would be right to see it also as having a primacy of causality: charity can be the source of faith. After all, the source of all life in the Kingdom is the Holy Spirit, principle of the risen life of Christ, that spirit which impresses itself on man in the form of charity. At the very root of the Christian life is the Holy Spirit, is divine love. The Spirit of God who is total openness and gift of self, opens man's heart to Christ, the Word of God, and leads man to give him his faith.

Though faith is the threshold, at the outset of our journey,[15] and charity is at its end, once man has attained charity, then that becomes the beginning: the pinnacle of the spiritual life becomes its living base. Thenceforward all virtue grows from that root and

[14] St. Polycarp, *Phil.*, 3,3.
[15] Yet there is in faith itself, as we have seen, a first element of charity which inclines the mind to accept divine truth.

is fed by it; the spiritual house is based on its summit and grows by means of it. We love in order to believe. You cannot have the root without the fruit that must grow from it, cannot have the Holy Ghost without faith and hope.[16]

The believer who loves hears the Word in his heart

As long as the believer was not yet established in the charity of the Kingdom, the word of God was mainly addressed to him from without, by the Apostles and the whole visible Church, those organs by which Christ in glory makes contact with the, as yet, alien world. Now the believer loves and is inside the Kingdom, Christ speaks to his heart directly and without words, in the depths of his soul where he now dwells. There are still words to be heard from outside by the body's ears, and they, the Church's words, remain the standard of faith. But while these words are taught from without, the Word himself can be heard within the heart. "He that believeth in the Son of God, hath the testimony of God in himself" (1 John 5.10).

God begets his Word in the believer and for him, in order that he may have faith in that Word. It is addressed directly to him, once he has become "one" (Gal. 3.28) with Christ in charity. In such a believer, the Church in the world achieves her goal; she has made him hear the *word* of God, and now it is the Word that he grasps. "Let the unction, which you have received from him, abide in you. And you have no need that any man teach you, for his unction teacheth you" (1 John 2.27).

Thus the believer will find the proof of his faith in his own heart. However it is expressed, whether by preaching or miracle or the example of the saints, the word of God always bears its proof within itself, a light which is its own witness.[17] And when the complete,

---

[16] This is the sense in which St. Alphonsus Liguori explained the text, "Charity believeth all things." Cf. *La Practica di Amar*, ch. 15.

[17] "The Light bears witness to itself; it opens eyes which are healthy; and it is its own witness, that the light may be known." (St. Augustine, *Tract. in Joh.*, 35,4; *PL*,35[165].)

personal Word is present in his heart, then the believer possesses the proof completely. We love in order to believe.

The believer who loves bears the realities of faith in his heart

All Christian truths belong to him: they are part of his being. He is indwelt by the Spirit, and therefore by the whole Trinity; by the Holy Spirit he possesses Christ, with whom he is identified; because of the Spirit's love and his communion in the body of Christ, he lives in the community of the saints, united to our Lady and the whole Church. All truth is substantially in the Christian, and he is in it.

The truths of faith become connatural to the believer. Though they may seem incredible to the unbeliever, they are in no way strange to the believer who loves, because he is not alien to them. They are, as it were, part of the family, and he is at home and at ease with them. There may be a thousand objections to which many believers could give no theoretical reply; but they will not leave this house, for it is home. It may seem from time to time, in dark moments, that faith contradicts what their reason tells them, that they must leave it if they are to be faithful to reason. But they will realize that such a course would be much more fundamentally unfaithful, for it would be unfaithful to their being, to what they know, in spite of everything, to be true, to what they live by. The saints have had deeper and more dangerous temptations against faith than those which have led less Christian men to stop believing. But none of them apostatized, for they would have been denying themselves, renouncing a reality which they bore with love in their hearts, the lord Jesus who had become their own.

A believer of this calibre no longer asks for outward signs, for miracles or revelations, words spoken outside himself. He says to himself: "It would be unfaithful to demand such signs, for a more genuine sign is imprinted upon my heart." When people kept asking for signs, Christ made that sad reply so often echoed by great

religious writers: "Unless you see signs and wonders, you believe
not" (John 4.48). The true believer is content to "do truth" (John
3.21), to remain faithful to the grace of the Father drawing him
(John 6.44), to have the testimony of God within him (1 John
5.10), to let himself be taught by the inner "unction" (1 John 2.27),
and thus to merit the blessing promised when our Lord said,
"Blessed are they that have not seen and have believed" (John
20.29).[18]

Feeding upon the Eucharist, in order to believe

All that was said of the risen Christ, the cause of our faith, is
clearly proved in the Eucharist, that "sacrament of faith." It is so
called, not because it presents more difficulties to faith than the
others, but because it actually contains the mystery of faith and
for that very reason gives us power to believe.

Two priests were speaking of the Eucharist. One of them admitted the great difficulty he found in believing it, but the other
declared that only in it did he find the power to believe it. It contains the whole mystery of faith, the mystery of salvation, and is
therefore the source and strength of the Church's belief, the sacrament of her faith.

On the south doorway of Strasbourg Cathedral are depicted the
Synagogue and the Church. The one is shown as an uncrowned
woman, her eyes covered, her sceptre broken—a broken woman.
The other is a regal woman with a clear gaze, made a queen by her
faith: the Church who draws her power to believe from the
eucharistic chalice she holds in her hand.

In times of persecution, Christians always try to take the
Eucharist to those who are called upon to confess their faith, to
console them, certainly, but more still to give them a share in the
power of the Kingdom, the power of doing great things, the first of

[18] When Christ says: "Believe that I am in the Father . . . Otherwise
believe for the very works' sake," he is showing us that the vital witness is
that given when he speaks directly of himself.

which is believing. The letter from the Churches of Lyons and Vienne tells how the deacon Sanctus, amid the most appalling tortures, "stood firm, without bending or flinching, firm in his confession, bathed and strengthened by the heavenly stream of life-giving water flowing from Christ's side."[19] Sanctus had been nourished by the Eucharist, for, in the Johannine thought so important in the Church of Gaul, it is in Christ's flesh received in the Eucharist that the fountain of the Spirit springs up. (Cf. John 7.37-9; 6.35.)

The Eucharist shows the believer the Kingdom that is to come and annexes him to that Kingdom. The heavens are opened to him and, like the dying St. Stephen, he sees "the Son of man standing at the right hand of God" (Acts 7.55). For the Kingdom, while opening itself to man and giving itself to him also opens man to the Kingdom, opens the eyes of his heart: "Their eyes were opened, and they knew him in the breaking of bread" (Luke 24.31-5). Thus the Eucharist turns the believer into the martyr—the witness before men of the coming of the Kingdom.

There is no denying the difficulty for the human mind in believing the Eucharist, any more than in believing in the mystery of the Kingdom. But for the believer the Eucharist, like the Kingdom, bears proof that it is true within itself. At Capharnaum the Jews had made the objection that Moses had fed the people with miraculous bread: "What sign therefore dost thou show?" (John 6.30). And our Lord simply proclaimed the true bread come down from heaven. Christ's sign was to be none other than the bread of heaven given to those who came to him.

Nowadays our faith can find hardly anything outside itself to support it; we no longer live in a believing society, surrounded by Christian ideas and ways of thinking. It is forced back to its pure state, to leaning only on its true object, on the mystery of the Kingdom. It could barely keep alive in us without the Eucharist, and the Church cannot depend on any of her faithful who do not receive it.

[19] Cf. Eusebius, *Hist. Eccl.*, 5,I; *PG*,20(417).

"Have the faith of God" (Mark 11.22) Christ tells us. And we reply: "I do believe, Lord: help my unbelief" (Mark 9.23). We have one model to help us—the model and succour of all the Church, the true daughter of Abraham, in whom God carried out the promise he had made to the patriarch. The Virgin believed that God could raise up offspring from a barren womb: and how great that offspring was—Jesus Christ, the Son of God, in whom all the new people has come into the world. Her merit was that she believed: "Blessed art thou that hast believed!" Her role now is to help us also to open our hearts to the Word.

7

The Charity of the Kingdom

Our Lord often proclaimed the Kingdom of Heaven, and spoke of it as a feast, a marriage feast. He often spoke of its coming as close.

A few days before his death, he sent two disciples to the town: "Go ye into the city; and there shall meet you a man carrying a pitcher of water, follow him; and whithersoever he shall go in, say to the master of the house, The master saith, Where is my refectory, where I may eat the pasch with my disciples? And he will shew you upstairs a large dining-room furnished with cushions" (Mark 14.13-15). In that room, upstairs, furnished with cushions, Christ that evening inaugurated the feast he had foretold, the feast on Mount Sion spoken of by the prophets, the feast which is the Kingdom of Heaven.

I. EUCHARIST AND KINGDOM

Our Lord had always pictured the Kingdom as a feast. In doing so he was inheriting the prevalent Jewish idea: "Blessed is he that shall eat bread in the kingdom of God" (Luke 14.15), exclaimed a Pharisee during a meal to which Our Lord was invited. And his reply was to tell the parable of the guests at the wedding feast, showing who are to be the elect of the Kingdom.

"Many shall come," said Our Lord on another occasion, "from the east and the west, and shall sit down with Abraham and Isaac, and Jacob in the Kingdom of Heaven: but the children of the Kingdom shall be cast out [of the lighted room] into the exterior darkness" (Matt. 8.11-12). The beggar Lazarus will come into Abraham's bosom; on the dining couch in the feast of the Kingdom he will recline as against his breast. "Enter thou into the joy of the Lord," says the Master to the good servant, join in the joyful feast. And the faithful servants, whose fidelity has not slept, will be brought into his house and made to sit down, and the Master himself will gird himself and serve them in turn. The five wise virgins hold their lighted lamps in their hands and enter the banqueting room, the room of their marriage. This marriage feast will last seven days, say the Rabbis, like every marriage; but each day will be an age.

Our Lord and his Apostles took their places. It was the decisive moment. There was an argument as to who should sit where, just as the disciples had once asked who should have the first place in the kingdom (Luke 22.24). They were alone with the Messiah of Israel and made up his paschal group, the "passahhaburah"; they were the companions of his pasch, "the Twelve," the nucleus of the Israel of the future, that "remnant" of Israel to whom the promises were given. Our Lord had assured them only a little while before: "When the Son of Man shall sit on the seat of his majesty, you also shall sit on twelve seats, judging the twelve tribes of Israel" (Matt. 19.28). Now Christ was renewing the promise: "You are they who have continued with me in my temptations: and I dispose to you, as my Father hath disposed to me, a kingdom; that you may eat and drink at my table" (Luke 22.28-30).

Now the long-awaited Kingdom was at hand, ready to be set up in the world: the feast was to begin. And it suddenly appeared under a totally new form, the form of that most sacred of all feasts, the messianic feast of the pasch: "With desire I have desired to eat this pasch with you before I suffer. For I say to you, that from this time I will not eat it [this Jewish pasch] till it be fulfilled in the

Kingdom of God" (Luke 22.15-16). The feast of the Kingdom was to be inaugurated that same evening; it was to be a paschal feast, not symbolically, but a pasch fulfilled.

All Christ had to say about his Kingdom, all the revelation in the synoptics, had come to its high point of brilliance and of mystery. At the end of time, the people of God were to be brought together as night fell, for the meal of deliverance. And God would preside over the feasters. But this meal was not to be a thing of shadows and signs, the eating of a lamb of one year taken from the flock, nor a feast for the exodus from one part of this world to another. The people would be celebrating the fulfilled pasch, the passover into the final land of joy, by eating the Lamb of God who taketh away the sins of the world.

While they were still eating the pasch of prefiguration, and Our Lord was handing round the ritual chalice, he said, "Take and divide it among you: for I say to you that I will not drink of the fruit of the vine, till the kingdom of God come" (Luke 22.17-18). The Apostles felt themselves to be caught up in a mystery, and anxiety was mingled with the joy in their hearts. Then Christ took bread and said, "Take ye and eat, this is my body delivered for you." He took the chalice and said, "Take ye and drink, this chalice is the New Testament in my blood" (Luke 22.19-20).

This then was the promised Kingdom, the divine Institution of the end of time; this was the feast of the Kingdom, the messianic marriage feast, the pasch fulfilled: the feast of Christ's body and blood, the marriage celebrated in union with that body and blood; a Kingdom made up of Christ and the banqueters round his table, of Christ in his redemptive immolation and the men who ate that lamb of sacrifice.

All the mystery of the Kingdom is contained and expressed in the Eucharist. Of course the Eucharist is not yet the total realization of the Kingdom; it is the sacrament of it, a realization adapted to this world, an imaged expression of its mystery. But the Kingdom will be nothing else. Christ revealed its everlasting reality to that group of men gathered round him for supper in the Upper Room.

The Church in this world finds her definition in the Eucharist she celebrates, the sacrament of herself; she is never more wholly herself than when celebrating it. When perfection comes in the fullness of heaven, the Kingdom will be nothing else than this assembly of Christ and his people in the feast of his pasch.[1]

II. *KINGDOM AND CHARITY*

Because the Eucharist is the sacrament of the Kingdom, revealing it and starting to realize it at the same time, the Kingdom appears as the Kingdom of divine charity, the place governed by God's love in Christ. For, in the light of the Eucharist, the Kingdom is shown to be a banquet—the fraternal banquet of Christ and his people. In times past there was a tremendous significance in sitting round a table together; it created bonds similar to those of kinship. Those who ate at the same table became brothers. This was not only because the joy of feasting together opened their hearts to one another, but because they were all drawing life from the same source, just as brothers get their blood from the same parents. To harm or kill anyone during a meal took on such grave seriousness that God himself was felt to be offended by it. Our Lord was well aware of this ancient idea, and bemoaned the fact that "one of you that eateth with me shall betray me"; "He that eateth bread with me, shall lift up his heel against me" (Mark 14.18; John 13.18).

The Church, the Kingdom of God on earth, is a banquet of brotherhood. The faithful sit at one table, eating one bread, drinking from one cup. "The chalice of benediction, which we bless, is it not the communion of the blood of Christ? And the bread, which we break, is it not the communion of the body of Christ? For we, being many, are one bread, one body, all that partake of one bread" (1 Cor. 10.16-17). For St. Paul, who gives these words a richness beyond their literal meaning, that "communion in the blood of

[1] Cf. Ignatius of Antioch, *Rom.* vii,3; Council of Trent, sess. XIII,6,8.

Christ," that "communion in the body of Christ," means the participation of all in that sacramental bread and in that cup, the union of all with that body, in that blood, and the union of all the partakers among themselves.

The old idea of the fraternal meal finds its "accomplishment" in the Kingdom, finds there the realization of all that it could only promise, and the promise itself exceeded. Moreover, all the first creation was "accomplished" in Christ, for it was simply the shadow cast ahead by a body—Christ's—still to come. The unifying power of this meal goes far beyond that of any other meal, the brotherhood it creates is of a kind unknown before. "For we that partake of one bread are one body." The members of the Kingdom are brethren in a metaphorical sense; but whereas to use a word metaphorically generally weakens its meaning (as with "brothers in arms," for instance), this new reality is scantily expressed by the word we use for it. These men are now brothers— not of course by having a common origin, but much more so. Because of this meal, they live a single life, in a single body, in the person of Christ in whom they are "all one" (Gal. 3.28). To have the same blood is a bond of union, yet it does not prevent men from going their separate ways; but the Kingdom saves them from their original separateness by uniting them at the highest point of their being, in the person of Christ.

Because the eaters of this meal are united to Christ in a single body, the Kingdom is a marriage feast. Christ spoke of the Kingdom as a feast of divine love, of which the closest and deepest earthly love is an image: "The kingdom of heaven is likened to a king, who made a marriage for his son" (Matt. 22.2). The fusion of two beings into one love and one body which earthly love tries to effect, is accomplished by God in the mystery of Christ and the Church, the mystery of the Kingdom. "They shall be two in one flesh. This is a great mystery; but I speak in Christ and in the Church" (Eph. 5.31-2). The new creation, the Kingdom which comes at the end, fulfills the promise which the first creation could never wholly achieve; it attains that union of which this world's love makes but a sketchy outline. A marriage is celebrated in the heights of heaven where Christ unites his bride to his own body in so close a union that she actually becomes his own body.

At the Last Supper, Our Lord showed himself the incomparable bridegroom when he said to his disciples, "Eat, for this is my body." He gives his body to his disciples, unites himself to them in his body, makes them his Church, the body "given" for us. "They shall be two in one flesh," said the prophetic definition. And St. Paul declares: "Because there is but one bread [which is the body of Christ], we form but one body, all who partake of that one bread" (1 Cor. 10.17). The marriage does not cease at the end of the eucharistic meal; the meal is the expression of a permanent nuptial mystery. The Church is Christ's body always, she forms with him "one man . . . one body" (Eph. 2.15-16). "You are all one in Christ Jesus" (Gal. 3.28). She is always the Church, because she unceasingly celebrates the marriage feast, consummating her union with Christ, in a single body. Thus the Church always lives in the moment of supreme love—of which the most intimate and generous mutual self-giving of two human beings is a far-off sign, a faint suggestion. The Church stands at the permanent summit of charity; it is there that she is herself, Christ's body. To fall from that summit would be to fall outside salvation and to cease to be. For she *is* in that she is Christ's body, in that she is the bride, in the moment of charity which joins them together in one body.

From the beginning, Our Lord described the Kingdom in the double image of a fraternal meal and a marriage feast. But before dying and inaugurating the Kingdom in his death, he went beyond these images, took them to the very limits of their meaning. Suddenly the Kingdom appears for what it is: the paschal banquet of redemption, and more than ever the banquet of charity: "I shall not eat this Jewish pasch more until I eat it fulfilled in the Kingdom." The meal in the Kingdom is the meal of the "given" body, of the "shed" blood: "This chalice is the New Institution in my blood," this chalice of blood, this body given in redeeming love, is the New Institution; the Kingdom of God is made up of those who eat the Lamb in his redeeming Pasch.

This Kingdom could not be a fraternal meal, a marriage feast, saving man from selfishness and isolation, without being a meal in Christ's redeeming death and new life. Men sit at table about the sacrificed Christ, and eat him in his death to the flesh, in his risen life. They, in turn, are drawn into that existence of death and of life in the Holy Spirit. They leave their existence "according to the flesh," opposed to the Spirit and his love, the fruits of which are hatred, jealousy, quarrels, and such (Gal. 5.20). They bring to the very roots of their Christian existence a condemnation of selfishness, pride, obduracy, of all that makes for separations.

And this death is like being drunk with a new wine that Christ drinks in the Kingdom of his Father, drunk with this wine, this joy, this new life which is the Spirit of God and his power. The man immolated in his "flesh" is animated by the Spirit, is transmuted into the Spirit, becomes, like the risen Christ, "spirit" himself, "one spirit with him" (1 Cor. 6.17). Now the Holy Ghost is Love; he is the unlimited openness of God, his infinite power of giving himself and receiving others into himself, his power of being absolutely himself in all of them. Wherever he rules, he takes man out of his limitations, makes him open to others at the very depths of his being, makes him capable of receiving God and mankind, of being truly one with others.

It is here, in this pasch of death and divine love, that we find the true marriage feast, the one true marriage that is the response to absolute love. Love dreams of death and eternity. The love that does not long for death and eternity is but a surface love. It wants both at once, both are necessary to it, however incompatible they may appear. If there is no desire for eternity, then there is no absolute will to love. And so it is with the desire for death. For man must die,[2] being unable in his present state to love eternally.

---

[2] God alone can love without "dying" because of his love, for he is spirit, he is love by nature. Whereas man is flesh.

The man Jesus and those who are his, die in a common pasch. He becomes the Bridegroom, his disciples the Church, the Bride in death, two becoming one in a single body.

Thus the faithful unite themselves to Christ in sacrifice, and become Christ more and more in that sacrifice, in the moment of his self-giving when he existed only for God and for mankind. The Church is Christ's body in the act of redeeming us; the children of the Kingdom live in the sacrifice of Christ; they are Christians because they are one with Christ in that heroic moment, at the pinnacle of the love in which he gave himself to the Father for the salvation of man. They are Christians, they are the saved, because they are in that love, in the movement that lifts them out of themselves up towards God for the salvation of all.

Peter and the other Apostles, and following them Paul and all true disciples, meet in the Upper Room and eat the paschal Lamb. And that is where they become Christians, in their union with Christ at the moment of his pasch. They have now no more right to refuse their life to others—"He hath laid down his life for us: and we ought to lay down our lives for our brethren" (1 John 3.16). Having died to themselves, they have no longer any right to think of themselves and forget others.

The redeeming charity in Christ's heart "presseth us" (2 Cor. 5.14); it becomes the Church's law of life and movement; it imprints upon her a whole new psychology, profound instincts, irresistible urges, "the desire of the Spirit" of life (Rom. 8.6). Had we the eyes to see the Church in her deepest mystery, as it is expressed in the lives of the saints, we should see there the body of Christ in its redemptive holocaust, "one body and one Spirit" (Eph. 4.4), the body of Christ the Redeemer in the fire of the Spirit.

When then shall we be Christians, shall we be saved? We must pray to Mary, in whom the mystery of the Church is wholly realized, to intercede for us unworthy Christians, and obtain that we may thus die and live, that we may be saved in love.

If charity is the law of the whole Church, it must first be the law of the Twelve who were in the Upper Room. They were made priests by the Eucharist, created in it, established in their function by the very institution of the Eucharist, by the setting up of the Kingdom of charity. They were created in the charity of the Redemption.

The apostles in the Upper Room symbolized the entire Church, her base and her summit; they were the Church in miniature, made up of those who ate the paschal meal together: they must be the base and summit of charity. They were the first to eat Christ's body, the first, in Christ's plan, to be transformed into that body that was to be given to millions of men, eaten by millions. Was Père Chevrier in fact saying anything new, when he said so magnificently: "The priest is a man eaten"? No, this says nothing not already quite clearly said in Scripture. No brilliant insight of any Christian thinker is ever anything but a new grasp of something absolutely fundamental and obvious and clearly stated in the Gospel, for it is always the Gospel which is least understood, most fresh to our mind.

III. *THE QUALITIES OF CHARITY*

We must love, then: that is the law of the Kingdom. But, "Who is my neighbour?" asked a doctor of the Law (Luke 10.29); and Our Lord's answer shows that love of neighbour means of all men, whether friends, strangers or even enemies. However, there are in our contacts with one another, differences of degree which, though they do not prevent charity from shining upon all men, give each ray a special kind of brilliance. Some have thought that the brother I should love most is not my neighbour in the faith, but the distant brother with whom I am linked only by our common human origin. St. Paul says no: "Work good to all men, but especially to those who are of the household of the faith" (Gal. 6.10). The Kingdom is where charity is in the world, and it is first of all within its frontiers that love must reign, among those who feast together in the Upper Room. It is to them that Christ says, "Love one another, as I have loved you" (John 15.12). Peter, John, James and Bartholomew must love each other as Christ loves them, with that charity that springs up in the heart of the Kingdom, in the Heart of the Lord. They must love each other, not simply with a kind of *esprit de corps,* not from loyalty to the group, but because they are united in the love of God, members of the Kingdom of charity.

Then too, Christian needs the charity of Christian more than anything else. It is hard to be a Christian, and no one could remain one without the love of his brethren. So Our Lord wills that his followers, "his little flock" (Luke 12.32), should be beloved, for they are the Lamb's flock, "little" as he was himself, humble as children before God and before the malice of the world. He sees them at the mercy of ravening wolves (Matt. 10.16), hated by the nations (Matt. 24.9), and, in his care for them, he wants these "little ones" to support one another, those who are naked clothed, those in prison visited, those who are thirsty given a cup of cold water (Matt. 25.35 ff). In each of these "little ones" it is he himself who is in prison, thirsty, naked, he who is the centre and totality of the Kingdom.

How can the Kingdom be a fire to warm the world around it, if its own coals do not glow together? Charity cannot reach a distant brother if it does not shine more strongly still on the brother who is close. I must first love those who sit with me round the Lord's table. It is more genuine and far more difficult—this everyday love of the brother in Christ who is always beside me.

But the Kingdom does not enclose its charity within the limits of its own boundaries. Its law is love, and its relationship with the world must fit that nature and be a relationship of love. The subjects of the Kingdom, united in the Body that is given for all, for the forgiveness of all men's sins, and transformed into the Body so that they exist now only in it, lead a life of universal charity, for the salvation of the world. Thus the believer will also love those who hate him: he will bless those who curse him; he will love with persistence, turning his left cheek to the man who has struck his right; he will heap the fiery coals of charity on his adversary's head. That is what loving my neighbour means.

And what is my charity? What manner of thing is it? It is a love; it says to its object: "I love you." In fact it is Love at its highest point, in all its perfection and power, the Holy Spirit who is the centre of all the love given in the world. Our charity is love; therefore it is a gift of one person to another. We do not love our neighbour on the rebound, so to say, of our love for God, because of another being whom we love with love; we love our neighbour in himself. It is there, in the very person of our neighbour, that we love and make contact with God and Christ, for it is in his person that our neighbour is united with Christ, or is destined to be united with Christ. And Christ's love is personal in the same way. Christ gives his body not to mankind in a lump, but to all men, giving it to each one, to me personally, to me—because I am me. It is the love of a brother, of a bridegroom: "Who loved me and delivered himself for me" (Gal. 2.20).

That is how he loved men even during his life on earth. Though some texts seem to suggest it, Christ did not cure people collectively: "But he, laying his hands on every one of them, healed them" (Luke 4.40). Each cure was a personal encounter, between him and an individual. He was not content merely to touch the patient with his words, but actually laid his hand on his infected body: "Jesus, stretching forth his hand, touched him, saying: I will, be thou made clean" (Matt. 8.3). For a leper it would have been the first time since the onset of his illness that he had felt the touch of a human hand.

One evening, Christ took a boat, crossed the lake on a stormy night, and reached the opposite bank when it was morning. He delivered a man there from the legion of devils that possessed him, and then Christ returned. He could have prayed God to have mercy on that man, could have commanded the legion from a distance. But the entire object of that rough voyage was to encounter this man who must be saved.

Charity is love; it is also an affection and tenderness, a "caritas" which makes our neighbour "carus," dear to us. In the banquet of the Kingdom which the faithful live by, Christ is total outpouring, wholly given and communicated. For he is wholly transformed into the Holy Spirit who is a giving. That is why the saints, as the Curé of Ars used to say, have "liquid hearts." That is how Christ loved on earth: "he had pity," the gospels so often tell us. He could not bear to see the widow overcome by the death of her only son. "Weep not" (Luke 7.13). He could not bear it, and raised up the young man because of this woman and his own heart. When the messengers told Jairus, "Thy daughter is dead: why dost thou trouble the master any further?", Our Lord was quick to forestall the man's despair: "Fear not, only believe" (Mark 5.35-6). He did not want to see such grief burst forth. His charity was deeply felt, wholly personal.

Yet it was not sentimental, not simply a natural instinct. There are some who confuse charity with the leanings of their affection —*Saepe videtur esse caritas et est magis carnalitas*: it often seems to be charity when it is really natural emotion[3]—whereas the Kingdom is a feast that takes place on Calvary, at which Christ's body is given to his disciples in death to "the flesh." Charity and joy unfold in death to the flesh, holy and pure, fruits of the Spirit which have ripened from the fire of sacrifice. St. John, who generally says that we love God if we love our neighbour, departs from his usual formula to say: "In this we know that we love the children of God: when we love God, and keep his commandments" (1 John 5.2). True brotherly love is judged by this criterion, for it is the holy charity of God extended over his Kingdom.

Thus, philanthropy by itself is not charity either, nor any other act of community or devotion: "And if I should distribute all my

[3] *Imitation of Christ*, I,I, chap. 15.

goods to feed the poor . . . and have not charity . . ." (I Cor. 13.3).
Charity is the divine reality, it is the presence of the Spirit communicated in the body of Christ, and is to be found only in the
Upper Room.[4] Therefore the precept of charity is not addressed
indiscriminately to all men. The rest, heathen and publicans, love
those who love them, salute only those who salute them. "But I
say to you that hear: Love your enemies, do good to them that
hate you" (Luke 6.27). Our Lord cherished no Utopian idea
of uniting all mankind in charity. Only the Kingdom is the realm
of God's love, and some will choose to remain outside it. Outside its boundaries people will still love in human fashion and
will still hate. Only the disciples of the Kingdom will love and love
divinely.

Charity could never carry its heroism to such a high point were
it not a divine reality. To love our neighbour as Christ loved (John
15.12), to turn the other cheek, to give our cloak to the man
who has already taken our coat, all this does not belong to the
domain of human reason at all; such behaviour presupposes a
different sort of nature. Charity is a new law in a new order of
things. The Father in heaven, who "maketh his sun to rise on the
good and bad" (Matt. 5.45), imposes his divine ways on the
members of his Kingdom, for he has made them his sons in his
own true Son, he has given them his nature and placed his own
Spirit in their hearts. Charity can do all things; it proves itself
to be the Spirit of God, the eschatological power of the Kingdom
which has appeared in the resurrection of Christ.

That power is active, it is a power of expansion; the Kingdom
spreads through the world by charity. The faithful are missionaries
—if they are true subjects of that Kingdom—because they love.
Sometimes the charge is made that their zeal is not disinterested,
that their charity has an ulterior cause, that they have a spirit of
conquest; yet what they are is simply men who love. The cause
they serve is that of all mankind. They want to make them all

---

[4] It is, however, true that the frontiers of the Kingdom extend beyond
their visible markings.

come in to the marriage feast, to give them all that best of all bread, the body of Christ, the only bread which truly satisfies man's hunger. "Your fathers did eat manna in the desert and are dead . . . the bread that I will give is my flesh for the life of the world" (John 6.45-52). Charity wants those it loves to have all the good things they need. But being a love in faith, a supernatural love, it longs above all to get them the "true good" (Luke 16.11). For its brethren in the faith who possess the Kingdom already, it desires an even greater possession. It watches with care over their fidelity and their progress in salvation: "Consider one another, to provoke unto charity and to good works: not forsaking our assembly as some are accustomed; but comforting one another" (Heb. 10.24-5). And there, kneeling in prayer, in the midst of the assembly, every believer must beg that all his brethren may become saints, true children of the Kingdom in charity.

8

Weakness and Power

Man is saved in the death and resurrection of Christ. If it is to be Christian and saving action, all that we do must be a participation in that death by which Christ went into life. Our Lord's death is the radical weakness of the sinful race of Adam, the poverty at the very root of human nature, man's denial of self and complete abandonment to another: an existential humility. This self-stripping is willed by Christ, is indeed loved, in response to the infinite power and abundant life of God. Our Lord's resurrection is the life-giving holiness and justice of God, the omnipotence of God, his creative power, invading the man Christ who is of himself completely poor, whose weakness lays him open to that invasion.

Death and resurrection, total weakness accepted by man and filled with the omnipotence of God—these are the two facets of the redemptive act. The first opens the door to the second. They are also the two facets of Christ's eternal existence, in which glory and power are possessed by an immolated humanity, laid open to God, abandoned wholly to him: the Lamb stands erect in his immolation. The two elements are not separated, with the immolation on one hand and the glorification on the other: the supreme humility of Calvary is eternal, linked with the glory and indistinguishable from it; it consists of God's domination in man who accepts it, in the total welcome given by weakness to glory.

The Christian in his turn is caught up in this double paradox; his life must be wholly conformed to Christ the redeemer who is glorified by dying to himself. On the one hand there is man's death, his poverty, his admitted and willed weakness. On the other, in equal measure, is his resurrection in God, the triumph of divine power, creative grace.

"Although he was crucified through weakness, yet he liveth by the power of God. For we also are weak in him: but we shall live with him by the power of God towards you" (2 Cor. 13.4).

Our resurrection is the work of God alone. It is for us to lay ourselves open to God's raising power, to recognize, with his help, our poverty and weakness, and to accept them—thereby accepting the salvation that comes from God alone, his glory that redeems us. By being united to Christ on the cross, we are made so poor in our own right that we die of it, in order that we may live in him by the power of God. This inward poverty is given various names. It can be called humility or renunciation, abandonment to God or spiritual childhood, or other names each with a slightly different shade of meaning. All are virtues which are described as passive, yet it is they that lift us up to the sovereign activity of God.

I. ACCEPTING WEAKNESS

Humility consists in recognizing ourselves for what we are and in lovingly accepting to be so. Spiritual authors never tire of telling us this: humility is a combination of a true realization of ourselves in God's sight, and a love of that truth. To be wholly poor in face of God's holiness, to recognize and love that poverty, in order that God may be wholly in us. Knowledge is not enough. "To recognize one's wretchedness is not humility, it is merely not being stupid."[1] Humility means accepting our poverty so as to be rich only in God. If we stop to think about it, we only need a

[1] St. Francis of Sales, *Les Vrais Entretiens Spirituels,* VI, p. 404.

little philosophy to feel ourselves as nothing before God's transcendence. But the kingdom is not promised to the wise of this
world, but to the little ones, and if we are to become little, knowledge must be accompanied by acceptance. Without that, humility
is not simply incomplete; it is nonexistent.

We must measure ourselves against God's greatness, against
the eternal majesty of his love and his glory. We must love that
majesty, love our own nothingness, and say in God's presence:
"I am dust and ashes" (Gen. 18.27). We must love both the
glory and the poverty, and we must rejoice in them. Some modern spiritual writers have omitted from their teaching this prostration before God's majesty, performed with the silence and recollection which are part of humility and adoration. By concentrating
too much on man, they would not open him wide to God. Hence
they are shallow and unhelpful.

Man, persuaded of his own nothingness, will also realize his
powerlessness to save himself or others; to be humble he must
accept, and rejoice in, that powerlessness, that the redeeming
power of God be made manifest. "Without me you can do nothing,"
said our Lord (John 15.5). If the mediator who alone is God's word
in the world, in whom alone is God's presence in the world and the
life-giving holiness of the Spirit—if Christ does not communicate
himself to us, how can we hear God, or see him, or live by him?
The distance between God and me is infinite, and God alone can
bridge it, because he is infinite.

As regards salvation, there is nothing men can do: not a thought
nor a word, not a wish nor even the shadow of a wish. "If any man
says that we can by our natural powers think as we should, or
choose any good relative to the salvation of eternal life, in other
words: consent to salvation or to the preaching of the Gospel, without the illumination and inspiration of the Holy Spirit who gives
to all delight in consent and faith in the truth, then he is misled by
a spirit of heresy, and does not understand the word of God in the
Gospel: Without me you can do nothing; nor the word of the
apostle (2 Cor. 3.5): Not that we are sufficient to think anything

of ourselves, as of ourselves: but our sufficiency comes from God."[2] Man must accept this basic poverty and the omnipotence of God which can alone effect salvation. He must rejoice in both, and love them with the same love with which our Lord put himself into the hands of his Father who alone could save him from death (Heb. 5.7).

In practice, unfortunately, we are all Pelagians, we all think we can work out our own salvation. We try to live our life as Christians without adverting to the fact that if we are to succeed, our souls must be totally believing, totally begging, totally opened to the glory of God in Jesus Christ. Sometimes, when we are aware of our lack of strength, of the heartbreaking thinness of our prayer and our love, we become discouraged and settle down at the level of the trivial, instead of desiring God's grace and finding it quite natural that our own ability is non-existent. We are both too self-confident, and too easily discouraged. Instead we should have no confidence in ourselves, and be filled with courage. We think by our efforts to save our brethren, though it would be easier to make the sun shine at midnight than to make the light of God shine upon them.

In practice we are Pelagians. We refuse to unite ourselves to the Christ who offered himself to the power of God in the weakness of death. We simply do not believe in Christ's cross, and in the power of God which alone raised up Christ in that death, in that totally accepted weakness. There should be nothing distressing in these thoughts about our poverty. To be nothing of oneself is the creaturely condition; and it is the very magnificence of the salvation offered us that makes it impossible for us to win it. When we realize that the void in us can be magnificently filled by God, then our poverty should delight us. But there *is* a distressing humiliation which makes our state lower than just that of creatures: we are sinners. We are not merely what is not, but what ought not to be.

We are all sinners: "If we say that we have no sin, we deceive

[2] Council of Orange, II can. 7. DB 180.

ourselves, and the truth is not in us" (1 John 1.8). It might be thought that when he said this, John, the most pure disciple, was not thinking of himself, but speaking in the name of the community that contained both just and sinners. The Council of Milevum declared such an interpretation of the text to be anathema[3]. Anathema too are those who declare that when the saints say, "Forgive us our trespasses," they speak not for themselves but for sinners. "For in many things we all offend" (James 3.2). Daniel, a holy and just man, made this admission: "We have sinned, we have committed iniquity"; and he ranged himself among the sinners, by continuing: "While I was yet speaking, and praying, and confessing my sins" (Dan. 9.5-20).

Even apart from actually sinful acts, we bear within us a disposition to evil, to the things that should be beneath us as men and children of God, and a sluggishness towards good. It is salutary to re-read Romans 7.14-24, and be forced to admit one's own wretchedness. By these fundamental tendencies, we remain virtual accomplices in all the works of pride and of the flesh, brethren of all the sinners in the world.

Even were man, by a merciful purification of his being, to be no longer torn by these lusts of spirit and flesh, he would still remain a being who of himself is capable of nothing but failure. Only God is good, only God is holy. We should always remain those whom God's grace had lifted above ourselves by lifting us above sin: we should be men reprieved.

The best Christians, the saints, have the most acute consciousness of the poverty of their nature and the evil bent of their lives. They call themselves the lowest and most wretched of men. St. Thérèse of Lisieux, whom we know to have been pure as an infant, with her perfect charity, wrote on one side of a leaflet she kept in her New Testament, "Lord, thou knowest that I love thee," and on the other, the prayer of the publican: "Be merciful to me a sinner" (John 21.17; Luke 18.13).

Such knowledge is not as yet humility, for it is merely know-

[3] DB 106.

ledge. Humility knows and accepts, and great humility rejoices. It rejoices not in sin, but in the weakness which is capable of no more than sin and in the infinite holiness of God which is given to that weakness. "How happy I am to feel myself imperfect, and to have such need of God's mercy. It is wonderful to feel oneself weak and small. I am glad always to find myself imperfect; indeed there lies my greatest joy," said St. Thérèse of Lisieux. She was repeating almost word for word something said by St. Francis of Sales: "Even when I feel most wretched, I am not distressed, and sometimes I even rejoice at it."[4] And this, in turn, echoes St. Paul's great cry, "Gladly therefore will I glory in my infirmities, for when I am weak, then am I strong" (2 Cor. 12.10).

II. *FAITH IN GOD'S POWER*

God's strength is given to man's weakness: "when I am weak, then am I strong." These astonishing, paradoxical words can only be explained in terms of the mystery of the death in which there is life, the mystery of the *tam beata Passio,* the blessed Passion. For Christ's death was an acceptance of man's weakness and God's dominion; it was a total opening to God's glory, which is the Holy Spirit, and to his infinite power. The supreme humility of Christ was a triumphal welcome given by prostrate man to the life of God. In our poverty is riches, in our weakness is divine strength; success may be brought about through our human failure, as long as that poverty, that weakness and that failure are accepted and loved so that God's grace may rule us.

The saints rejoiced in their sense of weakness, because they felt it to be open to God's omnipotence, because their own emptiness could be filled by his presence. As for Christ, whose death was crowned with life in glory, the moment of death coincided with the moment of glorification: "Father, into thy hands I commend my spirit." The saints felt the truth of the beatitude concerning pov-

---

[4] Letter to Madame de Chantal, March 4, 1608.

erty, and they realized from it that the Kingdom of Heaven was theirs.

This revelation came to St. Paul. When his authority was called in question, he re-established it by listing the ways in which God's power had been shown in him—the revelations he had been given, the labours, the ecstasies and the sufferings. But it would be folly to boast of such things. He found cause for courage and confidence elsewhere, at the very point in fact where the Corinthians he was addressing found only cause for scorn. Paul is weak, is humiliated. What had humiliated him he does not explain, for evidently the Corinthians already knew. He had a chronic illness, and to begin with he had seen this "angel of Satan who buffeted him" as an obstacle to his apostleship. Three times he had begged the Lord to deliver him from this trouble. But each time the answer came: "My grace is sufficient for thee, for power is made perfect in infirmity." The power of God flashes forth from the weakness of man. So he goes on to utter that cry which has echoed and re-echoed in the Church and will be heard till the end of time, overturning all the judgements of man concerning power and weakness: "Gladly therefore will I glory in my infirmities, that the power of Christ may dwell in me . . . For when I am weak, then am I strong" (2 Cor. 12.9-10).

One special, privileged example shows how all the riches of God lie in accepted poverty—the example of our greatest poverty, our wretchedness in being sinners. Through the New Testament runs this paradox that the wretchedness of sinful man, which in itself is the condition furthest from God, is, once it is recognized and accepted, next door to the salvation of eternal life, is a receptacle for divine grace.

St. Paul must often have spoken of the connection between grace and the poverty of sinners, for unintelligent listeners took his preaching as an encouragement to sin: "Why do not we say (as we are slandered and as some affirm that we say) let us do evil, that there may come good?" (Rom. 3.8). A little later he says: "Where sin abounded, grace did more abound" (Rom. 5.20). This must be taken in the sense, "Because sin abounded," for St. Paul goes on to forestall the objection to this: "What shall we say then? Shall we continue in sin, that grace may abound?" (Rom. 6.1). To prevent such a mistake, one must see exactly what the moral entity of the act of sinning is—failure to conform with the will of God. Seen thus, our act can only displease God. But there is also our weakness as sinners, our despairing poverty, our total inability to gain our own salvation. And this poverty can be a source of grace, a cause for hope. Christ has declared that the son of Man is come to save that which was lost (Luke 19.10). His coming, that majestic and supreme manifestation of divine riches, that coming which will one day remake the world in the glory and love of God, is a grace of salvation which has been given to man *because* he is a sinner.

Why is the grace of God thus rooted in our accepted weakness, in our poverty? Is it because God can only rule in us if our own personality is annihilated? Far from it. God is too great to be able to rule only over nothingness. But he only establishes the dominion of grace at the point where man, realizing his poverty, accepts the riches of his love, at the point where the poverty of the creature opens itself to the power of God.

Is there then some kind of co-operation between God and sin? "God forbid," cries St. Paul (Rom. 9.14). The co-operation is between the poverty of the sinner and mercy. For poverty, if it is recognized and accepted, lays man open to God's mercy. "I have habitually said that the throne of mercy is poverty," said St. Francis of Sales.[5] How blessed, then, is the condition of sinful man. God's mercy uses it as a foundation. "A faithful saying, and worthy of all acceptation, that Christ Jesus came into the world to save sinners, of whom I am the chief. But for this cause have I obtained mercy: that in me first Christ Jesus might show forth all patience" (1 Tim. 1.15-16).

Not only the mercy, but the power, of God is drawn to the weakness of sinful man, for when it is dealing with weakness, God's power is mercy. God proves the might of his arm by scattering the

[5] *Les Vrais Entretiens Spirituels*, **VI**, p. 22.

proud in the conceit of their heart, putting down the mighty from their seat (Luke 1.51-2). But the small and weak have no conceit: for them, "he hath showed might in his arm" by exalting the humble (Luke 1.51-2).

There is no activity more strictly divine, none that shows more clearly the power which saves sinful man: *Omnipotentiam tuam parcendo maxime et miserando manifestas*: Thou dost show forth thy omnipotence by sparing mightily and having mercy.[6] It is not before the justice of God that poor and sinful man must quake. If he but knew the true God, he would long for his justice to be executed upon him; his prayer is, *Judica me, Deus!* Judge me, O God! For God's justice is a gift that is given to the poor. In Scripture, where alone God's face is revealed, God's justice is shown as simply his holiness, his own infinite perfection. Justice of this kind is carried out only by communicating itself; it is a justice that makes others just, a justice of sanctification. Its work is not to reward the works of human justice, for there is no such thing. It is the justice of God which makes men just by giving itself to them; it is itself the cause of every good work we do, and when it rewards merit, it is simply completing the gift it has made. Nor is its job to punish. It only becomes punishment in the man who does not accept it, and only it can save him from that punishment. God's justice is effected by giving itself to the creature who is without it—by justifying him. If there were no poor men, no weak and little men, then justice would have no occasion to be displayed. Thus it may be bracketed together with mercy and power, for, like them, it is exalted and glorified in the salvation of men.

There is another reason why grace prefers what is weak. God watches jealously over the absolute freedom of his sanctifying action, over the total gratuitousness of grace. He allows man no claim over what is his sole possession; man cannot demand the salvation of everlasting life as his due. God's grace always remains a grace, a free gift, a help God gives us in his mercy, a love not owed, but freely given. That is why God chooses folly to confound

[6] Collect for the Tenth Sunday after Pentecost.

the wise of this world; that is why he chooses the weak, the things whose very existence is not admitted by the world, so that no creature can glory in his sight (1 Cor. 1.27-9).

The Jews were cast out of the Kingdom because they thought that their having performed the works of the Law gave them a right to enter it. Why are they not come to justice? asks St. Paul. Because they thought to attain it by works (Rom. 9.31-2). God had said to Moses: "I will have mercy on whom I will have mercy; and I will show mercy to whom I will show mercy. So then it is not of him that willeth, nor of him that runneth, but of God that sheweth mercy" (Rom. 9.15-16). "By grace are you saved, through faith, and that, not of yourselves, for it is the gift of God; not of works, that no man may glory. For we are his workmanship" (Eph. 2.8-10). When man knows that he is helpless and unworthy to be saved, and looks to God alone and his redeeming power, then salvation is given him.

If man lays himself open to grace by so far accepting his sinful condition that he actually rejoices in it, he has certainly escaped the temptation to Pelagianism; but is there not then a danger that he may regard God as the only actor in his salvation, and fall into quietism?

There will be no danger of this, as long as man remembers that God's power does not work upon us as inert objects, that God does not affirm his liberty by destroying ours, but by ennobling it and making it come alive. Thus the gift God gives us of his own holiness is not something to be received passively, but a love in which we share. St. Paul says: "By the grace of God, I am what I am" (1 Cor. 15.10); but he also speaks of corresponding to the measure of the grace given him, and says that "we are God's coadjutors" (1 Cor. 3.9), and that we are created for the good works we are to do (Eph. 2.10).

On the one hand is the poverty, recognized and loved; on the other a great effort. We say that poverty is recognized and loved, "that the power of God may dwell in us." In other words, we become open to the holiness of God in a consent to that holiness given by our entire being, fully and actively.

Every idea in our spirituality must find its place in the framework of the redemption that is in Christ, for our spirituality is wholly Christian, centred upon Christ and his action in redeeming us. No grace comes to us apart from the participation in Christ's death by which we rise with him into life. We must identify ourselves with Christ in his death, in his total self-renunciation, in order that we may share in the power and holiness of God. To experience our weakness and accept it in love is a real means of making ourselves die. No protests that we are nothing, no prostration before God's throne is as sincere or effective as simply the acceptance of our sinful weakness, of the humiliation which makes man blush to the roots of his being. The man who takes delight in his own poverty attains the perfection of humility: he has wholly given up seeking greatness for himself.

And this weakness accepted is a weakness in Christ, a sharing in his death, from which all the riches of the Resurrection flow. For what was Christ's death but the total acceptance of his weakness as man? "He was crucified through weakness" (2 Cor. 13.4). The first Adam lost all by trying to rise above his nature. Christ won salvation by accepting his human weakness right down to its final helplessness—death. This mortal weakness of Christ is simply the weakness of the sinful creature, of the man who has not got the immortal life of God, and his life-giving justice. "He was made sin for us" (2 Cor. 5.21); he had accepted human nature with its failing life, inherited from Adam, and bearing within itself condemnation to death, the seal of sin. And in Christ's acceptance of this weakness of sinful man lies salvation; from it springs the everlasting riches of the life and justice of God. Christ's sacred death in which the world's resurrection is to be found, was simply the total acceptance of his weakness as a son of Adam who sinned.

From henceforth, we can give ourselves over to the wildest hopes, as long as we realize our own weakness and accept it. "Let us not say let us do evil, that there may come good" (Rom. 3.8), for sin can never unite us to Christ's death, in which everything is love and holiness. But our weakness as sinners is another matter; that, if it is accepted, brings us to meet Christ at the moment of his own supreme weakness, and immerses us in his death, when he was received into the hands of his Father. The saints instinctively felt how close their weakness as sinners was to the sanctifying power of God: "O God, I am happy to feel myself small and weak in your sight, and my heart is at peace in joy," said Thérèse of Lisieux. Held above the bottomless pit of their own misery, with no ground beneath their feet, but secure in the hand of God, the saints feel safer than if they were established on the solid ground of their own works and merits.

St. Paul wanted to get rid of all sense of his own justice, "my justice," he calls it, that justice that could be felt and seen; what he had formerly seen as gain, he now rejected as dung, "that I may know Christ, and the power of his resurrection, and the fellowship of his sufferings" (Phil. 3.8-12). Blessed Claude de la Colombière wrote to a nun who, he had been told, was soon going to die: "I must tell you what would do most to give me confidence, if I were as soon going to render an account of myself to God as they tell me you are: it would be precisely the number and magnitude of my sins."[7] "If I were," he says; it is easy enough to say what one would do *if*. But St. Thérèse of Lisieux, actually on her deathbed, said, after a slight burst of impatience: "I confess that I am far happier to have been imperfect than if, supported by grace, I had been a model of patience."

In man are two poles: the weakness of sinful humanity, and the power of God; God's power will be in him in proportion as he accepts and loves his weakness in God's sight. The weakness and the majesty are so interlinked as to become almost indistinguishable: man's poverty, in as much as it is loved, is a receptacle of divine power; it is the grace of its reception, grace as a void to be

[7] *Complete Works of the Venerable P. Claude de la Colombière*, vol. VI, p. 475. Grenoble, 1902.

filled. So it was in Christ: his acceptance of his utter weakness as a man before God was simply the negative aspect of his life in glory.

What is essential is to be poor in God's sight, stripped of everything with Christ on the Cross. It is only Christ whom God raises to everlasting life. He raises us only insofar as we are in Christ and subject to his action in raising him ("we are risen together with him"). And God only raises Christ in death, in a complete acceptance of human poverty. To share in the Resurrection, we must share in the death. The law formulated by St. Paul holds good in all cases, and there are no exceptions to it: "If we be dead with him, we shall live also with him" (2 Tim. 2.11).

The essential is to be poor. There is the beginning of blessedness, there the narrow and low door to the Kingdom which becomes high and wide for those who are small. "Blessed are the poor, for theirs is the Kingdom," the Kingdom of Christ's resurrection. Blessed are the children, the little ones, for the Kingdom is theirs. There, in the poverty which calls for grace, lies the beginning of all fulfilment, of all miracle. Christ multiplied the loaves, because his Apostles had only five for five thousand people. He gave them the miraculous draught of fishes, because they had laboured all night and taken nothing.

All virtues begin with this. Faith, which is the acceptance of our own ignorance, and of the splendours of God's word. Hope in God, which begins at the very moment when we despair of ourselves.[8] Charity, which is forgetfulness of self and self-giving. Humility is the first and universal virtue which accepts the intervention in us of God's life, just as pride, which relies on self whether in satisfaction or discouragement, is the root of all sins. Here lies the mainspring of apostolic fruitfulness, when the apostle knows himself to be poor, and depends on God alone: "When I am weak, then am I strong." The essential is to be poor. But how hard it is to be

[8] "Not only can the soul which recognizes its poverty have great confidence in God, but it can only have true confidence if it does recognize it." St. Francis of Sales, *Les Vrais Entretiens Spirituels*, VI, p. 403.

totally poor![9] "It is one of the most marvellous graces we can receive from Our Lord," said St. Francis of Sales,[10] the greatest grace in a man's life, according to Thérèse of Lisieux. Indeed, it must be so, for it is the perfect transformation into Christ our redeemer, who accepted to be nothing of himself in order that the Father might be everything in him; it is the extending to us of the *tam beata Passio,* and its riches of resurrection. Though it is a totally free gift, yet we must work to acquire this poverty of spirit. It is a question not so much of reflecting how poor we are, but of totally accepting to be so on the manifold occasions when it is brought home to us, and of having perfect faith in the power of God.

Rather than be discouraged by the aridity of our relationship with God, by our distractions at prayer—to be discouraged by these things is in fact to compromise with them—we must accept our weakness and our fundamental helplessness, and hope that God will hear our prayer even though we are not worthy. What the small and weak know is that by giving our nothingness to God to fill, we can gain all things.

When we have failed, when we have sinned, we must not lash out at ourselves, and thus build up our own pride; we must accept that we are weak in God's sight, and must rejoice at it, that God's redeeming power may dwell in us. If we are to be saved from our sinful weakness, we need only recognize and admit it, just as Christ triumphed over death by accepting it. "Ought not Christ to have suffered these things, and so to enter into his glory?" (Luke 24.26). Ought not man to pass through the condition of a sinner, and so enter the glory of the Redemption? God permitted man's sin, and willed its punishment by the mortal weakness of man's flesh. And in Christ it is the acceptance of that weakness which wins for us a life that we should never have been heir to had man not sinned. God wills us weak, and he permits our failings and sins; and it is granted to us to find, in the acceptance of our weakness and the

[9] "One must consent to remain always poor and powerless, and that is what is difficult." St. Thérèse of the Child Jesus, Letter of September 17, 1896.

[10] *Op. cit.,* VI, p. 403.

humiliation of our sinning, the strength and holiness of God. We can only echo St. Paul's hymn to the ever-fresh, inexhaustible wisdom of God: "How incomprehensible are his judgements, and how unsearchable his ways!" (Rom. 11.33).

We must, then, accept our many failures, both in our own lives and in our apostolate, and must work ever more ardently, having faith in the power of God. If we do that then we will rise again, we will succeed through all these failures, even to the last and most complete of them—death. If it is accepted and loved, in order that God alone may govern us, our poverty will be our *vado ad Patrem,* our path to the Father in Christ who redeems us, who brings us into life. And if, when that final moment comes, we remember our sins, and our life passes before us in its utter emptiness, then we must say: "Lord, this is the moment for you to be the great, the holy, the just, the good God. Bless me, then, Father, for I have sinned."

9

Faithfulness to Prayer

Anyone who reads the Fourth Gospel with attention to symbolism, and awareness of the workings of suggestion and evocation, will soon perceive that it is intended to show Christ as the centre of worship for the new people of God. Here, unlike the account in the Synoptics, Christ's life unfolds almost totally in Judaea, within the sacred precincts of the Temple; and nearly all the incidents presented are dated in relation to a liturgical feast. Christ announces that the old cult is to be abolished, whether of Sion or of Mount Gerizim, and that the new worship is to be one of spirit and truth.

I. *CHRIST, TEMPLE OF THE CHRISTIAN PEOPLE*

Our Lord is the Temple of the new people. By coming into the world, the Word has established God's true dwelling among men. "The Word was made flesh and dwelt [set up his tent] amongst us, and we saw his glory" (John 1.14). In the past God had set up his tent in the Hebrews' camp, and had dwelt among his people. Christ dwells amid the new people, God's tabernacle among men. And as in the past, the glory of God, like a luminous cloud, rested over the tabernacle, as a sign of the presence and holiness of God, so we have seen the glory that covers Christ.

The book of Genesis tells how Jacob, fleeing from his brother, fell asleep in a place called Bethel, which means the house of God, and saw, in a dream, heaven opening above him, and a ladder connecting earth and heaven with angels of God going up and down it. When he woke up, he cried, "How terrible is this place! this is no other but the house of God and the gate of heaven!" (Gen. 28.17). When Our Lord went up from the banks of the Jordan to Cana, gathering his first disciples, Nathaniel, in his astonishment that he already knew him cried, "Thou art the Christ, the Son of God," and Christ answered: "Because I said unto thee, I saw thee under the fig tree, thou believest: greater things than these shalt thou see." And he added, "Amen, amen I say to you, you shall see the heavens opened, and the angels of God ascending and descending upon the Son of Man" (John 1.49-51). By thus recalling that mysterious dream, Our Lord must have meant to suggest the conclusion Jacob drew from it: "How terrible is this place!" Our Lord is the house of God, and it is in this place that the door of heaven is open to men.

Some weeks later, he drove the sellers out of the Temple. The priests called him to account: "By what right do you assume this power in the Temple?" and Our Lord replied, "Destroy this Temple and in three days I will raise it up" (John 2.19). The Jews destroy their temple, the home of prayer on earth, built of stone, of which the very presence of the sellers was a profanation! It was not long before they destroyed it. When Christ was put to death, the veil of the Temple was rent, the mystery of the Temple was made void, God left his dwelling-place on earth. "Behold, your house shall be left to you desolate" (Matt. 23.38). The fate of this temple, built with hands, this symbol of the old order, round which the Old Testament people gravitated, was bound up with that of Christ's earthly body. A few years later it fell forever: "Destroy this Temple."

The third day, this temple suddenly rose up in the midst of

God's people. "In three days I will rebuild it." He spoke of his glorified body. On Easter Day, Christ's body became the temple of the new people, the place where they gathered together, their point of unity, the dwelling place of glory where the multitude would rest in adoration, contemplating the face of God, and hearing his word. There they would come to offer the sacrifice of praise and expiation, they would adore and beseech. In the past, the Jews used to pray in a stone temple in Jerusalem. But the hour has come when the true adorers adore in spirit and in truth, in the glorified Christ, the true temple of God's holiness, and in the Spirit of God, the supreme truth and divine holiness, who filled Christ on Easter morning.

From its conception, Christ's body was consecrated in the anointing of the Spirit. But his Hour, the hour of the opening of the Temple, did not strike until his death and resurrection, till he left our profane existence and was given life in the Spirit, who is the holiness, the infinite openness of God. Then the doors of the Temple were flung wide to welcome the new worshippers. It is a temple they will never leave. They will never cease to be "in Christ," and Christ will be a temple forever. Even in the heavenly city, it will be in the Lamb, in Christ dead and risen, that the glory will be revealed, that the faithful will be assembled to contemplate and love God; "And I saw no temple therein. For the Lord God almighty is the temple thereof, and the Lamb. And the city hath no need of the sun, nor of the moon to shine in it. For the glory of God hath enlightened it, and the Lamb is the lamp thereof" (Apoc. 21.22-3).

II. *A PRAYING PEOPLE*

For the Christian, Christ is the principle of existence and of life. And since he is a temple, God's house among us, of which it is said that it is a house of prayer (Matt. 21-13), then it is a temple that Christians are living in, and their duty is to pray. For they are Christians through baptism, and, through baptism, they are in the temple of God. That is why the Church is a chorus of prayer in the world; a Christian's life can never be profane (that is, outside the sanctuary, outside the *fanum*), but is wholly a life of worship. From the first, the Christians were characterized by their almost continual prayer,[1] and even today there are missionary countries where to become a Christian is called "starting to pray."

The people are called by the same name as the gathering of believers who meet to pray—*ekklesia;* it is called the Church, because it is a praying assembly. The Church is aware that constant prayer is demanded by her nature. She hears in her heart the words of our Lord from the Gospel: "We ought always to pray, and not to faint" (Luke 18.1). And because she is, in most of her people, still caught up in the cares of this world, she sets some among them apart from earthly preoccupations, and dedicates them wholly to prayer. We should all be trying to attain this ideal of prayer. We have been united in the depths of our being to the sacred body of Christ in baptism, and we are in the temple. On the surface there are a thousand things to distract us from this consciousness of Christ's presence in our whole being. Our intellect and will, not as yet wholly belonging to Christ and fixed upon him, often stray to follow interests that are purely of this world, and the Christian can detach even his deepest being from Christ through these faculties. But prayer gathers our faculties together in Christ; it summons them back into the temple, and makes our Christian personality a united whole once more. By prayer, whether it be a hymn of praise or an anguished cry of need, a humble request for the bread of soul or of body, perfects and completes the grace of our baptism, the mystery of our identification with Christ: "They shall be two in one flesh" (Eph. 5.31), said St. Paul, comparing the union of Christ and his Church with the union of marriage.

[1] "The ideal of the Christian life was a perpetual communion with God, carried on by as frequent a prayer as possible. A Christian who did not pray daily, and indeed several times a day, was no Christian at all." Mgr. Duchesne, *Les Origines du culte chrétien*, 5th ed., Paris, 1925, p. 467 (available in an English translation, Greenwich, Conn., Seabury, 1954).

In prayer, Christ and his Church speak with a single voice, a single word: *Erunt duo in voce una*: "They shall be two in one voice."[2] "Two in one body," in the body of Christ with which the Church is identified. Two in one word, the word of Christ which the Church speaks in him. If we remember that Christ is the Word himself, we will realize how deep are the roots of Christian prayer.

The Word of God, the personal expression of God's perfection, has always been a word of praise of the Father. "In taking human nature, he had brought into this land of exile that hymn which is forever sung in heaven."[3] But his time on earth was still only the first step in the Incarnation. Then Christ was alone, a man among others, and his prayer as the Son was uttered only in himself. After his death and resurrection, the Incarnation was opened out, the grace of sonship was extended to other men, and with it the prayer of God. The single grain, buried and sprung up into life, has become a great people, an ear weighed down with the nations and their mass of prayer.

This prayer which the faithful utter from within Christ is what our Lord called "prayer in his name." To pray in Christ's name does not simply mean to use his name: "Through Christ our Lord." In Scripture, the name signifies the person, and the phrase "to pray in Christ's name" comes close to the Pauline expression "in Christ," which indicates the intimate communion between Christ and those who believe in him. Prayer in his name springs up from those depths of soul where the Christian is mysteriously identified with Christ, from that mutual compenetration our Lord spoke of after the Last Supper. The promise: "Whatsoever you shall ask in my name that will I do" is indistinguishable from that other promise: "If you abide in me . . . you shall ask whatever you will, and it shall be done unto you" (John 14.13; 15.7). Our Lord declared: "Hitherto you have not asked anything in my name" (John 16.24). How could they have indeed, for Christ's

[2] St. Augustine, *In Ps.* 1xi,4. *PL*,36(370).
[3] The encyclical *Mediator Dei*.

union with his people in a single body was only to come about in the glory of the Resurrection.

This prayer in Christ is always heard. When Solomon celebrated the dedication of the Temple in Jerusalem, he besought that every prayer uttered there would be heard (3 Kings 8.27-53). On the eve of inaugurating the Temple of the New Testament, our Lord promised that every prayer uttered in its sanctuary would be heard: "If you ask the Father anything in my name he will give it to you" (John 16.23) "My house is a house of prayer," we say in the mass of Dedication. "Who prays in it will receive, who seeks will find, and to him who knocks it will be opened."

Why is Christian prayer answered? Because a prayer in Christ is good. There are some churches which, we say, seem to be wholly a prayer, with every stone, every column, every arch, with the sense of a great mystery that pervades them. Christ is thus penetrated with humility, recollection and love; he really is a sanctuary that adores and that draws us into its prayer. He introduces us to the true prayer in which we adopt the attitude of a child, and say, "Our Father who art in heaven." A prayer in Christ can only be the prayer of a son. How, then, could it meet with a refusal, uttered in the bosom of the Father, in the Son whose plea the Father cannot reject without coming into conflict with himself?

III. CHRISTIAN PRAYER, A PASCHAL LITURGY

Above all, this prayer is good, and is answered, because it is spoken in Christ, thus prolonging his sacrifice with its "odour of sweetness" (Eph. 5.2). The Christian cannot be "in Christ" without sharing in the mystery of the Redemption. For the Christ of our Christian life is forever fixed in the fullness of that mystery, in his death wherein is his glorification; and every Christian act is a communion in that mystery.

The temple of the new prayer is the body of Christ raised up on the third day—"in three days I will rebuild it"—the body marked with the five wounds of its permanent immolation. Even in heaven, the temple of the faithful is the paschal Lamb, whom St. John saw as standing, even though slain (Apoc. 5.6). Here the believer meets God, adores him and prays to him, in the slain, the glorified body of Christ which is the "new and living way" (Heb. 10.20) that takes us to God.[4] The redeeming Christ is not just a temple of prayer, but is himself the prayer of Christians, a church at prayer, a prayer already complete, into which we enter. In his everlasting paschal mystery, he is wholly "God-directed," total self-offering; in the hands of his Father he is a prayer that is heard and a thanksgiving: a prayer which is not simply the "lifting up of the mind and heart to God," but the exaltation of Christ's entire being to the Father.

Christian prayer opened with the great cry Christ made at the ninth hour on Good Friday. It began at the moment when Our Lord, leaving his life in this world, entered the bosom of the Father, at the moment when Christ's longing and searching for his Father and his Father's help attained their summit and received their answer in the embrace in which his Father glorified him. At that moment the Church was born, and she continues in that moment, never leaving it. In that moment the Church's prayer was born, and goes on being born there, never leaving it. It extends throughout space and time the supreme prayer Christ said at the moment of redeeming us: "Abba, Father, into thy hands I commend my spirit."

All Christian prayer, whether humble supplication, or triumphant hymn of praise, is a communion in the redemptive act whereby Christ opened himself to the Father and was filled by him. Though it often asks things for itself, it remains always a gift of self to God at least in essence, and it is in Christ's pasch that the Christian dies to self and gives himself up to God. Prayer belongs to the great sacrificial liturgy of Christ which constitutes

---

[4] In building their churches in the form of a cross, the medievals saw them as images of Christ crucified.

the mystery of the Church. Thus it makes us ever more Christian. It perfects our baptism in Christ, immersing us more deeply in his death and resurrection. It keeps us all day long in the glow of the eucharistic celebration in which we are united to Christ in his death and glory.

Because our prayer is uttered in Christ our redeemer, in his death and his glory, it contains all the accents of man's distress, and all the joys of the Easter triumph. It is often sorrowful, a prayer rising from the depths of our anguish: "Out of the depths I have cried to thee, O Lord," a prayer that is painful to say, that belongs in the desert, arid and desolate. As long as we are in this world, and our death is not complete, our union with Christ's immolation will be painful. That we find the whole thing unspeakably wearying at times should not surprise us. This desolate prayer is Christ's, the tragic prayer of his loneliness and death: "Who in the days of his flesh, with a strong cry and tears, offering up prayers and supplications to him that was able to save him from death" (Heb. 5.7).

But the notes of sorrow are submerged in a great joy, the joy of answered prayer, of redemption accomplished, for even now death is swallowed up in victory, and Christians sing the canticle of the redeemed in the liturgy of Easter. In the midst of death, they say, *Resurrexi et adhuc tecum sum*: I have risen and now am with thee. Their most heartbreaking psalms terminate in the Gloria of gratitude; their calls for help, the *Kyrie eleisons* they will continue to repeat until he has mercy and comes, are borne along on an intense jubilation, and all their prayers rest on the certainty of the *Amen*.

For the prayer of Christians is said in Christ who has already been answered: they pray in the death of Christ and in his glorification, at the moment when his need and longing reached their goal, and he came to his Father in whom every need and longing is satisfied. Whether giving thanks or begging for help, they pray as men already answered, for they pray in Christ who is filled with the glory of God; they pray in the Holy Ghost (Rom. 8.16), the substantial gift they have received.

Prayer, then, is a sign of redemption, and there is always thanksgiving mingled with supplication: "Be nothing solicitous . . . by prayer and supplication, with thanksgiving, let your petitions be made known to God" (Phil. 4.6). Prayer is now only a sign that we are already heard, the sign of a redemption already made manifest in us, but is also what takes us on the road to the fullness of salvation; for the redeeming Christ, in whom we pray, is the way as well as the temple. His pasch, in which our prayer is a share, is a movement which has attained the summit and goal of its effort in him, and which leads us towards that goal. Prayer is itself the promise that it will be answered: it is, in us, the movement that bears Christ into the bosom of the Father.

Splendid indeed is the mystery of Christian prayer, the mystery of Christ and the Church joining together like two hands, in one great prayer of redemptive sacrifice. If it is true that everything finds its unity and completion in the paschal Christ, that everything else was created for him (Col. 1.16), it is also true that "all things are made for prayer."[5] For the redeeming Christ is a temple, his pasch is a prayer, and our prayer is spoken in that temple and that pasch. All is made for the glorified Christ, all is made for prayer. We should love prayer as we love the body of Christ, for it is to that that prayer unites us. We should love it as we love his death and resurrection, for it is in them that it makes us communicate. And we should believe in prayer and its power to save us, just as we believe that Christ is the beloved Son who was, in his death, taken up into the glory of God.

Foolish indeed is our indifference, as we enter prayer as if it were any ordinary place. Jacob cried at Bethel, "Terrible is this place!"; Moses took off his shoes to go near the burning bush. As we go into the houses of prayer on earth, the Church offers us

[5] St. Francis of Sales, *Sermons*, vol. III, p. 49. Edition d'Annecy, 1897, vol. 9.

holy water that we may "sanctify ourselves" before praying. She asks that we recollect ourselves and confess our sins before going up to the altar of sacrifice. And it is by every prayer we say that we enter the temple, the true temple, that we go up to the altar of the one sacrifice of Christ. Recollection and devotion (the gift of self) are inherent in Christian prayer. The Christian is drawn by his own weight towards recollection, even apart from when he is praying. Raised up above the things of this world, Christ on the Cross thought only of the work of redemption; and after praying for his executioners, answering the good thief, giving his Mother to his disciple, his mind drew away even from the men he was to save, to concentrate on the Father. He need consider them no longer; it was enough to give himself up to God to save mankind. And gathering together his whole soul, he gave it into his Father's hands.

The Church was born in this silence, at this high point of Christ's prayer, at the moment when he was caught up wholly by the Father. Every believer is immersed, is baptized, in this supreme recollection. That is where the Church lives, that is where we are Christians. Recollection is the Christian's natural element.

IV. *A SACRAMENT OF PRAYER*

"Lord, teach us to pray," begged the Apostles, and the Lord answered them. He first taught them the "Our Father," and later he gave them a sacrament of prayer, the sacrament of his body. The Eucharist gathers together the Christians of all time into the prayer of Christ. It sets the temple, the body of Christ, visibly in their midst. It calls men to prayer and makes it easy for them, for it is not only the temple, but the open door of the temple too. It is the sacrament of the sacred body, its presence and the means of its union with us: the sacrament of Christian prayer. Ever since Christ's death and resurrection the only valid worship is one in spirit and in truth. But since the death and resurrection of the faithful are incomplete, they still need a visible cult. This sacrament makes Christ's body, the temple of heaven, present amid the people, visible and tangible. Because it is present in them, even buildings of stone become sanctuaries of the true worship, places of prayer in spirit and in truth.

Every Sunday, which is a weekly celebration of Easter, the Eucharist brings together the people of Christ, and the invisible mystery of the Church is revealed: it is an assembly in the body of Christ, gathered on the mountain of his death and resurrection. It is Christ and his paschal mystery extending to the mass of mankind. But it is also an assembly of prayer, praying in Christ, in his death and his resurrection. The Mass is *the* prayer of the Church. It unfolds the mystery of all prayer, for it is always in Christ and in his paschal sacrifice that we pray. Every prayer we say unites us to this same mystery that we celebrate in the Mass.

Every Christian is aware of the treasures of prayer this sacrament holds for us. He instinctively sees that the Mass holds the primacy among all prayers. When he has received our Lord's body, he will linger over his prayer, in those special moments of an even more tangible presence in the temple of God. He contemplates the God who dwells in this place, and converses wordlessly with him. The very presence of the Eucharist in our tabernacles holds riches of prayer which we should use. This sensible presence among us of the centre of all prayer cannot fail to be effective. It is a sacramental presence, a presence of effective grace, acting upon all who are humble and believing.

To exhort the faithful of Magnesia to pray, St. Ignatius wrote: "Hasten to gather together, as in a single temple, as around a single altar, in the one Christ who has come from the Father and who is alone in him, and who has gone towards him."[6] This is how we are Christians, and this is how we pray: by being present in the temple, by communion at the altar of the one sacrifice. In

[6] *Ad. Magn.* 7.

Christ, and in communion with him in his death and resurrection, we go to the Father. The mystery of Christian prayer is the mystery of Christian life. To be faithful to prayer is to be faithful to our Christianity.

10

Christian Obedience

Christians nowadays have one cause of suffering not experienced —or not to the same extent—by Christians in the past. For them the road they walked was clearly marked out, a time-honoured path marked by solid traditions of doctrine and ascesis. For many Christians now, all this seems to have been called in question. Methods which it seemed would never change, and even ideas hallowed by tradition, are all in flux. The sure and safe roads seem to have disappeared. Many of our young Christians find themselves at sea amid the old traditions that are falling apart, and the welter of new ideas springing up.

Yet now, as in the past, they must follow the path of the baptized, the true road of holiness; they must realize the Christian ideal, firm in their faith in Christ and the one true Church. What, then, is that ideal, by what criterion are things specifically Christian? Scripture gives us the answer: Christian holiness is a holiness of obedience; our road lies in a wholehearted submission to God in the Church.

The Jews divided mankind into two categories—themselves and others, Jews and Gentiles. Christians, who came from both groups, knowing the new creation effected in them by God, called themselves "the third race." Each of the three "races" has not only its own special doctrine and cult, but also its ideal of life: Pagan, Jew and Christian all have their own ideal of perfection.

I. *THE GREEK IDEAL*

Pagan man saw perfection as belonging to the order of reason; he expected to find it in the fullest human development of his own faculties. This humanism found its purest expression in the Greek world. The Greek ideal lay not in holiness in the biblical sense—consecration, union with God's will—but in the autonomous development of all that is noblest in man. This search for perfection achieved its goal most characteristically in the hero and in the sage. The hero's heroism consisted in an affirmation of himself whereby he was superior to all adversity, a lofty kind of egoism. The wisdom of the sage lay in grasping the great principles of human life, and living in conformity with them. In both cases the result was complete freedom; each obeyed only himself, his own will to be great, the truths learnt from his own reason. Even when the Greek was obliged to carry his heroism as far as death, it remained always a heroism of fidelity to himself.

II. *THE OLD TESTAMENT IDEAL*

In the Bible, on the other hand, morality means submission, the person of man being subject to the person of God, obedience to God who has made known his will. The ideal is not heroism but holiness, which means submission to God's will until death; and that will does not always correspond with man's own wishes or the dictates of his reason. So much so that what is wisdom in Scripture may appear folly to the Greeks.

The law to which Israel submits is not the law of reason, as in Greece, but the Law of God. The commands of the natural law were also valid for the Jews, but only because they came from

God: it was God, not a man, who ruled. All Jewish law, whether moral or ritual, was given by God. In Scripture the law of reason is the law of Sinai, so that the Jews saw no distinction between natural law and positive law. Both were equally the Law of God, and the principle and peak of all perfection was "fear of the Lord," submission to his law.

The second book of Maccabees gives us a typical example of this morality. The old Eleazar and the seven brothers die because they are faithful, not to the dictates of reason, but to the Law of God, to a precept of ritual purity; they refuse to eat pork. The Greek king is amazed by their obstinacy in refusing to do something which, in the light of reason, is quite harmless: they die of their fidelity to God's law.

III. *THE NEW TESTAMENT IDEAL*

The master and teacher of the new covenant did not abolish the law proclaimed forever from Sinai, but "fulfilled it"; in other words, he reiterated its demands, but raised them to a higher plane of perfection. Christianity is wholly submission to God, but a submission now pushed to the limits of the possible, a higher submission in love. It too has its Sinai, of which the first Sinai was only a prefiguring. It has its tables of the law which, like the tables of Moses, govern man's whole life, subsuming the natural law and making all human activity religious, a direct submission to God. Our Sinai, our tables of the law, are Christ redeeming us, Christ in his death and resurrection.

An episode of great importance for Christian spirituality in the gospels is the transfiguration of our Lord. Looking back on that appearance on earth of Christ's glory, St. Peter wrote: "And this voice we heard brought from heaven, when we were with him in the holy mount" (2 Pet. 1.18). The Jews had two holy mountains: one belonging to the past, Horeb, with its lightnings and thunders, and one to the Messianic future, the gentle Mount Sion, which was to be Christ himself who, as we know from his own words, is the temple of the New Testament (John 2.17-19), Isaiah's cornerstone "in the foundations of Sion" (Is. 28.16) which our Lord took as his own title (Matt. 21.28). The people who went from Sinai through the desert to the hill of Sion marked out the path of the history of salvation, a history which reaches from one mountain to the other.

Christians often contrast these two mountains, the mountains of the two Testaments. St. Paul says that the first covenant came from Mount Sinai and contrasts it with the Jerusalem which is above (Gal. 4.24-5). "You are not come to a mountain that can be touched [Sinai], and a burning fire and a whirlwind, and darkness, and storm . . . But you are come to Mount Sion, and to the city of the living God . . . and to Jesus the mediator of the new testament" (Heb. 12.18-24).

Moses went up a high and lonely mountain, accompanied by some of the leaders of the people; the luminous cloud which manifested God's glory, came down over the mountain and enveloped Moses and his companions. His face became luminous. A loud voice was heard from amid the cloud, and thunder; and the terrified people asked that God should not speak directly to them again. God granted their wish, and promised, "The Lord thy God will raise up to thee a prophet of thy nation . . . ; him thou shalt hear" (Deut. 18.15). Moses was the man of the holy mountain of the past, the prophet of Sinai. Elias also gave his name to that mountain, for he too heard God's voice there in the murmuring of the wind.

When he was to enter upon the phase of his life that was to bring him to his final consummation when he was beginning to foretell his death and resurrection, our Lord took three of his disciples and, leaving the multitude below, "went up a high mountain apart." While he prayed, his face shone, as Moses' had in the past, and his whole person became luminous; a cloud of light covered the top of the mountain, the Glory of God (2 Pet. 1.17) enveloping our Lord and his companions. Two men appeared, the men of Sinai: the mountain of the past came to meet the mountain of the future. Then a voice was heard: "This is my beloved Son; hear ye him."

Like so many other scenes in the Gospels, this was still only an anticipation, a foreshadowing of Christ's glorification in his death and resurrection. His conversation with Moses and Elias gives us a clue to this, for in all this glory, "they spoke of his decease that he should accomplish in Jerusalem." In the glory and the death of his Son, God was promulgating the new law, just as he sealed the first covenant on Sinai. Christ himself, the beloved Son, dead and risen, is the Sinai of the New Testament; he is the table upon which God has inscribed his will. "Hear ye him." That is the law of the New Testament.

An inward law

This mountain from whose summit God promulgates his new law does not stand before the people, as Sinai stood in the desert; this table of the law is not read out for us to hear. We bear the law in our hearts, it speaks within us, it fills our lives; for the dead and risen Christ dwells within us and we live by him. We are "rooted in him" (Col. 2.7); he is the principle of our Christian being and our life. In him, the Christ of Easter, we have been baptized; in him we are placed forever, transformed into him in participation in his death and resurrection. Thus Christian morality is governed by a law coming from inside man, a living and existential law: the dead and risen Christ who is the foundation of Christian life.

A law of total submission

By his death and resurrection, Christ achieved the most complete submission to God that a man can. Throughout his life, our Lord went down by degrees until he attained the total submission of his being to God's will. The first movement of his human will was an act of obedience: "When he cometh into the world, he saith . . . Behold I come, that I should do thy will, O God" (Heb. 10.5-7). The first word of his that is known to us declares his submission to God: "Did you not know that I must be about my Father's business?" (Luke 2.49). The first act of his public life was a foreshadowing, a symbolic anticipation of his submission even to death. As he went down in the waters of Jordan to herald the baptism of his death, he replied to John the Baptist's protests: "It becometh us to fulfill all justice" (Matt. 3.15).

As he entered upon the Passion that crowned his life, he said: "That the world may know that I love the Father, and as the Father hath given me commandment, so do I; arise, let us go hence" (John 14.31). His redemptive action opened with the declaration: "Father . . . not my will but thine be done" (Luke 22.42).

Our Lord summed up and defined his life on earth and his mission in these words: "I came not to do my own will but the will of him that sent me" (John 6.38). And this summing-up was even better defined by an action, or rather an acceptance of God's will by a passion of obedience. Christ's death is the summing-up and definition of his whole life on earth. St. Paul knew our Lord's life on earth, he knew it as well as the Evangelists; yet in his epistles he never speaks of anything but his death, for to him the death was the characteristic event, recapitulating, crystallizing the whole of our Lord's life. And that death was an act of obedience containing every possible element of submission, an act "of obedience even unto death" whereby he gave himself up, literally, abandoned himself to give himself into his Father's hands: "Father, into thy hands I commend my spirit" (Luke 23.46).

This Christ is the source and the law of our life, this immolated Christ. It is in his death of obedience that we are baptized and that we live: "With Christ am I nailed to the Cross" (Gal 2.19). This Christ is not only immolated, but risen. And this divine life of the Resurrection is a seal that is forever placed on Christ's total obedience; it consecrates it, perpetuating and crowning it; it is God's total possession of this man who has handed himself over in order that only God's glory may reign within him.

In raising his Christ who had offered himself wholly to him, God has established his reign in him, has declared his will in him forever. For it is in the Holy Spirit that Christ was raised (Rom. 8.11). It is in the Holy Spirit that he is forever vivified, "enlivened in the Spirit" (1 Pet. 3.18) to the point of living only by him, of being so totally dominated by him and transformed into him that we may say that Christ "is made spirit" (1 Cor. 15.45; 2 Cor. 3.17). The Holy Spirit personified the will of God; to be vivified in the Spirit is to be vivified in the will of God.

Earlier on, Christ said that his food, and therefore his life, was to do the will of God (John 4.34). Now God's will has become his life in very deed, the physical principle of his life in eternity. In raising his Son, God has laid his hands upon fugitive man, man once obstinate and disobedient in Adam. On Easter morning, in the ecstasy of his glory, Christ said in his heart: *"Resurrexi et adhuc tecum sum, alleluja. Posuisti super me manum tuam, alleluja, alleluja!* I have risen and am with thee, alleluia. Thou hast placed thy hand upon me, alleluia, alleluia!" I am risen, and in me, Father, man returns to thee, man once obstinate, but now docile. Thou hast laid thy hand upon me, thou hast laid upon me thy weight of glory (2 Cor. 4.17), the weight of thy will, of thy will which is the Holy Spirit, the finger of the Father's right hand; thou hast laid upon me the yoke of thy glory, the Holy Ghost.

In his death, he ceased to live by himself and henceforth lives by the Holy Ghost who is the glory and power and freedom of God (2 Cor. 3.17), who is God's love. Christ's obedience even unto death was a consent to God's majesty, was a man's total welcome to God's love. Submitted to God's will, now the substance of the Kingdom of God in this world, Christ has been by this very fact raised up to the omnipotence of God and the fullness of the Son's liberty: "He was constituted Son of God in power by the resurrection from the dead" (Rom. 1.4).

Obedience as a Christian virtue

Christians live by this dead and risen Christ; they are Christian in so far as they live by him; their supreme law is obedience. Scripture calls them "children of obedience" (1 Pet. 1.14); those who do not accept to be Christ's are "children of disobedience" (Eph. 5.6).

The Church is Christ's body, but not in any undefined moment of his existence; it is Christ's body in the unique moment of the Redemption: in its death and glorification. It is with Christ in his obedience unto death, and it is joined to him in his resurrection, subject with him to the total possession of God. Yet the Church is still at a stage of imperfection: we are Christians in that we are Christ's body, sharers in his death and resurrection, but our share in it is still slight. The Church will achieve her perfection, the full stature of Christ, when "God is all in all" in her (1 Cor. 15.28), when she has attained total submission to God, in a total death and resurrection in Christ. Because it is Christ's body in which God's rule is established, it is God's Kingdom on earth where his will is done.

Obedience is the supreme law of Christian life. Therefore the criterion of our Christian conduct is not how admirable it appears to reason, nor how faithful to any given idea, but whether it accomplishes the will of God. The question we must always ask ourselves is whether we are acting within God's will, or obeying only ourselves.

Christianity is far from being a humanism, a fulfilment of man's potentialities; it is a divinization, a movement away from himself whereby man submits himself to God. At the base of all Christian life is the redeeming Christ, is submission to God. "When you submit to the bishop as to Jesus Christ, I see you no longer living like men, but like Jesus Christ who died for us."[1]

A morality of freedom in submission

Old Testament morality was also a morality of submission. Christ came to "fulfill" it, and by pushing obedience as far as it could go, found freedom: in dying to himself, he was filled by the life of the Spirit, which is the liberty of God.

[1] St. Ignatius of Antioch, *Trall.* 2,1.

Liberty in the Holy Spirit

The morality of the Old Testament was limited and incomplete. It imposed obedience to a principle outside man, and St. Paul describes it as servile. The transcendent God was outside man, and commanded him from a distance, from the height of Sinai. The Old Testament lay under the shadow of slavery. The Jew was not free, but spoke of himself as God's slave. In this, Mosaic morality was, it must be admitted, inferior to the ordinary human morality whereby man was governed by a principle within himself, his reason. But Christian morality is one of liberty as well as one of obedience.

The Greek, obedient to his own reason, was a free man, for in obeying an inward principle he was subject to himself. The Christian, even though he submits to the will of another, of God, remains free, for that will is not now uttered from the summit of Sinai, nor inscribed upon tables of stone. Christ himself is the mountain of the New Testament, it is upon the dead and risen Christ that the new law is inscribed—and Christ dwells in our hearts as the principle of our being and life as Christians. The law inscribed upon this table, delivered on the new Sinai, is simply the Holy Spirit, who is the will of God, the fullness of the law. The new commandment is called "the law of the Spirit of life" (Rom. 8.2), and the Spirit of God is "poured forth in our hearts" (Rom. 5.5).

Thus when I obey my God, I am submitting to the law of my own being and life, just as the Greek was submitting to his own interior law by seeking his ideal. I am simply doing my own will at its noblest and most personal. I can say with St. Paul, "All things are lawful to me" (1 Cor. 6.12); I have but to follow my own law, the law of the Holy Spirit who is in Christ. I am doing another's will and I am free; I am doing my will which God has welded into his.

The Christian acts according to the law of his being and his life, which is the law of his heart. He is freer than the Pagan who obeys the dictates of his reason, for he does what he likes. For the law of life, inscribed in the risen Christ and in our hearts, is "the law of the Spirit of life," and the Spirit of God is the love of God poured into our hearts. To do God's will, the Christian need only follow the instinct of his love. "That the world may know that I love the Father: and as the Father hath given me commandment, so do I" (John 14.31). *Dilige et quod vis fac*: love and do what you will.[2]

Every act of Christian obedience is an act of supreme liberty, for it is an act of love; it is free with the freedom of God. "Where the Spirit of the Lord is, there is liberty" (2 Cor. 3.17).

This freedom remains incomplete in this world

As long as the Church is in the world, these statements remain relative, and are in part anticipations. We are not yet wholly dead to self, not totally dominated by God. Since our submission is still imperfect, our liberty is too. In heaven we shall need only to follow the law of our heart, the Spirit, for he will then be our sole principle of life. Meanwhile, we are still partially under an Old Testament rule of life, in as much as we are, like the people of old, in "the flesh." God's will must still be intimated to us from without, by the Church and her institutions—the hierarchy, canon law, and individual religious rules. All these institutions are temporal, of value only during our pilgrimage on earth, as long as we remain imperfect, until we come "unto the measure of the age of the fullness of Christ" (Eph. 4.13).

But these institutions of the time of imperfection are also God's instruments for bringing us to perfect liberty. Though they are signs of this age of imperfection, yet they are also destined to bring it to an end, to bring us to the final consummation, for they make us die to ourselves, and submit us to God's will. Faith, too, is a sign of the time of imperfection, and suffering, and death, and all three make us die to ourselves and draw us into the life of resur-

[2] St. Augustine, *In I John. Tract.* vii, 8. *PL*,35(2033).

rection. The Church's institutions may be a cross we have to bear, but whoever takes it up, that cross is Christ's, "in which is salvation, life and resurrection."

The Church is established on earth to lead men to the consummation of the Last Day; her mission is to imprint upon them the movement that will take them forward from themselves towards the parousia of Christ. She does this by the kind of precepts she imposes and by the very fact of imposing them. How strange is the error of thinking that to disobey them is progress!

Our attitude to obedience gives us the standard whereby we can judge what we are. The Christian ideal is not purely human; the morality of Christ is not a morality proposed purely by reason, but a morality of submission to God's will. If we obeyed only our reason, our own principles, in preference to God's will, we should simply be Pagans.

Christian morality is submission in God's love. If we obey under constraint, by routine, without a child's spontaneity of love, then we are servile men, Old Testament men, for whom Christ has not yet died and risen. The Church has the mission to prepare in us Christ's last coming, by bringing to perfection our death to self and resurrection in the Holy Ghost. To refuse to submit to the Church is to persist in remaining in "the flesh," anchored to this world, to refuse to go to meet Christ or take others to him. Obedience is the criterion of our Christianity.

11

Christian Virginity

The work of redemption is the work of the sanctification of "the flesh." Saving history is a movement from the flesh to the Holy Spirit, from a creation that Scripture calls "this world," the world of "the flesh," to a heavenly creation animated only by the Spirit of God. It passes from one to the other, not condemning the first, not destroying it, but fulfilling it in a way quite beyond its own powers; for the second is fullness, the total reality which comes at the end and of which the earthly creation is but a fleeting shadow, a visible framework stained by sin. The Christian virgin is a figure of the Church already saved in the Holy Ghost, an image of the salvation wonderfully wrought in our flesh.

I. *A FIGURE OF SALVATION*

Christ has saved the Church by immersing her "in the laver of water in the word of life" (Eph. 5.26); he has made her die with him and rise again and, at that very moment, has united himself with her, as with a chaste virgin (2 Cor. 11.2), without spot or wrinkle or any such thing (Eph. 5.27), a bride dead to the flesh and raised to life in the Spirit of God. Salvation consists in this marriage celebrated in death and resurrection.

Dead to the flesh

The whole Church is dead with Christ, is dead to all the things to which he is dead. She has passed out of the earthly life which Scripture calls fleshly, whose nature is to be closed to God and his heavenly love and power of eternal life, and to be enslaved to self-seeking, weakness, and the tyranny of the powers that rule it, to the laws of this still imperfect creation. The Church is immolated with her Saviour, crucifying in herself the flesh and its lusts (Gal. 5.24). This death, though effected in mystery, is real, and the Church can no longer accept the tyranny of the flesh.

To sanctify one's body in the holiness of the Spirit is one of the capital demands of Christian morality, and St. Paul constantly returns to it. He does not base his exhortations on human dignity, on the necessity of subordinating the body to the spirit, as a philosopher would. The Christian demand is more radical; it explicitly requires not merely that we subordinate our instincts, but that we go beyond them altogether in a totally new situation, for it is based, according to St. Paul, on Christ's death to fleshly existence, and our participation in that death: "In that he died to sin, he died once . . . So do you also reckon that you are dead to sin . . . Let not sin therefore reign in your mortal body, so as to obey the lusts thereof. Neither yield ye your members as instruments of iniquity unto sin" (Rom. 6.10-13).

The whole Church has been baptized in Christ's death. But that death, though real, is only the principle, the seed, of a total death, and the faithful still live in fact in an earthly body. That is why earthly love and pleasure are still lawful and can be holy, for the believer, being immersed in his body in baptism and in the Holy Spirit, shares even in this life in the holiness of his glorified body; all bodily realities have become Christian, and can belong to the new world in which we are dead to sinful flesh. To be holy, it is enough that earthly love be not self-seeking, be open to the Spirit, to the charity of God which is a love that gives itself. Marriage remains the normal state of Christians in the world (Matt. 19.12; 1 Cor. 7.7), and virginity has never been considered a precept imposed by baptism.

Yet it is baptism which opens this way to the adventures of the summit, which utters this call to virginity. Man is wholly baptized, body and soul; in principle he is wholly dead with Christ. There are Christians who determine to live according to that principle alone; they renounce the flesh and its laws. Because they are baptized, they wish to be virgins. These are not unrealistic souls, happy in an illusion, living as though in another world which has not yet come. For, in Christ, that death is real, the end of this world is a fact, and the life of Christ has become that of the Christian.

They still must, of course, pay their tribute to the flesh. But the fact that they remain in an earthly state does not mean they are living an illusion; it enables them to give their own consent to the baptismal death God has wrought in them, to affirm it strongly in their whole being. They do not live as though their earthly body were dead; they try to bring to fulfilment what is already a principle and a longing for completeness. And since they know that the days of this world are numbered, they do not want to set out on the ways of the flesh. In Christ on the Cross, the world in its present form died; it has no value for eternity (1 Cor. 7.29-31; Gal. 6.14). We see it still standing in the splendour of spring, and its loves are by way of lasting forever. But the root of the tree is already cut, in Christ on the Cross; the world is in its death throes: "The fashion of this world passeth away" (1 Cor. 7.31). The Christian virgin does not misconstrue or despise the realities that must pass away, but attaches himself to reality, the true reality revealed in the risen Christ, of which all the rest are but a shadow.

Raised in the Spirit

Dead to the life of the flesh, Christians have entered a new sphere of life, the life of resurrection from the dead: "Buried with him in baptism, in whom also you are risen again" (Col. 2.12). On Easter morning, God re-created the world. By raising Christ, he brought into the world the last creation, foretold by the prophets, which was, in Christ, to extend to the whole world. Even in his body, our Lord has become a new man, the heavenly man (1 Cor. 15.47), set free from the laws of the flesh and transformed into the Holy Spirit: "He was made into a quickening spirit" (1 Cor. 15.45).

By baptism the Christian is raised with Christ; with him he is dead to the flesh and born into the life of the Spirit: "You are not in the flesh, but in the spirit, if so be the Spirit of God dwell in you" (Rom. 8.9). The Spirit of the Resurrection is God's holiness, and whoever is caught up in the action of God that raised up Christ is conquered by that holiness: "In that he died to sin, he died once; but in that he liveth, he liveth unto God" (Rom. 6.10). The baptized man will never cease to hear the words of Easter night: "If you be risen with Christ, seek the things that are above . . . Mortify therefore your members which are upon earth" (Col. 3.1-5). He will never again be able to give his body over to any purely earthly love, for he is subject to a law of holiness, of kingly love, which is bearing him towards perfect self-giving.

The Spirit, who is the expression of God's transcendence, the fullness of reality, by imposing his law upon us, abolishes "the flesh" in us. He does not set himself against the body, for that too is created by the Spirit, but he does set himself against "the flesh" —"for these are contrary one to another" (Gal. 5.17)—because "the flesh" is man closed in upon the weakness and selfishness of his material being, the man of this creation who will not give himself to the Spirit and who takes himself as the ultimate value, despite having been made for salvation in the spirituality of God.

Selfishness, in varying forms, some of which take on a guise of nobility, is inherent in him. He does not even aspire to the longed-for idea of love, the total receiving of another: the carnal body, bond of this world's unions, provides an obstacle to total love. He must die to this earthly "impenetrability," and rise again in the Spirit who is love in its fullness, the infinite love of God.

In baptism, the Christian is raised up in the power of infinite life, in the Spirit of God, who is the love of God now poured forth in our hearts. Dead to the flesh, the Christian is more than ever made to live and love. But the life and the love are not of this world.

Every Christian is committed to the law of holiness, to the effort of spiritualizing all his bodily activities. Even those in the world who are married, if their union is Christian, rise above any merely carnal love, put their bodies at the service of a far greater love, and make ready for the day when the body will be wholly risen in the Spirit. But there are Christians who go on to draw the ultimate consequences from their baptism. They are already risen, and they want to live completely in this new world they have won in Christ, of which it is said: "They that are worthy of the time of resurrection will take neither wife nor husband, for they are children of God [spiritual beings], since they are children of the resurrection" (cf. Matt. 22). They want to be virgins, because they are baptized. They demonstrate now what all Christians will become: "What we shall become, you have already begun to be; you possess even here below the glory of the Resurrection, and you go through the world untouched, as long as you remain chaste and virginal and even now like the angels."[1]

For these Christians, the Last Day, which is to be the day of their total birth in the Holy Ghost, is near. They are already taking part in that eternal birth by which Christ is divinely born of the Father in the Holy Spirit, in the glory of Easter. Virginity is youth, the youth of the Last Day. These Christians do not stay young in that their development is arrested, or in that they return to the past; they become young. Their youth is a going up to the spring which mankind has not yet reached, a going forward to the final point of history. For that final point is the resurrection of Christ in which the world will be born sons of the Resurrection. The youth and newness of this Christian childhood is at the same time the richness of age. (It may be noted in passing that if virginity is a sublime

[1] St. Cyprian, *De habitu virginum*, 22. *PL*,4(462).

childhood full of spontaneity, freshness and beauty, it is so because
of adult Christian effort. Religious infantilism would be a complete
negation of the mystery of virginity.)

The goal of all this is the Holy Ghost who is total reality, the
fullness of all things, the love of God. Christian virginity is not,
like natural virginity, a check upon the development of the human
being; it is a completion. It is marked primarily not by physical
integrity, but by love. When the Fathers sang the praises of virginal
integrity, they were speaking of it as a *heavenly* state of life. No
quality of the flesh could constitute the essence of Christian virginity, for it is a death to the flesh, a reality of the Spirit. This love will
not pass away, but belongs to the end; it is a fullness, for the Spirit
is God's transcendence and eternal actuality; he enables the Christian virgin to celebrate the marriage feast of eternity.

United to Christ

Christian virginity is thus different from all other kinds in that
it is not primarily achieved by bodily integrity. Merely to keep
one's virginity is not a Christian ideal; one must become a virgin.
Virginity is not primarily something to be given up, but something
to be accomplished; Christian virginity may be accomplished in a
marriage. To love and be loved, to give one's life over to the fruitfulness of that love—all this is no bar to Christian virginity, but
precisely what it demands, though at a different level.

Baptism makes us virgins, by taking us out of the carnal world,
raising us in the Spirit, for it is a nuptial sacrament: it unites the
believer with Christ's sacred body, to make him one body with
Christ. We die with Christ and we rise again with Christ, because
baptism unites us to his body in its death and resurrection: "In
one Spirit were we all baptized into one body" (1 Cor. 12.13).
"As many of you as have been baptized in Christ, have put on
Christ . . . you are all one in Christ Jesus" (Gal. 3.27-9). When
St. Paul speaks of the "bath of water" prepared for the Church,
he is referring to a nuptial ceremony that was customary in antiq-

uity. The Church becomes "holy and pure" in her marriage; she is made a virgin in her union with her Saviour's sacred body. Baptism is a nuptial sacrament.

The Church forms but one body with Christ in all her faithful. But there are some in whom the Church realizes her vocation as a loving bride better, some in whom she celebrates her marriage more gloriously: her virgins. It is to them above all that she owes the fact that she is bride and virgin, and in them that she is so more perfectly: "The Church flourishes as the true bride and as a virgin, by the flower of her chaste and pure virgins."[2]

Though dedicated to Christ, believers can devote themselves to another love, as long as Christ sanctifies it and lays it open to his divine charity. But Christian virgins want to live their baptism in its exclusive strictness: this admits of but one love, one union with their Lord. They love better, and they love one who is greater. "Peter, lovest thou me more than these?"—this is the ambition of Christian virginity. There is no one who is not required by God to love; but there are some whom he asks to love more. It does not appear that the Holy Spirit drew many people to virginity in the Old Testament. Since the bridegroom had not yet come, such virginity would merely have been renunciation. Neither renunciation nor death is willed for its own sake; what God asks is love.

The reality of that union with Christ

Scripture distinguishes two levels of reality. There are realities similar to the shadow cast by an advancing body. But there is another reality, which is coming at the end, and which casts its shadow right back to the origin of the world. The first are called carnal, and are of this world, ephemeral; the second is "heavenly,"

[2] Origen, *In Gen.*, hom. 3,6. *PG*,181.
"Virgins are a kind of public expression of the perfect virginity of their mother the Church, and the holiness of her close union with him"—Pius XII., the encyclical, *Sacra Virginitas.*

"spiritual." The author of both kinds of reality is the Holy Ghost, who is the reality of God himself, but only the spiritual is of the order of the Holy Spirit and his fullness of being.

The union of man and wife who, as Scripture tells us, together make two in one flesh (Gen. 2.24), takes place on both levels: on the level of the flesh and its imperfection is the union of two earthly beings; on the level of the Spirit the two are united in the fullness of being where Christ is united to his Church.

The believers in Corinth were told to stop imitating the Pagans. To couple with a harlot was to remove oneself from the body of Christ and become "one flesh" with her, whereas in Christ the believer is "one spirit" with him, a single spiritual reality (1 Cor. 6.15-17). In both cases there is a very real union in one body, but they are on two totally different levels.

In an exhortation on marriage, St. Paul takes up the text of Genesis 2.24: "This is a great mystery," he adds, "but I understand it of Christ and the Church" (Eph. 5.32). Great indeed is the mystery of marriage; from the origins of mankind, this earthly reality has been the prophetic image of the marriage which takes place at the end of time. The union of man and wife in one body is a kind of earthly fringe of a final reality, the image of Christ and the Church so united as to form but one body. In this union Christ shares his splendid mystery with his bride, making her live "his Hour," his supreme destiny; he makes her enter into his death and resurrection, divinely saves and sanctifies her. According to St. Ambrose,[8] Christ's body is the bridal chamber of the Church in which she sleeps with Christ in death and awakens with him in the Resurrection.

That is why the Church is called "the body of Christ." She is the bride united through every one of her faithful to Christ's sacred body, identified with him in his death and resurrection. How real, then, is this relationship, how intimate and profound this transformation into the unity of one body; no earthly gesture of love can be more than a shadowy outline of it. In the Spirit, the supreme

[8] *In Ps.* 118, *Sermo* 1,16. *PL*,15(1207).

reality, the shadow becomes a body; and the promise, impossible of total fulfilment in the flesh—"they two shall be one flesh"—is accomplished. Following upon the flesh, with the insuperable barriers it sets to love, has come the Spirit who is "communication," the principle of infinite openness, the source of unity in God himself. He gives the risen Christ infinite possibility of self-giving and receiving; gradually, he raises the Church to the same power to love. Once it has achieved this perfection, the union of Christ and the Church can be certain of an eternity of which this world's unions can only dream. "All flesh is grass and withers" (Is. 40.7-8; James 1.10-11), but the Spirit, in whom is all fullness, is eternal (Heb. 9.15).

To understand this mystery one must have a pure heart

"This is a great mystery," and only a heart whose eyes are unclouded—"the eyes of your heart be enlightened" (Eph. 1.18)—can understand it, or even gaze upon it. To unite herself to her bridegroom, to become one flesh with him, the Church—and in her the virgin—must share in his death to the flesh. The only point of meeting and union is in the act of the Redemption, in participating in the death, and in the infinite purity of the Spirit of the Resurrection.

Our Lord's coming into the world had already made purity blossom forth—in Mary his mother, in John the Baptist, in the beloved disciple. From the beginning, Christ's own purity was of a higher order; it was not merely that he did not give his heart to any earthly love. But now he has the purity of his nature, "like to the angels, being the son of the Resurrection." In the past, the disciples had been able to touch him with their hands; he had allowed the sinful woman to kiss his feet. Now he says to Magdalen: "Do not touch me" (John 20.19). The marriage feast of virginity is celebrated in faith, in the brightness of Easter morning.

Even though the allowances he makes for our earthly weakness have led Christ to unite himself to the Church in a visible form, it is in a sign, in the sacrament of bread, that he gives himself to her. Our communion with Christ in his paschal mystery takes place in the holiness of the Spirit, in faith and love, in a total death to the things of sense.

The sacraments of virginity

Virginity too has its sacraments. People sometimes try to exalt the sanctity of marriage by saying, "Even the religious life does not have a sacrament to consecrate it, yet Christ has conferred on marriage the dignity of a sacrament!" Yet consider! First baptism: virginity may fairly lay claim to that, for it is baptism that unites the believer to Christ in one body, makes him die to the flesh and raises him up in the Spirit.[4] Virginity in the Church is born of the waters of baptism. Again, it may call its own the sacrament of the Eucharist, in which Christ's body is given to the Church in order that Christ and his bride, being one body, may celebrate together the pasch of death and resurrection: "For we, being many, are one bread, one body, all that partake of one bread" (1 Cor. 10.17).

We are sometimes astounded when we think of the tremendous power the Church has over Christ's body in the Eucharist. She makes it present when she will, takes it where she will, feeds upon it whenever she wants! Yet there is nothing surprising in this. Married people have no more power over themselves, St. Paul tells us, each belongs to the other (1 Cor. 7.4). Christ's body belongs to the Church for always, and she rightfully makes use of it as her love demands. Because the Church is the bride in her virgins above all, the Eucharist belongs to them in a special sense. In the first centuries, on Easter night, the bishop used to place the host in the hands of the newly-consecrated virgins. They had consecrated themselves to the Lord, and the Lord in his turn was given to their love. The Eucharist is the virgin's glory and joy. The sacred body is his, and the mystery of the Hour which we

---

[4] Cf. St. Cyprian, *op. cit.,* 23. *PL,*4(463); St. Ambrose, *Exhortatio virginitatis,* 7. *PL,*16(348).

celebrate in the Mass is the mystery of his union with his Lord.

Thus virginity has its sacraments too. Indeed all the sacraments are sacraments of virginity, for all are sacraments of the body of Christ and his death and resurrection. Even Christian marriage, since it is a sacrament, is directed towards making earthly love virginal. In Christian partners, love is not the same as it is for Pagans; the body is already open to the life of the Resurrection, and the human love which unites them in the flesh has its head, as it were, in the clouds of the love of Christ and his Church, and their reverence for one another.[5]

Christ never allows his believers to unite themselves to the body of another in a merely human love, to become "one flesh" thereby. This would remove a member from Christ's risen body to become a member of a carnal body (1 Cor. 6.15). But the union of Christian marriage is most holy, because it is fulfilled in the union of Christ and the Church, and takes part in this divine agape. Thus, far from exalting marriage above virginity, St. Paul is simply admiring it as such a great mystery because it opens onto the mystery of virginity, whose grace and majesty it shares. The holiness of virginity is of the same order as that of Christian marriage, but it is the former which is loftier in itself, for it contains the Christian mystery in its essential purity. One cannot praise Christian marriage without singing the glories of virginity.[6]

To encounter Christ

The Church is truly dead to the world and living in the world to come, she is truly united with Christ in a single body. But these facts are in the nature of principles, of seeds not yet fully devel-

---

[5] Some Christian married couples come closer to the Christian ideal than some who are officially dedicated to virginity but in fact are dedicated only to solitude. The Christian ideal lies in love and fruitfulness.

[6] It remains that virginity, though it has its sacraments, is not itself a sacrament, while marriage is. The reason is obvious. A sacrament is a means; but virginity is the final reality already with us. Cf. B. Häring, *La Loi du Christ*, vol. III, p. 503, Paris, 1919 (*The Law of Christ*, vols. I and II, Westminster, Newman, 1961, 1962. Vol. III in preparation).

oped. The Church is far from free of the laws of this world and its downward pull, far from being assumed wholly into the next world. Scripture compares her not only to the bride, but to the betrothed still looking forward (Apoc. 22.17); completion will only come in the future, "when that which is perfect has come" (1 Cor. 13.16). That is why the Church is straining towards the blessed day when the Lord shall come and we shall meet him. She is, in the mass of her faithful, still journeying towards it; all that is Christian in them is working to make them more perfect Christians; all is movement as well as the beginnings of realization. They are Christians by their baptismal resurrection, and Christians because of the journey they are still making towards the Resurrection.

There are some in whom the Church is trying more than any to leave "this world" in order to encounter Christ: "Ten virgins went out to meet the bridegroom" (Matt. 25.1). These people live a life that is beyond "this world" whose "fashion passeth away" (1 Cor. 7.31), and, with nothing binding their hearts to earth, they utter the prayer which the whole Church prays in the world: "Maranatha!", that this "world may pass away and grace come."[7] "O Christ," they say, "thou art all things to me. I keep myself chaste for thee, and holding my burning lamp, I run to meet thee."[8] They are the sign of the Church's longing for the parousia.

II. *EFFECTING SALVATION*

It is the Christian's privilege that he cannot go alone to God, that he must always be working to save the world. The redemption of others is first of all a work of personal salvation. Christ himself won the salvation of the world only by realizing it in himself.

---

[7] *Didache*, 9,10.

[8] St. Methodius of Olympus, *Convivium decem virginum*, *Oratio* 11,2. *PG*,18(209).

It realizes in itself the salvation of the world

The Christian virgin is a good instrument of that redemption of the world wrought in the hearts of the faithful. "I sanctify myself," said Christ; I go out of this world of flesh apart from God, in order to be caught up by the life of divine holiness, that men may find that death and that life in me, and that "they also may be sanctified in truth" (John 17.19). Virgins are joined to Christ in this sanctification; they are virgins because they are united to Christ in his redeeming act; with him they leave the world of flesh and enter the divine life. The work of redemption, the work of "virginization," takes place in them and they can pray in their turn "that they also may be sanctified in truth."

Thus the Christian virgin carries out a function of the Church. The Redemption already realized in Christ becomes effective for mankind in the Church, and this in so far as it is presented in the Church. She is the body of her Saviour in which men find the salvation of Christ's death and resurrection. It is her vocation to be the presence of the Redeemer and his redemption, to be it intensely in all her faithful. That is why St. Paul, "a minister of the Church" entrusted with making the mystery of salvation fully present in her, speaks of filling up in himself what is lacking in the Church of Christ's sufferings (Col. 1.24). He tries to fill the gap, that it may overflow with the full measure of the Resurrection: "Always bearing about in our body the death of Jesus, that the life also of Jesus may be made manifest in our bodies . . . So then death worketh in us, but life in you" (2 Cor. 4.10-12).

Christian virgins work in secret for this presence in the world of the mystery. They give their whole being to Christ: They welcome renunciations, death to the world; and thanks to them, the Church becomes more and more the body of Christ the Saviour, the "pleroma" which contains the mystery of Christ in its fullness. It is a real crucifixion that virgins accept; they are nailed to their cross body and soul, and raised up lonely above the world so that, from there, the Church can draw all things to God. In her virgins, the Church is unceasingly celebrating her great Liturgy in which the one and only sacrifice of the pasch is offered day and night. At the point of death, they will sing, "I will go up to the altar of God," for then the mystery of their virginal consecration will be consummated in the wedding feast of the Lamb, the Lamb standing in glory, his flesh slain (Apoc. 5.6). But even in this world, they are "a pure victim," their soul is an altar where, each day, Christ is immolated for the redemption of his body."[9] Christian virgins have taken up their abode at the heart of the mystery, the point where the Church is united to Christ in the work of redemption.

Spiritual motherhood

The Christian woman vowed to virginity thus experiences in a hidden way that motherhood whose visible reality she has foregone. God created woman to be the "mother of all the living" (Gen. 3.20); motherhood is inscribed in every fibre of her being. In Christ, she is not deprived of this, her glory and joy: "Rejoice, thou barren, that bearest not: break forth and cry, thou that travailest not; for many are the children of the desolate, more than of her that hath a husband" (Gal. 4.27). Having become one body with the Church, Christ communicates to her the Holy Spirit by whom he was filled at Easter, and who is God's infinite fruitfulness. In his Church, Christ becomes the new Adam, "the Father of the world to come" (Is. 9.6), who begets the multitudes of the nations to God.

The Church, no mere collectivity but a community, realizes her motherhood in every Christian, to the extent that each one is faithful to the Church's calling, to its union with Christ in the mystery of salvation. In the Church there is one Christian who contains within herself the whole vocation of the Church—our Lady. That is why all God's children lovingly call her "our

[9] St. Ambrose, *De virginibus*, L. 2,2; cf. L. 1,11. *PL*,16(211,206).

Mother." It is only virginity that can bring God's children into the world. Every girl in Israel cherished a longing to become the Messiah's mother; but Christ was born of the one who had chosen to forego earthly motherhood. "By the power of the flesh," woman gave sons to Adam; but to bring God's children into the world, Eve had to become Mary and conceive by the Holy Ghost.[10] Every Christian mother realizes this: to bring up the children born of her flesh as children of God, she must continually be raising herself up to the Spirit.

In the early Church, the consecration of virgins sometimes took place during Christmas night. St. Ambrose reminds his sister Mercellina that it was then that she received the veil of virginity from Pope Liberius. There is no better feast, he says, for consecrating virgins than this day upon which a virgin brought forth a child.[11] In this way woman's two claims to honour are celebrated, the grace of her youth and of her motherhood. She is a mother, and she remains forever a virgin, becoming ever more so. She shares the glory of her who was privileged by God above all other women.

A foretelling of the world to come

In the world not yet redeemed, the world of the realities of sense, grace is not satisfied with being present only in the heart of the Church. To pave a way for it among men, it must be preceded by signs that foretell it. The world needs to see these signs before it can believe: "You shall be witnesses unto me" (Acts 1.8), said our Lord. Virginity is such a sign. It bears witness to Christ redeeming us; it proclaims the mystery of Easter. It announces the death of Christ and the end of "this world." For the fact that Christians forego marriage is because "this world" is already condemned in the death of Christ. Why fasten oneself

[10] St. Augustine, *De Sancta Virginitate*, 6. *PL*,40(399): Married women do not give birth to Christ, but to Adam, and hasten to have their children born again by baptism.

[11] St. Ambrose, *De Virginibus*, L. 3,1. *PL*,16(219).

with this world's bonds when "the fashion of this world passeth away" (1 Cor. 7.31), when this world is already crucified upon Christ's cross (Gal. 6.14)? They have broken out of the enclosure of "this world"; they are living above it. In her virgins, the Church proclaims openly to men the truth she tells herself in secret in the Eucharist: she "shows the death of the Lord until he come" (1 Cor. 11.26). Men feel vaguely that "this world's" foundations are shaken; they perceive that the Church constitutes a threat to it, and so those who cling to "this world" start to hate the Church.

What so many men, alas, do not realize is that the Church is proclaiming the world's resurrection as well as its end—not its destruction, but its transformation. This may perhaps be because so many dedicated believers make the Resurrection too little visible, the death too much so—too much because it is not real enough, not accepted in the full joyfulness of love.

The Church proclaims Christ's resurrection as well as his death; she introduces into time the new era in which to live means to love far more. Already the sons and daughters of the Resurrection are to be seen among men. "The day star has arisen in their hearts"; "the day is at hand" (2 Pet. 1.19; Rom. 13.12); the charity of the new world has already begun to shine. "Rejoice," they say to their brethren, "again I say, rejoice . . . The Lord is nigh" (Phil. 4.4-5). Their joyous cry stirs up the torpid, creates a restlessness in the world, draws those who want to fasten themselves to the world that is passing away towards a more generous love. Like the eucharistic body of Christ, they are a leaven of virginity in the world of the flesh.

It is useful for an apostle of Christ to be free of the burdens of a family, unhampered by material shackles. But to see such liberty as the prime motive for the perfect chastity of an apostle is to misunderstand the mystery of the apostolate and of the Church. There are, after all, many laymen who exercise a more active apostolate than some who are vowed to virginity. But the world needs to see men and women who live by God alone; even Christian families need them as a reminder to their love not to sink into the bog of this world. Virginity does indeed guarantee that the apostle is free; but it is more than this, for it is in itself an apostolate.

Virginity liberates, but it mainly does so in the depths of the soul: it liberates love. "The flesh" is closed in upon itself; carnal man cannot make himself intimately present to anyone else. His love is weakness—like the flesh itself—shut in by the limitations of selfishness; to achieve any kind of fullness, it must concentrate on a single being. But divine charity is free; it is born in man when he dies to the bonds of the flesh; it spreads outwards; it enables the apostle to make himself intimately present to the world he has left, to enter the very heart of mankind to save it. For its nature is that of the Spirit who penetrates all things.

Far from being spread thinner, the intensity of this love for each person it goes out to, increases with the number upon whom it can be bestowed. Christ was alone when he lived according to the flesh, but once he attained salvation, once he entered the life of the Spirit, he began to be incarnate in all mankind. For the apostle, virginity is a condition of redemptive incarnation.

III. *VIRGINITY'S SAFEGUARDS*

As long as the Christian is in the world, his consecration remains on the way to being accomplished, and remains in danger. He is involved in the great temptation of the Messianic age—from which we pray God to deliver us—and to the very end he is faced with a choice. Virginity too must be accomplished daily, and is daily in danger, until the "day of redemption" with its meeting face to face.

Charity

To realize virginity and to protect it, one needs love, for its whole essence lies in total love. One must love in order to achieve intimate union with Christ; love with the force that projects man towards his encounter with Christ; love, because the new life in Christ is nothing but the Spirit of love. One must love God and one's neighbour. The man whose soul is now overflowing with charity is wasting his time in jealously preserving his bodily chastity, for he can have no part in the mystery of virginity.

Mortification

So fine a thing as this charity cannot but be threatened in hearts that linger in "this world" of the flesh. It must be protected. We must die more and more to this world; though we remain in it, we must cease to live by its laws: "They that are Christ's, have crucified their flesh, with the vices and concupiscences" (Gal. 5.24). One element of virginity is a constant putting to death—just as in Christ death to the flesh is inseparable from the life of the Resurrection. A daily purification of our hearts, of our sight and all our senses, accompanies and conditions each day's love. But this death is never sought for its own sake; the virgin only turns away from the "world" because he has eyes for nothing but the One. The world has its attractions, but "I love something better."

Humility is another element of this mystery in which the virgin is buried with Christ in death. His "life is hid with Christ in God" until the day when Christ shall appear (Col. 2.3-4). There is no virtue that the Fathers recommend more consistently to virgins.[12] Without humility, virginity is not simply in danger; it is already lost. The virgin has gone back on Christ's death, returned to the world of flesh whose prime characteristic is pride, "the pride of the flesh." "If anyone can remain chaste to honour the flesh of the Lord, let him remain in humility. If he glorifies himself, he is lost; and if he makes known his vow to any but the bishop, it is vitiated" (in other words, he has lost chastity).[13]

[12] Cf. St. Augustine, *De Sancta Virginitate*, 7. *PL*,40(412-427).
[13] St. Ignatius of Antioch, *Polyc.* 5,2.

Prayer

Love of God and renunciation, which are the two facets of the consecrated life, are a grace which, if it is to continue being given, must continually be longed for in prayer. On earth, virginity is in a state of prayer. It is going forward towards the bridegroom it does not yet possess fully, towards the mystery of death and resurrection that it knows only in part. It sighs, "Come, Lord Jesus" (Apoc. 22.20), and goes to meet him by its movement of longing; it comes to him by opening its heart.

Virginity in the world is a movement forward of the world. If there is no vigil and prayer in the darkness, there is no virginity. All these means whereby virgins preserve their consecration amid the world—holy charity, renunciation, prayer—all are simply virginal consecration in its deepest reality as expressed in their life. It protects itself by what it is, for it is a life in the Spirit of love, a death to the world and a movement towards fulfilment.

All the roads whereby we explore the mystery of virginity lead us back to baptism, that sacrament of the Redemption whereby the Christian life always finds its beginning. Virginity is no esoteric practice, no ascesis of supererogation; it is a striving towards what is essential, a realization of the Christian vocation in its characteristic purity, as it will be revealed at the Last Day.

For all believers, the Christian life is a long process of "virginization"; its mainspring is the sacred body of the dead and risen Christ, to which we are united by baptism and the other sacraments. In marriage, man and woman are given to each other, by Christ, to be pure: in other words, to love each other, for purity which is set against the rule of the flesh is simply real love. But by calling some of his followers to virginity, Christ wills to make them a prophecy of the Church as she will be when she has attained the goal of her redemption, the eschatological image of the Christian in whom the mystery of the Church, Christ's paschal bride, is accomplished.

Virginity lies at the heart of the Church, together with the feast of Easter, with baptism and with the celebration of the Eucharist. It belongs to the mystery of the Church, not as one part of a whole, but as the whole mystery lived out in certain members.

Easter Day used also to be the feast of baptism, of the Eucharist, and of the consecration of virgins. "It is Easter Day! Throughout the world the mysteries of baptism are being celebrated, and dedicated virgins are receiving the veil."[14] St. Ambrose reminds each virgin that during this Easter night, she came forward amid the neophytes dressed in white, carrying a candle, as a betrothed girl coming to her king, her bridegroom.[15] For her place was there, among the newly baptized; by consecrating her virginity she was descending to the depths of the Christian mystery. The Church, the gathering that celebrates the pasch, is there for the whole world to see, for angels and men. Virgins are an image of it, a witness to it. They must be careful that they be, before angels and men, an image of the salvation wrought by God in the world.

[14] St. Ambrose, *Exhortatio virginitatis*, 7. *PL*,16(348).
[15] Id., *De lapsu virginis*, 5. *PL*,16(372).

12

The Longing for Salvation

I. "THE KINGDOM OF HEAVEN IS LIKE TO TEN VIRGINS, WHO TAKING THEIR LAMPS WENT OUT TO MEET THE BRIDEGROOM." (MATT. 25.1.)

Ten virgins went out to meet the one bridegroom, bearing in their hands the lamp of their vigilance, the lamp which must not be allowed to go out: the kingdom of Heaven is like them. The kingdom of God on earth, the Church, is wholly in movement. It is not a static reality, anchored to this world, moving at the tempo of this world. Like the wise virgins, the Church is going out to meet the bridegroom. For the fulfilment, and indeed the very being, of the kingdom of God on earth lies ahead in the last days, in the glorified Christ who is at the end of time: it is essentially orientated towards, and drawn by, the reality that is to come. That is why it is in a state of longing, of desire, like the virgins who went to meet the bridegroom. Our Lord compared the Church to a merchant who sought the world over till he found a pearl of great price, and having found it, sacrificed all that he had to gain it.

According to the Epistle to the Hebrews, the Church, like Abraham, is always on the march, a stranger and pilgrim on earth. Like Isaac and Jacob, it dwells in tents, and still awaits the "city that hath foundations; whose builder and maker is God" (Heb. 11.9).

The first Christians compared themselves to people crossing the sea and wandering in the desert, travellers whose dominant idea was longing for the Holy Land. All the verbs St. Paul uses to characterize the life of Christians in this world are verbs of movement. The Christian "walks," "runs," strains to go forward. "So run," he urges (1 Cor. 9.24). "You did run well," is his congratulation (Gal. 5.7). He says of himself: "I follow after, that I may apprehend . . . I do not count myself to have apprehended [Christ]. But one thing I do: forgetting the things that are behind, and stretching forth myself to those that are before, I press towards the mark" (Phil. 3.12-14). And, at the end of his life, he can say of himself, "I have finished my course" (2 Tim. 4.7).

The Christian is on the march, not with his feet, but with his heart, his longing, his will to find.[1] "The true Christian's whole life is a holy longing."[2] In fact, when the Church gathered to celebrate the Eucharist, and thus to express her whole life, the essential prayer in the early liturgy was, "Come, Lord!" And the bride in the Apocalypse never ceases to sigh, "Come!"

We have here a fundamental law which obtains as long as salvation is not complete. Our Lord himself gave it to us in the Sermon on the Mount: "Blessed are the poor in spirit, for theirs is the kingdom of Heaven . . . Blessed are they that hunger and thirst after justice, for they shall have their fill" (Matt. 5.3-6). Blessed are all those whom this world cannot satisfy, to whom the earth is unjust, and who look to God alone for help and justice—the kingdom of Heaven belongs to these men with their longing.

Christ gave a description of two men. One glorying and self-satisfied, wishing nothing better than to be the Pharisee he was, faithful in observing the law with its tithes and fastings. The other, a publican, humbled and begging God to save him, "Have mercy on me a sinner!" And the latter alone was justified by God (Luke 18.14). Publicans and harlots went into the Kingdom before those who were officially "just" under the old law, who

---

[1] Cf. St. Bernard, *In Cant., PL,* 183(1185).

[2] St. Augustine, *In I Joh., tract.* 4,6. *PL,*35(2008).

were self-satisfied, shut in and happy in their own sufficiency, just and wise according to the letter. God, who came only for the sick (Luke 5.31ff.), the poor in soul and body, those who needed and wanted his help, had nothing to give these just and wise men, who were so pleased with themselves. All the gospel story illustrates the law expressed by our Lady: "He hath filled the hungry with good things, and the rich he hath sent empty away" (Luke 1.53).

When Christ appeared among his people, they were divided. A great many of the Jews attached themselves to Christ and entered the Kingdom; the rest rejected both him and his Kingdom. This "sorting out" of souls did not take the form of dividing those who were just according to the Law from the sinners, with the former accepting, the latter rejecting the Kingdom. The division lay between those who were satisfied with themselves, who felt no need of salvation; and those, who, finding nothing in themselves or their lot to be pleased with, went wholeheartedly towards the God of salvation.

Among them were some great saints, like Mary herself, filled with humility and longing; there were also sinners. What saints and sinners had in common was that both wanted God and his salvation. On Calvary, our Lady and the good thief came together in that desire, and together entered the Kingdom. The rich went away empty-handed; and the ordinary people, the poor, the sinners, were filled with good things—the Magdalens, the Zachaeus's, the good thieves. For their prayer was, "Have mercy upon me a sinner!" (Luke 18.13); "Lord, remember me!" (Luke 23.42). Of Zachaeus, we are told that he "sought to see Jesus" (Luke 19.3).

An "unwritten saying" of our Lord's runs: "I found them all drunk, and none among them were thirsty."[3] A longing for God and his salvation is the fundamental law of salvation for us.

---

[3] Cf. *Revue Biblique*, 56 (1949), 445.

II. *THE OBJECT OF OUR LONGING*

The object of this longing is the salvation God gives us in Christ. We desire salvation to come, the saving grace of God transforming us into God's life-giving holiness. St. Paul speaks of "the hope of salvation" (1 Thess. 5.8), "the hope of justice" of God (Gal. 5.5); of "looking for the blessed hope" (Tit. 2.13), which means simply our full transformation into Christ, that holiness, that "consummation" of which Scripture tells us.

The object of our desire is the same as the goal towards which Christ was going in his pasch, when "with a strong cry and tears" he went "to him that was able to save him from death" (Heb. 5.7). We want for ourselves God's life-giving glory which shines forth in Christ. For it was in that great cry that the Church was baptized; she is immersed in Christ's pasch, she is born there, and lives there, in that great movement in which he "died out of this world towards God."[4] Christ in us is a dynamic principle, for he is the Christ of the pasch. He is the *prodromos* (Heb. 6.20), the forerunner who draws us along with him.

That is why the Christian people is a journeying people, a people in whom the exodus prefigured in the past must be accomplished. We lead a Passover existence, an existence of passage, going from one ontological place to another; otherwise it would not be Christian at all. On earth, it can never be satisfied with itself, for it never arrived. Its longing hastens towards the final resurrection. It is a people forever "mobilized," having nothing here to call its own save the road along which it is speeding.

Even in heaven, the Church will be animated with the dynamism of the pasch. Even having attained the goal of its blessed fulfilment, Christ's movement towards his Father did not cease, but was made eternal at its highest point, in the paroxysm of longing with which he rejoined his Father. When the Church, in its turn, attains the fullness of resurrection in Christ, its desire will

[4] Ignatius of Antioch, *Rom.* ii,2.

be filled without being destroyed, its desire will reach its goal without losing its life. It is a longing that opened out, during this life, till it could take hold of the limitless gift God has given us in Christ, and it will never close. The Church will never move beyond the moment when the vehemence of its desire encounters the object that satisfies it. Man's happiness lies not simply in possession, but in seeking as well. In heaven finding will not do away with seeking, but each will be totally fulfilled through the other.

Meanwhile, the Church goes forward towards this twofold fulfilment of longing and satisfaction. "In all things [she] grows up in him who is the head" (Eph. 4.15). For the history of salvation is still in its beginnings in every one of us, still going towards its goal. Baptism is but the principle and promise of its fulness, as is the Eucharist. "We are saved by hope" (Rom. 8.24). Though caught up into the mystery of salvation even in this life, the Christian does not yet experience all its effects. We still groan in "this body of sin," in this existence "according to the flesh," which is an existence according to sin and damnation. We still need the glory of God (Rom. 3.23), the gift of the Spirit who is the life-giving holiness of God, in whom we are saved: "God hath called you unto salvation, in sanctification of the Spirit . . . whereunto also he hath called you unto the purchasing of the glory of our Lord Jesus Christ" (2 Thess. 2.12-13). We shall be saved when we are holy in the fullness of the Spirit, in Christ in glory. Salvation lies in holiness, and it is this that the Church longs for.

As God only gives salvation in Christ and in his mystery, and as God's holiness, the glorious life of the Spirit, is found nowhere in the world save in Christ and in his mystery, it is towards him that the Church's longing is directed, towards the Christ who, through his redeeming mystery, stands at the end of time. St. Paul was straining forward with all his might to grasp him (Phil. 3.12-14), and the whole Church moves towards him with the longing of betrothed love: "We look for our Saviour" (Phil. 3.20). "We look for the blessed hope and coming of the glory of the great God and our Saviour" (Tit. 2.13). When he comes for her, to unite her to himself in the glory of the Spirit, the Church will be saved.

The longing for the parousia, the longing for the salvation in Christ that belongs to the last days, for our total fulfilment in him, is so essential to the Church that, without it, the Church would cease to be Christ's church on earth. For the Kingdom is like ten virgins who went to meet the bridegroom, and the Church's whole life is spent in desire and expectation: "And you yourselves be like to men who wait for their lord" (Luke 12.36). Without this longing we should no longer be a Church at all, for to be a Christian means to be a man of hope (1 Cor. 15.19); we are, in St. Paul's words, they "that love his coming" (2 Tim. 4.8).

"Thou hast made us for thee,"[5] said St. Augustine, and this is above all true of the Christian. We are Christian by the movement that bears us towards God; Christian because we are caught up in Christ's passover in the movement which thrusts him into the Father. Quietism is something totally foreign to Christianity. The most genuine Christians, the saints, from Paul to Thérèse of Lisieux, have all been consumed with longing for the "coming," for their "gathering together unto him" (2 Thess. 2.1). That magnificent Christian, Ignatius of Antioch, at the opening of the second century besought his brethren in Rome to let him go, not to prevent his dying, for only then would he be a truly Christian man.[6]

All this is the work of the Spirit, who is the principle of creation and the agent of its history: he governs the world from its first creation until its eschatological fulfilment. St. Ignatius of Antioch felt the Spirit in him like a spring of water thrusting forward and murmuring, "Come to the Father."[7] It is also the working in us of the glorified Christ: "Christ in you, the hope of glory" (Col. 1.27). He has attained to the Father, he is the goal of human development, and his presence in the Church makes her totally "mobilized" for the Last Day.

---

[5] *Confessions,* L.1, c.I.
[6] St. Ignatius of Antioch, *Rom.* 6,2.
[7] *Rom.* 7,2.

III. *WHY LONGING IS NECESSARY*

No one can attain salvation without longing. Salvation is wholly God's work and his alone: "You are saved . . . not of yourselves for it is the gift of God; not of works . . . for we are his workmanship" (Eph. 2.8-10). What is there left for us to do but to desire salvation and receive it? Yet surely God calls upon man to use all his faculties to collaborate with grace? Indeed he does, but this wholehearted striving towards salvation consists solely in desiring and receiving it.

No effort of ours can give us God, but our efforts are needed if God is to give himself to us. Our co-operation lies in opening ourselves to salvation, in actively receiving it. With God's help, man creates in himself a capacity for receiving, he works to make himself ready, he hands himself over to salvation. This work of opening, this effort to prepare oneself for grace, is accomplished by having a sincere and active good will towards God; we may call this good will desire, giving the word the sense of a call from man's deepest self by which he accepts God's action entering him. Man's effort to collaborate consists simply in this total desire for God to reign in him: "Grace is God's share, the desire for grace my share."[8] That is why prayer is so necessary, and infallibly promises us salvation: "Ask and you shall receive" (John 16.24), for prayer is only the expression of our longing.[9]

Do we pray to tell God what we need? No, answers our Lord, for "your Father in heaven knoweth what is needful for you" (Matt. 6.8). Do we pray to make God more kindly disposed towards us? No indeed, for "God is love" (1 John 4.8), and ever disposed to save us; he is "God our Saviour" (Tit. 2.10-11), whose grace is ever besieging our frontiers, whose "nature is ever to show

---

[8] Psichari, cf. R. Maritain, *Les Grandes Amitiés,* p. 351.

[9] "The word 'prayer' includes all the rules of holy desire." St. Agustine, *De perfectione justitiae hominis,* c. 8. *PL,*44(300). "For thy longing is itself prayer." Id., *En. super Ps.* 37,14. *PL,*35(404).

mercy and forgiveness."[10] Prayer does not dispose God to give us grace, but it disposes us to receive it; it lays man open to the invasion of God. "He wills that in prayer be exercised our desire which enables us to receive the gift he has prepared for us. For it is a great gift, and our heart is small and narrow, and he has to say to us: Be you enlarged" (2 Cor. 6.14).[11] "Disposed to give to all, God only gives to him who asks, lest he give to him who is unable to receive."[12]

IV. *SALVATION AND SANCTITY ARE ALREADY THERE IN THE DESIRE FOR THEM*

If desire is man's share, and God's share the gift which is of necessity granted to that desire, then desire for holiness is in fact holiness. If it is true that the Church is like ten virgins who went out to meet the bridegroom, like the men who waited for their master; if in truth "the whole life of a genuine Christian is a holy desire," and true Christians are those who "love his coming," then indeed holiness is, on man's side, nothing but a great longing. It is through this longing that the Church realizes her definition and thus her perfection. "Our present justice is that by which we run, in hunger and thirst, towards perfection, towards the fullness of justice which will wholly satisfy us."[13]

Thus, when our Lord demands supreme perfection of his followers: "Be ye perfect as your heavenly Father is perfect" (Matt. 5.48), he is not asking them to realize that perfection by their own efforts—for they never could—but to desire it; their perfection will consist in the magnitude of their desire. When he asks that they love God with their whole heart, and with all their strength, and their neighbour as he loves him, he is not demanding that they themselves succeed in attaining this tremendous love. He

[10] Mass of the Dead.
[11] St. Augustine, *Ad Probam. PL*,33(500).
[12] Id., *En. in Ps.* 102, *PL*,37(1324).
[13] St. Augustine, *De perfectione justitiae hominis*, c. 8. *PL*,44(300).

is the Son of God, and no one will ever attain the perfection of his love for our neighbour. Man's job is simply to desire that love.

Our Lord commanded us "always to pray" (Luke 18.1; 1 Thess. 5.17). Only the rarest saints can produce that masterpiece of the spiritual life, a prayer that never stops. But our Lord does not demand that we succeed, but only that we will to attain the perfection of a holy and uninterrupted prayer. Does he demand that we actually avoid all sin? No. This would call for exceptional grace, such as is given only to a few privileged souls. But our hearts must have a longing, never-ending and ever-renewed, to live without sin. Does he, in fact, require us to succeed in spreading his Kingdom on earth? If we think this, then we are claiming power over God's rule. What our Lord wants of us is the longing which prepares us for his action, our work in order that "his kingdom comes." What God considers is our heart, our good will—not the success we achieve by our efforts. He looks not at the size of the widow's mite—except perhaps to pity her poverty—but at her generous heart, and says that she has given more than anyone. When he thus applauded the widow, he canonized good intention. "Never forget that God places a higher value on this humble good will with which one offers oneself to him, making one's life an oblation for his honour and glory alone, than for all the service we render him, however great."[14]

Christian perfection consists wholly, on our part, in desiring that perfection. Whoever desires it with all his heart has achieved the perfection God requires of him. Before God "we are more what we will to be tomorrow than what we are today."[15] Even the most exacting of the saints have never sought to find any perfection outside that of good will. Our present justice is that by which we run, in hunger and thirst, towards perfection. They are convinced that this justice is granted to our desire even in this world: "He

[14] St. Francis Xavier, Letter of Nov. 5, 1549. Cf. *Etudes* XII (1952), p. 319.
[15] J. Mallet, *Lettres à sa fiancée*, p. xxi.

who desires God with a sincere heart already possesses him whom he loves."[16]

"Oh, how far better it is to deal with God than with the world! To gain this world's goods . . . is it enough to want them? When we fail, then our desire merely increases the pain of failure. With God, how different it is! To want his love and his grace is already to possess them."[17]

The Church is a traveller in this world. Her role is to go from the pasch that marked her birth, to the parousia that marks her consummation. And the risen Christ is "He who comes." His role is unceasingly to meet the Church who desires him, from Easter, whence he brings the first-fruits of paschal glory, until the parousia, when he fills her with their plenitude.

Desire is equivalent to sanctity on two conditions: it must be a great desire, and a sincere one. The desire must be great, in proportion to the holiness which God has enjoined upon us; our heart must open to the perfection God wants to fill it with: "For this is the will of God, your sanctification" (1 Thess. 4.3). Yet to want divine sanctity for ourselves as we see it in the great saints, would seem to be madness, an unreal fantasy; these are fine words which might enchant the heart of a child, but not an adult who has seen life, who knows human nature, knows how rare are saints. Indeed, is it not damnable pride? No, indeed. The longing for real sanctity is neither naïvete nor pride, but the strictest duty.[18]

The Church is essentially orientated towards the Last Day, towards the fullness of her union with Christ, towards her total resurrection, her entire transformation into the living holiness of Christ. Her whole meaning and vocation would be vitiated if she

---

[16] St. Gregory the Great, *Hom.* 30 *in Evangelia. PL*,76(1220).

[17] St. Alphonsus de Liguori, *Vera Sposa*, c. 4.

[18] "Céline, do you think St. Teresa received more grace than you have? . . . myself, I would not tell you to look for her *seraphic holiness*, but rather to *be perfect as your heavenly Father is perfect*. Ah, Céline, our *infinite desires* are far from being dreams or chimeras, for Jesus himself has so commanded us." Letter of Thérèse of the Child Jesus, May 1890.

did not strain towards the parousia, towards her total union with Christ, "the Holy One of God," if she were not animated with longing for complete sanctity.

Christ imposes on all Christians, even the least, so lofty an ideal that the most ambitious desires could want no greater: "Thou shalt love the Lord thy God with thy whole heart." Could one ever have too great a desire to love? Christ also imposes upon us such an ideal of fraternal charity that the most ambitious desire could long for nothing nobler than what is demanded by this strict duty: "A new commandment I give unto you: that you love one another, as I have loved you" (John 13.34). How can it ever be said that our desire is too great, if that desire, however great, does not even achieve the level of what we are strictly bound to? However we increase our desire, far from surpassing the ideal willed by God, it can never even attain it: "Be ye perfect as your Heavenly Father is perfect." Our desire would have to be as boundless as God's holiness for us to respond to Christ's demand.

As for the mediocrity of his life up to now, that should never discourage a Christian, nor does it dispense him from having a great desire. A man's life is only mediocre if his desire is mediocre. There is neither childish naïvete nor pride in having a great longing for God. For God has already given us such a gift in Christ that we can only receive it by opening our hearts to limitless desire. What then has he given us? In baptism, and in every Mass that is said, he has given us his Christ and all the force of the Redemption. We have received the Christ of Easter who is the Christ of the Last Day in his power to sanctify all things. We have been given his riches of redemption, yet we do not yet possess them. God, Christ, his death and his glory, are things too enormous for us to grasp, too great to be contained in us. We must always want them more, open our hearts to take possession of the grace we have already been given. The Church must open herself wide so as to possess, at last, on the Last Day, the mystery of salvation which has been given her since the first day, since Easter.

Christians need never be afraid that they are asking too much when they pray. The greater the graces they ask, the more certain are they to be heard; for then only do their prayers fulfil God's will. "Ask for great things, and the lesser shall be given you in addition"—so Christ is supposed to have said according to a "logion agraphon." For thou, O Lord, dost always exceed our merits and our desires.[19]

The second condition will also be realized in this way: that the desire be sincere. For no desire for God is fully sincere unless it turns towards a total possession. The desire which is equivalent to sanctity must be no mere wish: "The sluggard willeth and willeth not," says Scripture (Prov. 13.4). He wants to get up and wants not to get up: "As a door turneth upon its hinges, so doth the slothful upon his bed" (Prov. 26.14). He says he cannot go out, because there is a lion in the road! (Prov. 26.13). In fact, he does not want to get up, but far prefers to remain in bed.

Man must unceasingly force himself to be sincere. For often the expression of his longing does not correspond with what he really wants, and he prays as though he did not wish to be heard. So it was with St. Augustine in his youth. He was fifteen; his father wanted to send him to the school of rhetoric in Carthage, but had to wait a year to save enough money. In that year of idleness, Augustine fell into the vicious ways in which he was to remain for fifteen years. He knew it was wrong, and he prayed, but he admitted later that he did not want his prayer granted: "Give me chastity and continence," he would say, "but not yet." "I was afraid to find my prayer heard too soon, and to be cured of this trouble," he explained.[20] God will not listen if there is no note of sincerity in our prayer.

Often, Christians are afraid of grace, afraid of being loved by God, afraid of what that mighty love will do to their self-will, though in it lies their happiness. In his retreat of 1872, Mgr. d'Hulst noted: "I begged Mary for some saints to [convert] Paris.

[19] Collect for the 11th Sunday after Pentecost.
[20] Confessions, book 8, s. 7.

Once again I felt stirrings of that question which always disturbs me: Why don't you ask this for yourself? and I am afraid to say such a prayer, because I am afraid it will be heard. That is the difficulty." Later on, grace triumphed over these hesitations, and he prayed daily to God for this.

We say the same words as the saints, the same prayers which won for them the graces of sanctity: "Thy kingdom come, thy will be done." For us they remain words only, a surface desire. We might be frightened if God took us at our word, and cry, as God's kingdom rushed upon us, "Stop, Lord, I did not ask for this!" For the saints, this prayer comes from the depths of their souls—*de profundis clamavi*. The saints are not moulded of a different clay from the rest of us. What distinguishes them is the magnitude and sincerity of their desire.

"Francis was already nailed to the cross with Christ . . . when he said to the Brethren: let us begin to serve God our Lord, for we have hardly done so up till now . . . And, with Christ as leader, he set out to accomplish great things."[21] We are drawn forward by the example of their freshness of heart. "I clearly realized," wrote St. Teresa of Avila, "that God never fails to reward our slightest good desire, even in this world. Let us never whittle down our desires. We must believe firmly that with God's help and our own efforts, we too can come to acquire what so many saints have succeeded, with God's help, in obtaining."[22]

And Bernanos, writing at the end of his life: "And I, my dreams, I wanted them boundless—what else is the use of dreams? And that is precisely why they disappointed me. Were I to begin my life again, I would try to make them greater still, for life is infinitely greater and more beautiful than I ever believed, even in my dreams, and I am far smaller."[23] More than all these words and examples of great Christians, is the great revelation of the value of desire to encourage us: "Ask and you shall receive."

[21] St. Bonaventure, *Legenda S. Francisci*, c. 14. Opera VIII, p. 545. Ad Aquas Claras, 1898.

[22] *Libro de la Vida*, c. 4.

[23] Bernanos, *Paris*, pp. 11 & 26.

What we must do is to place our soul in a state of desire, to say with the psalmist: "I have longed for thy salvation, O Lord; and thy law is my meditation . . . I have gone astray like a sheep that is lost: seek they servant" (Ps. 118[119].174-6).

On the eve of his death, Christ promised his disciples that he would come: "I go and I will come." He referred to his parousia, his final and glorious parousia, but also to his intimate parousia within the Church. From Easter onwards, our Lord never ceases to come to his own in the Upper Room, and all our life is under the sign of his coming. But every parousia can have a double effect, can give grace or damnation, according as we await this coming with longing or do not want it at all. Blessed are those servants who expect and desire the coming of their Master. Blessed the virgins who go out with lamps of desire. "There is laid up for me a crown of justice . . . and not only to me but to all them that love his coming" (2 Tim. 4.8). May the Lord grant us the grace of longing, the *supplicandi affectum,* the love of supplication spoken of in one of our Lenten "Prayers over the people."[24] We pray above all to the greatest of the "wise virgins," her whose "lamp is brightest."[25] May Mary, the Virgin of longing, share the oil from her lamp with all mankind.

[24] Monday after Laetare Sunday (4th in Lent).
[25] Petrarch, *Canzone* VII.

13

The Christian's Prayer
in the World

By immersing his Church in his own baptism of death and resurrection, Christ has taken her out of this time and space and brought her into eternal plenitude, where he sits at the right hand of God (Col. 3.1). Thenceforth the Church is Christ's body, dead forever to this world and raised in God. Why, then, must the Christian ask God for salvation if he already possesses it? Why beseech, why declare our need and our poverty, if we have already entered the promised land of the end of time, if we already "sit together in the heavenly places, in Christ Jesus" (Eph. 2.6). The Talmud tells us that "in heaven there is no more prayer [of petition], only thanksgiving will be heard."

St. Paul was certainly looking at the Church prophetically when he spoke of our being seated in heaven; in all such statements he is in part anticipating, for salvation will be complete only in the future. But it is certain that the Church on earth is linked to the world above; it communicates in the riches of eternal salvation, and though she has not yet, so to say, caught up with her final salvation, she is fed and nourished from heaven by the word of God and the sacraments, the two channels of eternal life.

Though he still needs grace, all the Christian need do is open the ears and eyes of his heart to hear and see "the good word of

God" (Heb. 6.5), and his mouth to receive Christ's body and all
the wealth of the Holy Spirit contained in it. A sense of sure
possession and of gratitude, a serene assurance must lie at the base
of all Christian prayer, just as baptism and the Eucharist are at the
base of all Christian life.

Yet we still need the prayer of petition. Indeed it is the prayer
that characterizes the Church on earth precisely because she is
still on earth. Petition, the prayer of poverty and humility, the
prayer that suffers and labours that the salvation of God may
come, corresponds, despite the grace we already possess, to an
essential element in our earthly situation—its incompleteness. To
neglect this would be to falsify our whole spirituality, to betray
and misunderstand the Church on earth whose goal is to advance
God's salvation in our hearts and in the world. The prayer of
petition is the prayer of man in this world to whom salvation is
given but not yet perfected. He prays by the power of grace, by
the gift of the Spirit, and thus as one who initially possesses salvation. But he asks that this salvation be granted to him in its
fullness.

That was how our Lord himself prayed as long as he was in this
world far from God: he prayed like a man in whom God's total
salvation has not yet been realized. Most of our Lord's prayers
that we know about are prayers of petition. He prayed for himself,
for he had yet to go to the Father and receive the fullness of life,
the divine and holy life of the Resurrection in which man's salvation consists. He besought that salvation with a tremendous power
of supplication, with tears, "with a strong cry . . . to him that
was able to save him" (Heb. 5.7). For his mortal humanity in
which he was like sinful mankind (Rom. 8.3) he asked glory of
the Father, he asked for that life of power and immortal holiness
in which man is saved (Rom. 3.23): "Father, save me" (John
12.27), "Father, glorify thy Son" (John 17.1).

His prayer for himself had universal echoes; it was the prayer of the world's redemption. This suppliant, with his arms outspread on the cross, is "the mouth of our nature";[1] he asks for his own glory in order that all flesh may be given life in him (John 17.1-3). The act of redemption was a supplication of Christ's whole being, a thrusting towards the Father, a desire that was also an act: "I go to my Father." Both in spite and because of already being God's son, he still went to the Father and was received by him.

Having himself prayed thus, our Lord taught his disciples to ask whenever he told them to pray: "Ask and you shall receive" (Matt. 7.7). "All things whatsoever you ask . . . believe that you shall receive: and they shall come unto you" (Mark 11.24). "Whatsoever you shall ask the Father in my name . . ." (John 14.13). The three prayer parables—the importunate friend (Luke 11.5-13), the Pharisee and the publican (Luke 18.9-14), and the unjust judge (Luke 17.1-8), all speak of the prayer of petition. St. Luke sums up the last of them thus: "He spoke also a parable to them, that we ought always to pray, and not to faint" (Luke 18.1). The unceasing prayer recommended in this parable is prayer of petition. At the disciples' request, our Lord formulated a prayer that was to be a model for all Christian prayer: "When you pray, say: Our Father . . ." That model is wholly and throughout one of petition.

All this remains valid, despite the fact that since then God has brought salvation into the world by the death and resurrection of Christ. The final salvation sought by the oppressed widow of the parable (Luke 18.8) has been realized in the redeeming Christ. But it is only realized in us in so far as our death in Christ and our resurrection are real. Though dead and risen in Christ, we are not wholly so, indeed often scarcely at all: "salvation in hope" (Rom. 8.24), in principle, in mystery. Petition is a prayer of need, and mankind still has great need of salvation. Encircled as we are with sin, weakness and death, "we are waiting for . . . the redemption

[1] Theodoret, *Com. in I Cor.* xv, 27; *in Heb,* ii,5-8. *PG,*82(360, 692).

of our body" (Rom. 8.23). We need spiritual help from God if we are to live as sons of God, for we still necessarily (and sometimes more than is necessary) live in the flesh of sin. The injunction: "Pray lest ye enter into temptation" has lost none of its force, for the flesh is as weak as ever. The great messianic temptation, the risk of letting salvation slip through our hands, is with us till we die.

The grace of the Holy Ghost which is our salvation and the motive of our assurance and our thanksgiving, is not something we possess as of right: it is a gift, and we must remain ever in the state of receiving it. That is why St. Augustine says that prayer alone can guarantee that we will persevere in that grace, for it is prayer that opens us to God's gift.[2]

Apart from our own personal need, there are the immense needs of the Kingdom. In his Church, Christ remains in agony till the end of time, continuing to utter that "great cry to him who can save him from death" (Heb. 5.7). St. Paul prayed "night and day" for the faithful, that they might persevere and be sanctified (1 Thess. 3.10; 2 Tim. 1.3). He prayed that the word of God would run and spread (2 Thess. 3.1). The Church is wholly advancing towards a salvation which she possesses as yet only partially, but which will come in response to her desire. She awaits God's help and the blazing out of grace. Christians are those who hope (1 Cor. 15.19). "We groan within ourselves, waiting for the adoption of the sons of God" (Rom. 8.23). "We look for the blessed hope and coming of the glory of the great God and our Saviour Jesus Christ" (Tit. 2.13).

The prayer of petition is simply the expression, even though sometimes unconsciously so, of the Church's longing for the parousia, her desire for the help that comes from God. Christians beg that God and his Christ come, and intervene throughout their lives to effect salvation, right up to the final intervention of the Last Day. The Church's supplication is a sign that her children have hope, that they long for the coming of the kingdom of God

[2] *De Dono Perseverantiae*, c. 6. *PL*,45(999).

their Saviour, both in themselves and in the world. The Our Father, the paradigm of all prayers, is a prayer of petition, and the petition is for the parousia: it is a prayer motivated by the incompleteness of God's reign in the world, and directed towards its fulfilment. It begins by asking: "Hallowed be thy name. Thy kingdom come." Its other requests, for forgiveness, for deliverance from temptation, even its humble wish for daily bread, all are directed towards the parousia in the wake of those first great petitions for the coming of the Kingdom.

When our Lord urged us to pray unceasingly, he pictured a widow oppressed by her enemies, asking a judge for protection and justice. If she only goes on importuning the judge long enough, he will grant her justice. "And will not God grant justice to his elect who cry to him day and night?" God will not be slow to help them, to bring them messianic salvation (Luke 18.7). In this parable, it is clear that all the Church's groanings are directed towards her final salvation, towards the day of God's tremendous and final intervention in the world. "Will not God grant justice to his elect who cry to him day and night?" All that Christians need, materially or spiritually, results from the fact that they live in a world of sin, death, and hatred, a world in which mankind's redemption is incomplete. And all the help we ask, and God gives, is related to God's intervention in that world to redeem us, which intervention he will crown when salvation is ultimately and wholly manifested, at the parousia. "Ask . . . that your joy may be full" (John 16.24).

The prayer of petition is the characteristic prayer of the Church on earth, the sign of her initial salvation as well as of her presence in a world of sin and death, and the expression of her orientation towards final salvation. Salvation, already realized in part, yearns to be fulfilled in us: "grace makes us ask for grace";[3] the Spirit, salvation given unto us, makes us long (Rom. 8.26) for the fullness of the salvation given us to be achieved. Thus, having received the body of Christ in the Eucharist, and the redemption that is in it, we

[3] Dz.-B., 176.

still ask "that our salvation may increase,"[4] that our hold upon the mystery already given to us may grow tighter. The prayer of petition is part of the paschal liturgy on earth whose purpose is to realize the pasch of Christ more and more fully in the Church; for his pasch was a mighty supplication, an opening of Christ's whole being to the being of God, that God might come, that he might reign: "I go to my Father." This prayer can only cease in our hearts when we are wholly raised to life, on the Last Day.

If there are some Christians who ought, more than others, to be men of expectation, of longing and of prayer, men who watch and wait for the dawn, they are the leaders of this people on the march to salvation, the leaders of its exodus to God, the apostles of the Church. They must "love his coming" (2 Tim. 4.8); they must be at the head of this great supplication, summing it up in themselves, bearing it forward to Christ, that he may come, that he may hasten "the time of refreshment" (Acts 3.20), that the Kingdom may come. Here too they must *be* the redeeming Christ in the world, the man of universal supplication, whose death was one vast longing, an uprush of love, a *clamor validus,* bearing him out of this world of sin into the glorifying embrace of the Father.

The mystery of the salvation of the world is wholly accomplished in Christ; the resurrection of all, the last judgement, all the events of the parousia, are already contained in the risen Christ. But while Easter was fully a reality for Christ, it is still only a possibility for the Church who must open herself to accept this redemption in its entirety. The apostle must impress upon the faithful this movement of prayer, this supplication. For to develop the need and habit of the prayer of petition in the Christian people is to promote in them an authentically Christian spirituality, the essential spirituality, paschal and eschatological.

Of all prayers, the prayer of petition is the most modest, a prayer that suffers, where praise and thanksgiving spring from the

[4] Postcommunion for the Mass of S. Tiburtius, April 14.

serenity and joy of a salvation already accomplished. In the scale of values we are accustomed to give it last place: we call it selfish, focusing on our individual profit, whereas the other forms of prayer, having attained the summit of encounter with God, leave behind all self-seeking, and contemplate God alone in his adorable perfection. It is true that petition often centres too much upon the self; but is it so imperfect in itself? Are the standards we judge it by the same as God's? The Son of God when he was on earth begged and besought, and in his glory, continues to do so without ceasing (Rom. 8.34; Heb. 7.25). If the Son of God himself so prays, then it must be that the prayer of petition can also attain to the supreme perfection of prayer.

Christ prayed for himself and for others. Even when he was praying for others, it was still himself that he prayed for, for he was the Redeemer of mankind, not by any outward calling, but by the exigency of his own being; so much so indeed, that the salvation of mankind filled the need of his own perfection. Yet this "self-seeking" prayer is also the prayer of the Son of God, and holy with God's own holiness. It is dangerous always to be trying to pray disinterestedly. Only God has need of nothing.

The love that receives can be as great as the love that gives. To love is to open oneself, to accept the gift of another, and it is to give oneself. Thus it is in receiving that one gives oneself best. God proves his love as much by taking us into himself as by giving himself to us. Love is a mutual communion. The Church's longing for the parousia is a longing to love: "The Spirit and the Bride say: Come" (Apoc. 22.17). The prayer of petition, though it begins by being selfish, ends by being pure charity. It is thus indeed the prayer of the Christian in this life, for it can suit itself to him in the selfishness of "the flesh" and lead him to the fullness of the Spirit. The road of the Christian on earth is the road of his prayer of petition.

And we may perhaps say of God that he finds a joy in such prayer that he does not find anywhere else. He hardly needs men to praise him, when he hears within himself an infinite praise, in his Word, he who created only to have those to whom he could give. Though creation was a free act, yet God had to create to have someone to whom he could give. Man is praise of his Creator by the gifts he receives from him, and by receiving those gifts. Thus, for Christians, participation in the "sacrifice of praise," the Eucharist, is most perfectly expressed by acceptance: they receive the body of Christ. The Church is the glory of God (Eph. 3.21) because she is the pleroma of Christ (Eph. 1.23), she is that which is filled with Christ's fullness.

Our Lord spoke of the great joy of finding the lost sheep. God's joy in men is the joy of a saviour. He can receive nothing he has not already got; he receives something only when we accept his gifts. The joy of our Father in heaven is the same joy a father has on earth when his child asks his help humbly and lovingly. When we pray, God receives what he wants. Thus it is a prayer truly meet and just, truly holy, that the Church utters when she asks God for salvation. Every petition calls to us the Kingdom in which God will be "all in all" (I Cor. 15.28), in which all things will be filled by him.

PART IV

OUR MASTER IN THE CHRISTIAN LIFE

14

"Know the Lord"

Hearing that Christ was going to go through their city on his way to Jerusalem, the people of Jericho gathered before the gate of the town to see the prophet. There was a short man there called Zachaeus, an important revenue official, "the chief of the publicans." In order not to be lost in the crowd, he climbed a sycamore, for "he sought to see Jesus who he was" (Luke 19.3). A few days later, our Lord made his entry into Jerusalem. Some Greeks, men who "feared God," who had come up to the holy city for the feast, approached Philip, one of the disciples: "Sir," they said with respect, "we would see Jesus" (John 12.21).

Curiosity about our Lord, a desire to penetrate his mystery, amounting often to a passionate and anguished longing, has continued for two thousand years. To see Christ! What multitudes of men have felt the wish felt by the Greek proselytes and the chief publican of Jericho, with a confused sense that their own existence is in some way bound up with this man, and that he can satisfy their highest longings. "Blessed are the eyes which see the things that you see," said Christ, knowing that he held within himself mankind's happiness. "Many prophets and kings have desired to see the things that you see, and have not seen them" (Luke 10.23-4).

If man can achieve total joy, it can only be through the highest part of his nature, what makes him most a man: his knowledge.

Indeed, our Lord said: "This is eternal life, that they may know
. . ." (John 17.3). Yet when the light enters man, it must not be
a light without life that touches his intellect alone, but a living and
life-giving light that penetrates the whole man: "Father, the hour is
come, glorify thy Son, that thy Son may glorify thee. As thou hast
given him power over all flesh, that he may give eternal life to all
whom thou hast given him. Now this is eternal life: that they may
know thee, the one true God, and Jesus Christ, whom thou hast
sent" (John 17.1-3).

The whole Christian life may be defined as a knowing. "To know
God" is a phrase used in Scripture to contrast Israel with the
Gentiles "who know not God." The Christian people is defined by
its knowledge of God and of him whom God has sent. This does
not mean that the Christian has two different objects of knowledge,
nor two separate "knowings" each bringing salvation, one of
God, the other of him who is sent. To know Jesus Christ alone
is sufficient. Who knows Christ knows the Father. To Philip's
demand, "Lord, show us the Father and it is enough for us," our
Lord replied, "Philip, he that seeth me seeth the Father also"
(John 14.8-9). For the Father is revealed only in the Son
and wholly in him. He is the "invisible God" (Col. 1.15); he
"inhabiteth light inaccessible, whom no man hath seen, nor can
see" (1 Tim. 6.16). He reveals himself to the Son, but to him alone,
for in him alone is he well pleased. To the Son he opens all his
mystery, keeping nothing secret from him. It is not simply that
he projects upon him the light of his divine being; the Son is
himself that projection, "the image of the invisible God" (Col.
1.15), "the figure of his substance" (Heb. 1.3), the stamp of the
divine seal. And that Son, among men, is Christ Jesus: to know
Christ is to know God. "Eternal life is to know thee, Jesus, Son
of God" (John 17.3).

I. *THE OBJECT OF CHRISTIAN KNOWLEDGE*

This knowledge gives life and salvation, because its object is Christ the saviour; it is by its object that it saves us. Christian knowledge is not of a Son of God quite unrelated to us, the Son who is inaccessible, but of Christ who is God's son for us and for our salvation, who is by his very nature our Redeemer: the God-man, dead and risen for us.

This Son of God is a man, and to separate him from his humanity, to consider him apart from the Incarnation, is not to know him at all: "That which was from the beginning . . . which we have seen with our eyes . . . and our hands have handled . . . we declare unto you the life eternal" (1 John 1.1-2). St. John says we must not "divide Christ," that reality forever indivisible, which we cannot know apart from his human and divine unity: the man Jesus, the mediator of God who dwells in inaccessible light, the visible image of the invisible God, in whom God reveals himself. Except in the Incarnation, the Son of God is not begotten for us, the Word is not spoken for us, but only for the Father. If a man were to fasten his contemplation upon the Word in his divinity alone, he would never come to the Word at all, for we can only hear the Word as it is spoken for us, and it is spoken for us only in this man.

Christ must not be divided, and it is important to realize that this man is truly Son of God. The Jews saw Christ only with the eyes of their body, and did not know him, or they would never have crucified this Prince of glory (1 Cor. 2.8). Even before they crucified him, the Jews divided him, destroyed him in their minds, for he did not exist save through his divinity. We cannot see Christ as he is with the eyes of our body, and in this world he was not seen as he is. He only became visible when he had disappeared from sight.[1] He whom to know is salvation for men, is the man Jesus in his mystery of glory, revealed at Easter, the man who is Son of God.

Of course the mystery of Christ *was* already revealed during his time on earth, but only as dawn reveals the day. It is often said that his disciples "did not understand until he was risen from the dead." They understood neither the words, nor the deeds, nor the person. Their eyes did not see. "When you shall have lifted up the Son of Man, then shall you know that I am he" (John 8.28). Easter Day marked the beginning of the total revelation, and brought knowledge. A light they had not known before shone for them and "their eyes were opened." By raising Christ, and by the very action that raised him, the Father begets his Son fully *for us:* "He raised up Jesus, as in the second psalm also is written: Thou art my Son, this day have I begotten thee" (Acts 13.33). This Word, once hidden, is now proclaimed with power (Rom. 1.4), it is heard by all who listen. The Light coming into this world (John 1.9) has reached its zenith, for our advantage. Now there has come about what Christ promised: "You shall see me" (John 14.19).

Before he died, our Lord begged the Father to grant him glory in order that his divine generation be made known, and the Son be made visible. By seeing the Son, men would recognize the Father and be saved. This is the work of universal resurrection that Christ must achieve in all flesh, for eternal life is to know God and him whom he has sent. Henceforth Christ is present to the world in his total reality, and not merely according to his earthly body as the object of sense-perception, of physical hearing. "We know Christ according to the flesh no longer" (2 Cor. 5.16) but as Son of God. He is present and preached to us in the light of his glory; he is known in faith. Even the story of his life on earth was written by the Evangelists and is read by us in the Upper Room—amid the assembled believers, in the manifestation of Easter. "The light of the gospel of the glory of Christ . . . shines" throughout the world

[1] Ignatius of Antioch, *Rom.* iii,3.

(2 Cor. 4.4), a countenance illuminated by the transcendence of God, utterly human and close to us, and more wholly human, more fully present within us, because it is divine.

God presents this face for our contemplation that we may be saved in its radiating glory. For the face is our Saviour's, the glorious image of our own salvation (2 Cor. 3.18). It would not be offered to us to contemplate, nor could it be, were it not the face of our Saviour, the image of our salvation, for this blazing glory that reveals his being is a fire of holocaust devouring a victim—devouring the man Jesus in his oblation for us.

The deepest mystery of Christ is revealed only in that immolation, in the work of our salvation. The Incarnation would be hidden from our eyes, would remain unknowable by us, were it not for that work, for it is profundly a mystery of redemption, essentially directed towards our salvation. Thus it is only declared, only revealed, in the saving death. The Son of God is known when he appears as a Saviour. He is the Redeeming-God-Man.

In their essential reality, the Incarnation and Redemption constitute a single saving mystery. "God so loved the world, as to give his only begotten Son; that whosoever believeth in him may have life everlasting" (John 3.16). God has given his Son, sending him into the world (3.17), and delivering him up to die (3.14) in one act, in one movement of his love. That is why Christ is loved by his Father, that is why he proclaims himself as Son, giving himself up for our salvation: "Therefore doth the Father love me: because I lay down my life, that I may take it again. . . . This commandment have I received of my Father" (John 10.18). Why does he not give the eternal mystery of his divine Sonship as the reason for God's love of him? Is he not loved as the beloved Son in whom God is well pleased? He is. But it is in the work of salvation that the Father recognizes Jesus as his Son, for that is the goal of the Son of God in his human nature. He could have said, "The Father loves me because I am his Son sent into the world," but this would have been to say the same thing. The Father had proclaimed his love by

the Jordan at Christ's baptism and on the Mount of the Transfiguration. But both baptism and transfiguration were anticipations
of the Death and Resurrection, prophetic images of the Redemption. God's words of love were spoken of the man Jesus "delivered
up."

The only knowledge of Christ that is of value to us is the knowledge of him as Saviour. Paul declared: "I judged not myself to
know anything among you, but Jesus Christ, and him crucified"
(1 Cor. 2.2). Thus has he shown him to the Galatians, "before
whose eyes Jesus Christ hath been set forth, crucified" (Gal. 3.1).
Christ's wounds are sources of knowledge as well as of salvation
—for salvation and knowledge go hand in hand—the open gates of
the mystery. Upon the Calvary of Christ's death and resurrection
the saints meditate, contemplate, and learn to know their Lord.
That is the true mount of transfiguration, upon which the coming
of the Son of God was revealed, and the divine filiation affirmed,
when Christ was delivered up for our salvation.

There came a Roman soldier who drew near Christ and struck
him with his lance, thus defining man's picture of the Son of God.
From generation to generation, till the end of time, they will look
upon this eternal likeness of God, "him whom they pierced" (John
19.37). The mystery of God is at last revealed, with these wounds,
this death, this heart being pierced. God's majesty is seen upon a
face that has been mocked and covered with blood through hours
of agony for us, in a body that has been pierced. God is now known.
Crosses are set up along all the roads of mankind, "trees of knowledge" whence comes the knowledge of God. Lifted up above the
world, like the serpent in the desert, on the Cross and in his glory,
the Son of God sheds the light of God among God's people. In the
heavenly city, the Lamb will still be the eternal lamp of knowledge,
the Lamb in his glory and his immolation (Apoc. 21.23) in whom
God reveals himself. In anticipation of that day of redemption, our
Lord said to Philip, "Who seeth me seeth the Father."

Upon the New Testament Horeb, God reveals his eternal name
in the burning bush, which he revealed to Moses but which could
not be then understood: "When you shall have lifted up the Son of

man, then shall you know that I am" (John 8.28). That I am God who is and who is to come, who has promised and will keep his word: the everlasting love in whom is the salvation of men. God is called by a new name, unknown before: "I have manifested thy name to men" (John 17.6), "not the name by which thou art called God, but that by which thou art called my Father."[2] He is the father of our Saviour, he is love.

Man could never have raised himself to the knowledge of God. A work may lead us to the knowledge of its author, because there is a connection, an analogy between them. An intelligent being who was not a man might come to guess something of man's nature by studying an implement man had made. And in this sense God may be seen in his creation. But what in fact could be known of the human mystery from so small a clue as something made by man's hand? And there is even less likeness between God and his creation than between man and his workmanship. The mystery of God can only be known in his Son, and that Son has revealed himself in the passover of his death and his glory. God is the Father of the dead and risen Christ, "Thou art my Son," he says at Easter, "this day have I begotten thee" (Acts 13.33).

Revealed at last, God appears to defeat understanding, expressed as he is by contradictions—in the Christ of glory and of power made nothing in a total gift of self. God in himself is not the same as the man Jesus dead and risen; but translated into the language of the Incarnation, God's fashion of being is defined in that nothingness and that life. This God is love (1 John 4.16), and that is something we cannot understand. God, revealed, is more of a mystery than ever. He is different from us, for since the Resurrection this man Jesus, God's image, is quite different from us. Between Christ's earthly life, lived like ours, and his Lordship of glory, lies death, a radical negation, an infinity of difference. The man of "flesh" has been destroyed, excluded from the divine definition. God reveals himself in this man, but only to show that he is utterly different from men. He is different, Holy, "separated from sinners" (Heb. 7.26), "dead to sin" (Rom. 6.10), for he is Love.

[2] St. Augustine, *Tract in Joh.*, 106. *PL*,35(1909).

The role of death, in God's terms, is to deny, but at the same time to affirm. It affirms most strongly; it affirms by the very fact of denying, expressing a total gift of self, a gift which exhausts all the possibilities of giving, to the point of totally denying the self. There was no other means but death which the man Jesus could use to express in himself that God is infinite in love. Death further proclaims what, in the terms of the Incarnation—in other words, in Christ—may be called God's humility: the fact that in God there exists a kind of humility unto death, the humility in its total purity that is proper to infinite love. Death tells of God's infinite love by its emptiness; Christ's glory tells us of it by its fullness, by the Holy Spirit who fills Christ and who is the fullness of God. All the divine attributes are personified by the Spirit: he is the expression of God's mystery, of his glory; he is the personification of love in God who is love. Christ is transformed into glory, into the Spirit, into the love of God. He is no longer merely good as he was on earth, but goodness itself, love itself, for it is he who is the outpouring that is given, that is communicated to his own, in the Spirit of God. From him there radiates power unlimited, but it is a power to create and to save; and there radiates too the justice of God, but a justice that is given for the justification of sinners.

This glory which gives him his true appearance, as "Son of God in power" (Rom. 1.4), which makes him the image of the Father, this glory is wholly for our benefit: "He rose again for us" (2 Cor. 5.15), "for our justification" (Rom. 4.25). This glory both proclaims that God is our Saviour, and effects that salvation. Look at your Shepherd, dead and at the same time glorified for you, and "fear not, little flock" (Luke 12.32).

II. THE NATURE OF THIS KNOWLEDGE

A knowledge of faith

The image of God revealed in Christ redeeming us is a supernatural one, hidden from the eyes of the flesh; to see it one must die to the flesh. Scholars may spend a lifetime studying the man Jesus; but this man is a mystery, and there is no road that will take them to it: he is in the bosom of the Father. Only the Father knows his personal secret, the Son in his bosom. Only the Father and those to whom he reveals his secret: "I confess to thee, O Father, Lord of heaven and earth, because thou hast hid these things from the wise and prudent, and hast revealed them to little ones. Yea, Father; for so hath it seemed good in thy sight. All things are delivered to me by my Father, and no one knoweth the Son, but the Father: neither doth any one know the Father, but the Son" (Matt. 11.25-7).

Christ was not surprised when the Jews failed to understand him. "It is written in the prophets: And they shall all be taught of God" (John 6.45). The Jews did not believe because they were not taught of God. To know Christ, one must belong to the flock of his disciples: "I know my sheep and my sheep know me"; for such knowledge is divine, a knowledge of God the Father and of his Son: thus "the Father knoweth me, and I know the Father" (John 10.14-15). Only God knows Christ, and they to whom he gives his own knowledge.

Blessed was Simon Bar-Jonah, because he was among the little ones, and recognized the Son of God during his life! Blessed they who see him—whether at midday on the road to Damascus, at the evening meal in the inn at Emmaus, when he came to supper in the Upper Room, or when he comes individually to supper with the believer (Apoc. 3.20). Blessed is the disciple, for "I will manifest myself to him" says Christ (John 14.21).

The disciple recognized the Son of God during his life, not by the eyes or ears of the flesh, but by the grace of his Father in heaven. "Blessed are the eyes that see the things which you see" (Luke 10.23), but still more blessed "are they that have not seen and have believed" (John 20.29). For the eyes by which we see the Son of God are not those of the flesh. Man must die to "the flesh," and rise on the plane of the Spirit. At first Paul had only a knowledge of Jesus of Nazareth according to the flesh, and judged him in the fashion of men; but after God had revealed him to Paul's heart, he knew him no longer in that way (Gal. 1.16), but came to contemplate him in his death and resurrection.

The man of flesh knows the realities of the flesh, but only the man of faith knows those of the Spirit too (1 Cor. 2.14). Christ has entered a divine sphere of life, the life of the Resurrection as Son, and since his resurrection he has been visible only to those who share that life: "You shall see me, because I live, and you shall live" (John 14.19), to those who "eat and drink with him" (Acts 10.41).

A knowledge of charity and of life

Knowing a person is never the same as simply knowing a fact, an act of abstract intellection. To know someone involves a full perception, a total knowing, in which the whole of our knowing being surrounds the object of our knowledge, so that we penetrate it from all sides and take possession of it. It is a knowledge of compenetration, something we experience, and is most fully realized in friendship. Anyone we cannot love remains a mystery to us, a house closed and impenetrable. Christ is a mystery too, but rather for the infinity of his openness, his unlimited comprehensibility. (The word "mystery" has, in fact, two diametrically opposite meanings.)

Our knowledge of Christ is a vital reality; it is as much an embrace as a knowledge, a profound experience; it is knowledge, through possession, of a person who already possesses us, a mutual taking hold granted to us by the goodness of the Lord. Christ says: "I know my sheep and my sheep know me" (John 10.14), and that "my" is the key word in the sentence: sheep and shepherd know each other in possession—as the Father and Son know each other (v. 15), as the Father and the Son who is in the Father's bosom.

St. Paul longs to "apprehend" Christ, as he is himself known and apprehended, to win him, to be in him, and thus to know him, in the most intimate communion, in the self-same death and resurrection (Phil. 3.10-12). Christian knowledge involves a real and mysterious *presence* in us of him who is known. Just as only those in whom the Spirit dwells can know the Spirit (John 14.17), and those who dwell in God can know God (1 John 2.3-6), so only those in whom Christ dwells can know him: "That Christ may dwell in your hearts, that . . . you may be able to comprehend" (Eph. 3.17-18).

In order to manifest himself, Christ begins by establishing a dwelling-place in us. He comes there not as into a house, but by taking possession of us, by a work of unification and identification, like a lover who wants to be in the beloved, to become one with her inseparably by a new, unifying creation. With men, love longs for such a union, but cannot create it. In Christ, love is the Holy Spirit by whom God creates all things, a creative love which effects what it wills. Having become one, Christ and his faithful know each other in this union. "In that day you shall know, that I am in my Father, and you in me, and I in you" (John 14.20). "In that day" the disciples will know it, in the era of the Resurrection, when they will possess and be possessed, when they will know, by a communion of being and of life, in the Holy Spirit.

The time of ignorance, when the disciples did not understand, before he was risen from the dead, is now over. "You shall see me, because I live and you shall live" (John 14.19). But the world will not see Christ in glory; it will never know him, because it does not possess him (John 14.17), because it has not eaten and drunk with him after his resurrection from the dead (Acts 10.41). Knowledge begins in secret, at the very centre of our being: "When it pleased him who separated me from my mother's womb . . . to reveal his Son in me. . . ." (Gal. 1.15-16). It springs up from the invisible point of contact in charity, where we are one with him. We know mysteriously the mystery of Christ. That is why St. Paul speaks of "the eyes of the heart." The Christian's eyes are open at the very centre of his personality, in his heart: "I will give them a heart to know me," says Jeremiah (24.7); "In that day you shall not ask me anything" (John 16.23), said our Lord. The disciples will no longer ask "What is this that he saith to us?" (John 16.17), for the Word will dwell in their hearts, and the Word is himself the answer to every question. "The unction which you have received . . . teacheth you" (1 John 2.27).

What we see with our eyes, what we hear with our bodily ears, remains outside us. Abstract intellectual knowledge takes place at the surface of our being. But knowledge of Christ shines into the furthest depths of our being, to the point at which we are most fully ourselves. Thus it is also our salvation, a light which fills us. This knowledge in the heart is inexpressible, for it is a personal knowledge shared by the two beings who come together in it. No word of ours is connatural to it, none is born from that knowledge. Only God has a word for it, in the knowledge he has of his Son, the Word himself, who is identified with that knowledge.

From its central starting point, this knowledge extends outwards in different forms, in certitude, in joy, in experience of the Lord's goodness and beauty. Man recognizes Christ and wonders, feels enriched by that realization, and loves. He is aware that his Lord does not simply possess many qualities that are good, but that he is good simply by being; that infinite Love is, so to say, made substance in this Redeemer dead to himself and living in the Spirit. He has learnt nothing new, but understands all; he understands all the Scripture that tells of Christ, and realizes that it is true. From this deepest point, the light can glow right up to the surface of the soul, taking shape in a variety of ideas, more expressible and fragmentary, refracting and changing in the prism of every individual in different ways, according to the character and activity peculiar to each.

III. *THE WAYS OF KNOWLEDGE*

The Church learns to know her Lord, when she unites herself to him and becomes one body with him. This union is achieved by communion in one death and one resurrection. They know each other in their union, and are united by their shared pasch: Easter is the day of their mutual knowledge. Our Lord was not knowable as long as he was in the order of the flesh, for the flesh is impenetrable and obscure; there is no true communion through the flesh. How much was he known on earth? Was he not known fully by his Mother at least? Certainly less so than he could be known in his death and glory. He sought to make himself known to his Mother from the beginning, calling her to die more and more to the flesh of her own Son, leading her from the first up towards the summit of death and of knowledge. Then did Mary truly know her Son, when she united herself to him in his mystery of death and glory.

Our Lord was not known before, nor did he "know" his Church before with this kind of knowledge, through union in one body in the Spirit. He had to give himself up for her, and draw her along with him in his death, in order to establish this knowledge of mutual and total self-giving: "I know my sheep, and mine know me . . . and I lay down my life for my sheep" (John 10.14-15). They know each other above the flesh, joined together in the instant of dying to themselves, in the charity of the Spirit. "The flesh" is closed, so it must die if we are to strive to love truly; our eyes are opened in death, in that moment of knowledge, when the light is no longer hidden from us.

The Lord dwells forever within the mystery of the Redemption; that is his filial mystery, in which he became before our eyes what he had always been (Rom. 1.3-4). "Where dwellest thou?" asked two of the disciples (John 1.38), and Christ took them into his tabernacle: "Come and see!" The tabernacle in which he dwelt among his disciples was his body in death and glory: "Come and see," he said, and drew them towards union with his sacred body, making them take part in his saving mystery. And the disciples knew their Lord in that tabernacle. When the Church consents to dwell together with her Lord, to live with him in death to herself, then she will know him, in love. She will take hold of him as he has already taken hold of her, will know even as she is known, in a mutual giving: "I will espouse thee to me in justice and judgement, and in mercy, and in commiserations, I will espouse thee to me . . . and thou shalt know that I am the Lord" (Osee 2.19-20).

By baptism, Christ brings men into the mystery of his death and resurrection, in the union of one body; and baptism is a *photismos,* an enlightening. Long ago, our Lord sent the man born blind to the pool of Siloe—"Siloe is interpreted, Sent," so that he was sending him to himself, to wash his eyes in the pool; thus he foretold enlightenment by the water of baptism.

Our Lord gave his disciples the Eucharist, and this, more than any other, is a sacrament of knowledge. On the road to Emmaus, the disciples' eyes were "held," they did not recognize their companion—indeed they had never truly known him. But in the evening, at the inn, "they knew him in the breaking of bread" (Luke 24.15-35). One evening, at the end of the road, they will sit down forever at the table of bread and wine, they "will sup with him" (Apoc. 3.20), and will see him "as he is" (1 John 3.2).

The ways of knowledge are the ways of love, in a total giving of self. "The flesh" and the Spirit are completely opposed, the flesh closed in on its natural selfishness, and the Spirit who is love. Charity opens our heart, "the eyes of our heart": "He that loveth me . . . I will love him, and will manifest myself to him" (John 14.21; cf. Eph. 3.17-18). Apart from charity, there is no knowledge; "If I should have all knowledge and have not charity, I am nothing" (1 Cor. 13.2), for I would not even have the knowledge. To love and to consent to die, "to be found in him . . . that I may know him" (Phil. 3.9-10)—here lies true knowledge.

The Church, needing always to know better, calls upon the Holy Ghost. She turns instinctively to him for knowledge, though it is not he whom Scripture calls the light. He is power, the omnipotence of God; but though he is not the light, it is still he who makes it possible for us to see, who gives us the power to know the Lord. He gives it because he is love, he is union with him whom we long to know.

Knowledge involves a close working together of wills, it requires faithfulness to the Lord's commands. "He that hath my commandments . . . I will love him and will manifest myself to him" (John 14.21). That is how Christ himself knows his Father: "I do know him, and do keep his word" (John 8.55). Sin, on the other hand, destroys all knowledge: "Whosoever sinneth hath not seen him or known him" (1 John 3.6). For sin divides, whereas knowledge is born of communion.

The paths of knowledge attain their end quicker when they go by way of humility, humiliation and suffering. It was in humility, humiliation and suffering that Christ united himself to his Church, by them that he loved and knew her. True love must always include this death to self, for it is necessary if one is to have union with and knowledge of another. But humiliation and suffering are short cuts, so to say, to love; in them death becomes true death. That is the moment of truly "dying with" Christ, of mutual knowledge. The light is then so pure and so deep that it is not even seen. But gradually there can be discerned in the depths of the soul the sacred face marked with humiliation and glory. St. Paul took this path of mortification. As a Pharisee, he had judged according to the flesh, and had not known. Then he was caught up, cast back upon himself, and cut off from all the roots he had lived by. He renounced all the claims of self, all causes for self-congratulation (Phil. 3.8-9), and, his heart stripped bare, he knew Christ and his power of resurrection, in a communion of suffering.

Humility is necessary for knowledge for the further reason that the mystery of Christ is a mystery of sonship; we can have no part in it without that loving humility which is how the relationship of Son to Father is expressed in the man Jesus. Christ's divine sonship could only be revealed in death, in a humility belonging to his whole being. "Thou art my Son," says his Father then, for the world to hear, "this day have I begotten thee," this Easter day (Acts 13.33). In the same way, whoever accepts to die to his false importance and to become God's child, will also be begotten by God and will know Christ: he will know Christ by being born with him—the words are almost the same in French, for knowledge is *connaissance*.

The Christian who is humble and loving enters the beatitude promised to the clean of heart who will see God. For only those who love God and their neighbour and have humility are truly clean of heart. Only they are true, genuine, without fault or alloy, without stain, pure as clear water; and it was of them and their purity that our Lord spoke when he said, "They shall see God."

IV. *SALVATION LIES IN KNOWING CHRIST*

"Blessed are the eyes that see," the hearts whose eyes are open. The springing up of light in the heart is the beginning of salvation; when that knowledge attains its peak, perfection has come. Between these two, the beginning and end of salvation, lies progress in our knowledge of Christ.

It was thus that St. Paul became a Christian: "by the revelation of Jesus Christ" (Gal. 1.12); his new life began "when it pleased God . . . to reveal his Son in me" (Gal. 1.15-16). "There fell from his eyes as it were scales" (Acts 9.18), the veil was drawn back, and Paul turned to look on the Lord's face (2 Cor. 3.14). Salvation came through his eyes. "Mine eyes"—the eyes of my heart—"have seen thy salvation." Christians experience their new life as a light which has burst upon them, and in the early centuries they used to speak of their conversion and baptism as an "illumination," calling themselves "seers" *(epoptai)* of Christ the Saviour, just as the three Apostles were "eye witnesses" *(epoptai)* of his majesty at the Transfiguration (2 Pet. 1.16-18).

Born in light, the Christian life advances by steps of knowledge. All the inward re-making of man is an advance towards knowledge: "stripping yourselves of the old man with his deeds, and putting on the new, him who is renewed unto knowledge" (Col. 3.9-10). And St. Paul longs for his Christians to have the fullness of knowledge which will enable them to be filled with the fullness of God himself: "That you may be able to comprehend, with all the saints, what is the breadth and length and height and depth: to know also the charity of Christ, which surpasseth all knowledge, that you may be filled unto all the fullness of God" (Eph. 3.17-19). He wants them to come "unto all riches of fullness of understanding, unto the knowledge of the mystery of God the Father and of Christ Jesus: in whom are hid all the treasures of wisdom and knowledge" (Col. 2.2-3). Sure of the riches of knowledge, St. Paul sacrifices all things, renounces all things "to win Christ;" all other goods seem to him loss compared with the supreme good of the "excellent knowledge of Jesus Christ my Lord" (Phil. 3.7-8). He unceasingly turns towards the face of the Lord; he exposes himself to his light, and feels himself "transformed into the same image from glory to glory" by the light of his face (2 Cor. 3.18).

But why must one pay such a price for mere knowledge, why must we yield up our life in communion with the mortal sufferings of Christ? No price would be enough to buy this knowledge "which surpasseth all" (Eph. 3.19), which is life in death itself, a fullness of possession and of experience, the experience of Christ in us and of the "redemption that is in Christ Jesus" (Rom. 3.24).

One day Christ will come, and will manifest himself, and will majestically keep his promise: "I go away, and I will come unto you." "A little while and now you shall not see me: and again a little while, and you shall see me" (John 16.16). "In that day you shall see" (John 14.20). We see him already in this life, but imperfectly, and we are saved by that coming and that knowledge, but imperfectly. During our life on earth, the face that shines upon us is still veiled—for our eyes are veiled—and is beginning to transfigure us "into the same image from glory to glory" (2 Cor. 3.18). Suddenly his light will blaze out before our eyes, and complete our transformation: "When he shall appear, we shall be like to him, because we shall see him as he is" (1 John 3.2).

This supreme knowledge will be something quite new, quite different from this world's knowledge, and different too in its effective power to redeem us. Our earlier knowledge will cease to be (1 Cor. 13.9-11). But it will go in the same way as the child's knowledge gives way to the adult's (ibid). Even in this world, our knowledge is real and living, born out of a living union with its object, in love. But here the believer sees and knows Christ only imperfectly. The object of our knowledge in heaven will be the same as the object of our knowledge on earth: Christ our Saviour in whom God reveals himself. Even, and indeed, especially, in heaven, Christ our Saviour will be the centre of life, our nourishment for eternity. It will not be a kind of heavenly tête-à-tête that man has with God in heaven, but the banquet of the Kingdom. St. Paul longed "to be absent from the body, to be present with the Lord" (2 Cor. 5.8); for him, the vision that is to succeed our earthly knowledge by faith will be of Christ (2 Cor. 5.7-8). Heaven is a Kingdom, where Christ is Lord, centre, all; it is a banquet of communion in the paschal mystery. This does not mean that our vision of God will be indirect, reflected in Christ as in a mirror. The faithful will see God's own face. But they will see it in this living and knowing union, in their identification with Christ in the Spirit, in the communion of the people of God in the paschal Christ who sees the face of his Father. Heaven is Christian. "I have risen and am with you"[3] will be the cry of the whole people gathered in their Lord.

Israel of old came "to see" Yahweh in his temple in Jerusalem. Henceforth, God is to be seen in the temple not made by the hand of man: in the dead and risen Christ. The goal of the Incarnation is achieved, the mystery of the Word come into the world to enlighten all men.

"Know thyself," said the philosophers of old, for there lies wisdom, there salvation. But how could salvation be found in man, in man's own movement to study himself? Since in his heart there is a thirst for salvation, how can he find salvation by searching there? Salvation is in the Saviour whom man finds, by getting out of himself, in the depths of his own heart. "Know the Lord," says Scripture.

[3] Introit for the Mass of Easter.

15

Christ the Way of Humility

That there is a virtue of humility is due to Christ. It has been said of humility that it is "the sign of Christianity,"[1] its characteristic mark, which presupposes that it must first be the sign of Christ. And indeed he did say: "Learn of me, because I am meek and humble of heart" (Matt. 11.29).

If a Christian looks for motives of humility, he will find two. The first comes from his creaturely condition, which places him wholly in God's power. In this, man's humility is a glory; it is the recognition of dependence that makes man great. For he is created, he is a man, he is a son of God through this dependence. The second motive comes from his sinful condition, which places him even below the creaturely condition: this is the humility of poverty, the recognition of debasement.

Christ's humility presents two similar aspects. It is founded upon his condition as man, Son of God, wholly dependent upon God. But in its other aspect, it relates to sin. In order to save sinners, he accepted the condition of sinful man which made him lower than he was, just as sin makes us something less than ourselves. In its first aspect this humility is natural, a humility of greatness, born of Christ's divine exaltation in his human being. The other aspect is not a humility of Christ's nature, but of his redeeming function, a humility which was on earth a humiliation.

[1] Ps.-Marcarius, *Hom.* 15 and 26, *PG*,34(593, 681).

I. *THE HUMILITY OF THE INCARNATE SON OF GOD*

Christ is the man-God, the man who is Son of God, and this glory produces in him an essential humility.

The humility of the God-man

We can look at the Incarnation in two ways—either as the Word's coming down to mankind, or a human being's being raised to substantial union with God from the moment of his conception. Some spiritual writers see the coming of the Word into the world as a tremendous abasement of the Godhead, an incredible humiliation of God. But such a view has no basis in Scripture; the Incarnation is not a humiliation of the Word, for God cannot abase himself. St. John does not say: "And we saw his humiliation"; he says: "We saw his glory" (John 1.14).

On the other hand, if we contemplate the man Jesus raised to the dignity of God, we find a great storehouse of humility. The power of the Holy Spirit which created a man-God in the womb of Mary, created an essentially humble man. So closely is that man united to the godhead that he is "taken up" into it, as it were "sucked in" by the Word, subsisting in him. God himself concludes his being and makes it personal. This man, then, exists wholly in relationship with God, is totally offered to him and his will, all openness and appeal to God. Nothing in him is closed, nothing folded in upon itself; he sets up no personal autonomy against God's possession of him: "All things which thou hast given me are from thee. . . . All my things are thine, and thine are mine. . . . As thou, Father, in me, and I in thee" (John 17.7, 10, 21).

The perfection of all humility is in this man, for nothing holds him back within himself; his whole being is a movement towards God, with no going back. There can be no more total submission, no more open receptiveness, than we see in the man Jesus, who subsists in God. This humility of Christ's is no abasement of man; it is a submission and an openness, the condition and the result of his exaltation; it is the substantial imprint of the glory of God. Christ's humility, rooted in the mystery of his divinity, will never be over. Death brings to an end the humiliations of this world, but this fundamental humility is not suppressed, but developed to its fullest, by death. Receptiveness to God's grace, and the imprint of that grace, become deeper than ever through the supreme exaltation of the glory of Easter.

On earth, the divine exaltation of this man was not complete in every sense, for God's power in him had not achieved all its effects. Christ came "in the likeness of sinful flesh" (Rom. 8.3), which is marked out by its lack of the glorious life of God (Rom. 3.23), by being closed, in an autonomy of weakness and poverty. He needed a more total bodily submission to the possession of God; he had to humiliate himself more profoundly at God's hands, to be more given, to be "sanctified" (John 17.19). He must do away with all likeness to "sinful flesh," with all that held him away from the Father, until he could say in his resurrection: "Thou hast laid thy hand upon me, Alleluia!" Christ's essential humility achieved its fullness in his death and resurrection. The man had opened all his frontiers to God's invasion, and Jesus was to remain forever fixed at the moment of his death and resurrection, in the moment of welcoming infinite glory.

Having attained its glorious perfection in Christ, the grace of the Incarnation now extends to the world, and with it comes humility. The work of redemption is accomplished in a way exactly the opposite of the attempt made by the first Adam: it divinizes us in humility. Christian humility is given to us by our insertion in the God-man. It is a baptismal virtue, inherent in the grace of baptism of which it is a kind of sign. Its presence in us is a criterion of genuineness, whereby we can judge our life, our charity, our prayer, all our Christian activity: nothing in us is Christian, unless it bears this imprint. It is given to us, but it is also demanded of us, for it must deepen in us along with the grace of baptism, until the moment of death when, in a total acceptance of God, man attains the fullness of his divine grace. Death will be, for the Christian, the feast of his humility, a feast he has been preparing for ever since baptism.

Filial humility

Our Lord is God and he is Son. He is wholly Son, in his divinity and in his humanity. He receives everything from the Father, yet in the Godhead is in no way inferior to him. But as man, the Son is subject to the Father. On earth, our Lord recognized this: "The Father is greater than I" (John 14.28); he accepted it lovingly, and directed his whole life towards the Father who is greater: "I go to the Father: for the Father is greater than I" (John 14.28).

From this fact of being less than the Father, he drew all the consequences of adoration and obedience. The Father alone kept the initiative in the scheme of redemption: "But of that day or hour no man knoweth, neither the angels of heaven, nor the Son, but the Father" (Mark 13.32). "But to sit on my right hand, or on my left, is not mine to give to you, but to them for whom it is prepared" (Mark 10.40).

Our Lord becomes the servant of that Father who is greater, the "Servant" spoken of by the prophet, in whose hands "the will of the Lord shall be prosperous" (Is. 53.10), and who dies for his sovereign Master. "Yea, Father, for so it hath seemed good in thy sight" (Matt. 11.26). "That the world may know that I love the Father, and as the Father hath given me commandment, so do I: Arise, let us go hence" (John 14.31).

The two ideas of the "Son of God" and the "Servant of God" are so close that they sometimes run together. The divine word spoken when the Spirit came down upon Christ by the Jordan: "Thou art my beloved Son, in whom I am well pleased" (Mark 1.11), is but a repetition of the prophet's phrase: "Behold my servant, I will uphold him: my elect, my soul delighteth in him. I have given my Spirit upon him" (Is. 42.1). In the Acts of the Apostles the two titles, Son and Servant, are joined together, *Pais Theou,* so that they cannot be distinguished.

Since the Father is the stronger, our Lord asks his help in carrying out the divine plan. He prays for the power to work miracles (John 11.41), for the glory from the Father which will enable him to give life to men (John 17.1-5). For, of himself, he can do nothing (John 5.30). He wants honour from the Father alone: "I honour my Father, and you have dishonoured me. But I seek not my own glory" (John 8.49-50). Whatever honour is given to him, he passes on to the Father: "None is good but one, that is God" (Mark 10.18).

For Jesus loves his Father. His humility towards him is nothing but love. Though his attitude is one of submission, it is of submission to a Father: "Abba, Father!" "Yea, Father!" "I give thee thanks, Father," "Father, the hour is come." Every great act of obedience opens with a reference to the Father: "That the world may know that I love the Father, and as the Father hath given me commandment, so do I: Arise, let us go hence" (John 14.31). The total submission of death was total love, a giving of himself into his Father's hands, a child returning to his Father. "Did you not know that I must be about my Father's business?" he had asked, long before (Luke 2.49). And now, his longing being fulfilled, he says, "I go to my Father."

Christian humility is a virtue of love, a virtue of sonship, and all true humility must be Christian, for there is only one Son, "Jesus Christ, his Son beloved and blessed."[2]

The glory of Easter did nothing to efface this filial humility; it fixes it forever at its highest point of adoring submission and love, on the Cross. Indeed we may say that Christ died in order that the Father should be more his Father than ever, and he more his Son, more begotten than ever: "This same God hath raised up Jesus, as in the second psalm also is written: Thou art my Son, this day have I begotten thee" (Acts 13.33). His glory places him, in the

[2] *Martyrdom of St. Polycarp,* 14.2.

whole of his being, at the first moment of existence, in his divine
begetting, and fixes him in the perfection of his attitude as Son.
Even in his body, he is with the Father in the divine intimacy in
which the Son is begotten.

Christ's pasch, his passage from this world to his Father, is the
Son's mystery at the height of its glory. The Word's being is total
movement towards the Father;[3] he is Son because he exists wholly
in relationship to the Father. Separated from the Father, held down
by our carnal condition, the man Christ was lowered beneath his
filial condition, he was not wholly "towards the Father." In dying,
our Lord said, "I go to my Father." And thenceforth, he is fixed
in this passover, in this death and glorification, this movement
towards the Father and union with him; he is wholly "towards the
Father." "He was constituted the Son of God in power by the
resurrection from the dead" (Rom. 1.4). Thus the humble Servant
is exalted in the Resurrection: "Behold, my servant shall prosper,
he shall be exalted, and extolled, and shall be exceeding high"
(Is. 52.13). But his exaltation consists in being made smaller than
before, more than ever the Father's little one.

Men grow when they leave the womb that bore them. But Jesus
rises above all things and grows supremely by entering more and
more into the womb of God, by letting himself be absorbed by it,
begotten by it even to his bodily life. From this time on, he is
greater than all the world, because he is more than ever the Son of
the Father; he becomes the source of the universe, the origin of all,
because he is wholly fixed in the origin itself, in eternal generation.

John the Baptist indicated him by saying: "Behold the Lamb of
God." And in his glory, in the Apocalypse, he is still the Lamb. In
the flock of sheep he is the little Lamb, and is thus able to save
the flock: *Agnus redemit oves,* the Lamb has redeemed the sheep.
He walks at their head, leading the vast flock to the springs of life
(Apoc. 7.17), because he is the Lamb. There is no contradiction in
the fact that Scripture urges us to become like both Christ and little

---

[3] John 1.1 should perhaps be best translated: "And the word was *towards*
(pros) God."

children. For in putting on Christ, we are born children of God; the more we become identified with him, the more like children we are.

From the glorious fullness of his own sonship, Christ extends to mankind his filial being and his attitude as a child of God. The grace of baptism is a grace of birth, of childhood. As the perpetual beginning of our Christian life, it makes us more and more born in God, children ever more humble and submissive, until we reach the very "springs of the waters of life," the springs of childhood, to which the Lamb is leading us. Our glory is to be sons, and our humility is the measure of our greatness.

II. *THE HUMILITY OF THE REDEEMER*

Christ's humility, which is inseparable from his condition as God-man and Son of God, is simply the welcome he gives to grace, to God's invading power; it is man's acceptance of God's glory. Because he was to redeem mankind, our Lord was not only humble, but actually humiliated. He accepted a condition of life lower than he need have; he abased himself beneath himself. To a Christian community unsettled by ambition and discord, St. Clement of Rome wrote: "Christ is of those who abase themselves, not of those who set themselves above their flock. He, the sceptre of God's majesty, the Lord Jesus Christ, came in no display of pomp and arrogance, though he might well have, but with humility."[4]

Before his day, when the Philippians were disputing among themselves, St. Paul urged them to strive to be superior in humility (Phil. 2.3). He set before them the example of Christ who, though of divine condition (a man who was God), laid no claim to divine honours, but lowered himself, took the condition of a slave, becoming like other men and, to all appearances, merely a man (Phil. 2.6-8). The Philippians must, therefore, also yield their rights, as Christ did—not making any merely temporary concessions to

[4] Epistle to the Corinthians, 16,1.

charity, but an essential concession, whereby he accepted from the first a life quite unrelated to his true dignity: "He emptied himself."

"The holy one of God" who is by rights "the heavenly man" (1 Cor. 15.48), the Lord who is Spirit (2 Cor. 3.17), in whom dwells the fullness of all reality (Col. 1.19) and all the riches of the "Spirit of glory" (1 Pet. 4.14), he whom the princes of this world would never have crucified if he had not hidden the glory of his countenance (1 Cor. 2.8)—he accepted to be an earthly man, a man "according to the flesh" of this world, needing the glory of God as we sinners do (Rom. 3.23). He bore upon him the imprint of man's sin: the weakness of death. He, the Son, found himself placed lower than the angels (Heb. 2.9). It was no Son's existence that he led: a slave among slaves, subject to the burden of our earthly nature, subject to the laws of the Jews (Gal. 4.4), subject to political authority (John 19.11), he had given up all his divine freedom. The contrast between what he had a right to, and what he in fact chose, is glaring: "Who being in the condition of God. . . . emptied himself, taking the form of a servant. He humbled himself . . . even unto death" (Phil. 2.6-8). For ordinary Christians, humility means acceptance, a recognition that they are men and sinners; for Christ on earth it was a renunciation.

Christ did not want humiliation for its own sake. As man he had a great urge towards life, and nothing in him sought negation. It cost him horribly to die, and to die such a death. He accepted death for one reason only. He set his face to Jerusalem as to the future: "And it came to pass, when the days of his assumption were accomplishing, that he steadfastly set his face to go to Jerusalem" (Luke 9.51). He foretold the Resurrection in the same breath as the death, and saw beyond the humiliation to the glory. The moving power of his humility on earth was his redeeming love. He loved his Father who saved and mankind who were to be saved. "That the world may know that I love the Father . . . let us go hence!" St. Paul defines Christ's motive for humility in a single sentence: "Being rich, he became poor, for your sakes" (2 Cor. 8.9).

Though it was a renunciation, our Lord's humility, as expressed in his abasement in this world, sounds much the same as his essential humility as a man who is Son of God. It was an acceptance of God and of his will, an acceptance of his own condition in the world as a result of God's will—of his poverty and mortality. That is why St. Paul identifies our Lord's humility with his obedience: "He humbled himself becoming obedient unto death" (Phil. 2.8). And Christians following in his wake, have accepted to be humiliated to something less than they are, falsely accused and scorned, but always as Christ was. Love must govern all voluntary humiliation, all submission. Otherwise, man is placing too high a value upon himself, and that is not God's will. Unless we love, there is no reason to obey, to renounce, or to be poor.

Because it is a humility of love and acceptance, it makes our Lord appear touchingly, genuinely human. Like everything animated by divine love, it is completely natural, a humility totally devoid of pride. It is without excess of any kind. It does not seek abasement for its own sake, for that would be paying an honour to the flesh (Col. 2.23), would close man to God, would in fact be pride; humility is not abasement, but openness; it is the soul's call to the Holy Ghost. Nor does it attempt a rigid stoicism which would set it above ordinary human weakness. The Father willed that in his earthly humanity, Christ should be "so much a man as to be nothing more." He does not overrate himself, taking up heroic attitudes. He is saddened by ingratitude; he shrinks from the agony he must undergo; he cries out like other men in pain.

It is a great comfort to us to see our Lord bearing his cross so "weakly."[5] "It would have been possible for him to take up extreme attitudes, to vaunt his heroism, and die as one consumed in a fire of life. But that was not what he chose. A sorrowful acceptance of death itself, falling crushed to the ground, that extraordinary sweat of agony; thank you, Jesus, for choosing thus, among all possible human reactions. Blessed be thou for having deigned to suffer like ordinary men do, poor broken men" (Charles du Bos). And in the accepted weakness of this man, the world was saved.

[5] St. Thérèse of Lisieux, Letter of Feb. 28, 1889.

Humility is Christian, for its only model is Christ. No philosopher had been able to show how man's greatness lies in accepting his weakness, and in loving. The humiliation even unto death which Christ accepted was a total welcome given to God's glory. The love which demanded that humiliation, in the same instant did away with it, filling it with glory as with a hidden fruit. For charity is the breaking through into man of the divine, the presence of God's mystery; it is the Holy Spirit, who is the infinite glory of God, communicated to us. What we call renunciation becomes, in love, a taking possession.

Though the humiliation was all that could be seen by men of flesh and blood, yet the humiliated Christ was in the act of achieving glory. His glorification did not follow upon his abasement; it filled it invisibly till the moment when the abasement was total and it could blaze forth. "For which cause God also hath exalted him, and hath given him a name which is above all names" (Phil. 2.9). When the abasement reached its final point in total acceptance, at the moment of death, Christ was lifted in the might of God, placed at the summit of the universe, and given possession of all things.

The humiliation had made way for the breaking through in Christ of the life-giving love of God. The glory of Easter, the power of the Resurrection, these are simply the Holy Spirit, the Charity of God, to whom Christ opened himself completely in death. For it was in the Holy Spirit that he was raised (Rom. 8.11). The Redemption took place through the humiliation which opened the way to God's charity. In the death of Christ, the man was filled with salvation, with resurrection, with the holiness of the Spirit. It is through weakness, through humiliations, that we must offer ourselves to the power of the Spirit.

Death and resurrection divide Christ's redemptive life into two phases—one of humiliation, the other of sovereign power. There is a sharp contrast between the two, yet there is an underlying force drawing them together—humility.

Christ's glory is a glory of redemption. It raises him higher than the whole world in order that he may serve the whole world; so much so that the universal lordship of the risen Christ is simply a universal service. For the whole of the Incarnation is redemptive; right up to the end of the world, Christ's coming has no power of lordship except for the world's benefit: "I came not to judge the world, but to save the world" (John 12.47). This is the law of the Kingdom: whoever is greater shall serve the rest, and his exaltation and his power depend on his mission to save: "The princes of the Gentiles lord it over them: and they that are the greater exercise power upon them. It shall not be so among you, but whosoever will be the greater among you, let him be your minister, and he that will be first among you, shall be your servant. Even as the Son of Man is not come to be ministered unto, but to minister" (Matt. 20.25-8). In the Kingdom, then, greatness is service; it is measured by service, by humility. And in the Kingdom, the greatest is Christ.

In the Upper Room, he gave a prophetic image, a sacrament of the Kingdom with the King as the food of his subjects. "He that is the greater among you, let him become as the younger; and he that is the leader, as he that serveth. For which is greater, he that sitteth at table, or he that serveth? Is not he that sitteth at table? But I am in the midst of you, as he that serveth" (Luke 22.26-7).

On earth, in his existence of humiliation, our Lord was at the service of his brethren to the furthest point that a man can be—to death. If, in the Kingdom, devotion is the criterion of dignity, where is the devotion, where the humility of Christ, in his divine exaltation? Between Christ's heavenly devotion and his earthly humiliation lies the same distance as between the life of glory and the abasement of this world. On earth, he carried his service to the limits of human possibility; now they stretch to the possibilities of God. Christ becomes the food and life of all mankind, not only sacramentally, but for eternity. Even in heaven, "he girds himself, and makes us sit down to meat, and passing, will minister to us" (Luke 12.37).

It could not be otherwise. Christ was raised up to the new life in the Holy Spirit. The omnipotence conferred upon him is the

Spirit's, his Easter glory is the glory of the Holy Spirit. Christ was transformed into the Spirit and has no majesty but in him: "He is the Lord who is the Spirit" (2 Cor. 3.18). The Spirit is love, outpouring, the humility and freedom in giving of God himself. Christ is great through love: "separated from sinners, and made higher than the heavens" (Heb. 7.26), he was at the same time raised above this flesh of weakness closed in upon itself, with its insuperable barriers to self-giving, its innate creaturely pride.

St. Paul sees it as suddenly lifted up, in God's raising power, above every creature in heaven and earth, above every name; and there, at this majestic summit, Jesus is given as head of his Church (Eph. 1.18-23). He is given, he is ours, a Lord who belongs to us, *our* Lord Jesus Christ.

We can help ourselves along the way to humility by meditating upon the majesty of God and the nothingness of all created being. But to seek humility by this road is fraught with dangers. God's countenance may seem so terrifying that we cannot bear its splendour; if so, man must simply cast himself face down on the ground in fear, and may well fall into pusillanimity. It is not for the Christian to lie prostrate and motionless before God; through the pasch of Christ in which he communicates, he must "go to the Father." Any merely intellectual way to humility is bound to remain lifeless and to fail of its effect. Humility is a virtue of the heart filled with the charity of the Spirit, and the Spirit "is the truth" (1 John 5.6) and cannot fail. To be humble, what is essential is to live in the love of God who is in Christ Jesus.

The surest road to humility is Christ. For he is "the way" (John 14.6). The Christian soaks up humility as a sponge soaks up water, if he lives in Christ. After the poverty of earthly man, trying to be a god by closing himself in upon his own littleness, becoming a god only in reverse, there has now come the man from heaven, Jesus, the Lord of humility, in the glory of his openness to God. Born into the pride of Adam, we are begotten to humility as well as to divine life in our Lord Jesus Christ. It is because he has become our way to humility that he is our Saviour. If we did not accept Christ's humility within us, we should have no part in salvation: "If I wash not thy feet, thou shalt have no part with me" (John 13.8).

To make certain of a Christianity of union and humility, St. Paul simply urged that we live intensively in Christ: "Let this mind be in you which was also in Christ Jesus, who . . . emptied himself . . . , humbled himself" (Phil. 2.7). To be humble, one need only live by Christ. There will gradually cease to be any least trace of pride in those who live only by Christ. Theirs will be a branch on which only humility and charity blossom: "I know that you are not swollen with pride, for you have Christ Jesus in you."[6]

[6] St. Ignatius of Antioch, *Magn.* 12.

16

The Heart of the Lord

Before they celebrate the Eucharist, the people ask the Lord each Sunday for a sprinkling of water to purify them. They recall the first aspersion of baptism, which brought them into the redeeming mystery of Christ's body, and they ask that it be renewed in them. On Easter morning, when the Church gathers to celebrate the mystery, she does not need to ask for it; her prayer has been heard, and she sees gushing up in her midst that water of purity. In the joy of this heavenly gift, she sings: *"Vidi aquam . . .* I have seen the water coming out of the Temple, from the right-hand side, Alleluia! And all who have been touched by that water are saved." What stream is it that "delights the city of God"? What Temple holds this treasure? What is the opening in the wall on the right-hand side, whence the stream flows?

I. *THE SPRING FROM THE RIGHT OF THE TEMPLE*

Water, image of the Messiah's good things

In the parched and thirsty East, water is an image of man's life and joy. Wherever there is a spring, there is life: "The wilderness shall rejoice, and shall flourish like the lily . . . it shall rejoice with joy and praise" (Is. 35.1-2). Man, wearied from his journey, covered in dust, weak with thirst, drinks deep, bathes, and finds his frame filled with a new life. Water, the image of life, of man's strength and joy, becomes for the prophets a rich symbol of the Messianic goods which Yahweh will one day bestow on his people.

When God brings his people back from exile, springs will appear all along the road of their exodus, as they once did at the foot of Sinai. Israel will know a new time of exodus, a return more wonderful still.

"Behold I do new things . . . I will make a way in the wilderness, and rivers in the desert . . . I will give waters in the wilderness and rivers in the desert, to give drink to my people, to my chosen" (Is. 43.19-20).

"They shall not hunger nor thirst . . . he shall lead them to the fountains of water" (Is. 49.10).

God will strike the rock as before, and make a spring gush out of it:

"They will not thirst in the desert when he leads them out: he will bring forth water out of the rock for them; he will cleave the rock and the waters will gush out" (Is. 48.21).

The land promised by God, flowing with milk and honey, yet having known so many years of barrenness, will now be transformed, to become a new and hopeful land:

"I will open rivers in the high hills and fountains in the midst of the plains; I will turn the desert into pools of waters, and the dry land into streams of waters" (Is. 41.18).

The whole people will be brought back to life, in the land made young again:

"Thou shalt have strength, and thou shalt be like a watered garden, and like a fountain of water whose waters shall not fail" (Is. 58.11).

When later they came to contemplate the future in apocalyptic terms, the prophets were to see the people as gathered together in Jerusalem, the holy city, in a worshipping assembly. A powerful torrent will come from the Temple, or from the holy city which will be wholly the house of God, and will water all the deserts round about:

"A fountain shall come forth from the house of Yahweh, and shall water the ravine of the Acacias" (Joel 3.18).

"It shall come to pass in that day, that living waters shall go out from Jerusalem: half of them to the east sea, and half of them to the west sea: they shall be in summer and in winter" (Zach. 14.8).

Ezechiel contemplates this Temple of the new Israel at some length. One day, Yahweh took him to the entrance of the house, at the right-hand side, facing east, and the prophet saw springing up from under the threshold a stream whose water flowed eastward towards the desert. The man who was with the prophet followed the spreading path of the water, and having measured a thousand cubits with his line, told Ezechiel to cross it, "and he brought me through the water up to the ankles." After another thousand cubits, the water came up to his knees. Another thousand, and he had water "up to the loins." And after a final thousand, "it was a torrent which could not be passed over . . ."

And when this river came to flow out into the Dead Sea, the lifeless mass of water in the sea was at once made healthy and alive and swarming with life, so that fisherman could sit on the bank, casting their nets.

And as he went back to the source, the prophet saw trees in the desert, all along the path of the torrent, trees with unwithered leaves which bore new fruit every month, "because the waters thereof issued out of the sanctuary" (Ezech. 47.1-12).

At Easter, Ezechiel's vision is shown to the whole Christian people in the splendour of its full realization, and they cry: "Vidi aquam egredientem de Templo a latere dextro, Alleluia! Et omnes ad quos pervenit aqua ista salvi facti sunt."

Sitting beside the well at Sichar, Christ told the Samaritan woman that the hour was come: God would give his people to drink and that water would be in every one of them a fountain springing up to life everlasting (John 4.14).

Water, image of the Holy Spirit

In the years of captivity and exile, in silence and prayer, the messianic hopes of Israel deepened. God himself became the object of their longing for salvation, God who was to dwell amid his people on the holy mountain, who was to give Jerusalem its true name: "The Lord is there" (Ezech. 48.35). Salvation for Israel will lie in the holiness of belonging to God.

From that God there will flow, for all who belong to him, a fountain of life-giving water. Israel has in the past rejected the spring that wells up in Sion (Is. 8.6), "the fountain of living water, and have digged to themselves cisterns, broken cisterns, that can hold no water" (Jer. 2.13). But when the time of grace comes, that fountain will spring up more abundant than ever from the very womb of God; the life-giving holiness of Yahweh, which is the Holy Spirit, will come upon his grace-filled people.

God will give his Spirit in a measure hitherto unknown. He will make him rest upon the messianic king in all the fullness of his manifestations (Is. 11.2), and will pour him out upon the whole people: "And it shall come to pass after this, that I will pour out my spirit upon all flesh . . . in those days I will pour forth my Spirit" (Joel 3.1-2; *Douai* 2.28-9).

This abundance of water promised for the era of grace was the image of a tremendous outpouring of the Spirit of God in the land of Israel.

It is not a stream that springs up from the depths of the earth but simply the Spirit of God flowing out from within Yahweh himself. Because this water comes down from the heights of God, the prophets coined the phrase "to pour out the Spirit," "outpouring of the Spirit," which the New Testament also used, and which was to become part of the Christian vocabulary.

This marvel of fountains springing up, which was to accompany the people in their new exodus, was to be simply the outpouring of the Spirit:

"I will pour out waters upon the thirsty ground, and streams upon the dry land: I will pour out my Spirit upon thy seed" (Is. 44.3-4).

"Until the Spirit be poured upon us from on high, and the desert become a forest" (Is. 32.15).

Surging up from the depths of divine holiness, this water will cleanse the people from all stains:

"And I will pour upon you clean water, and you shall be cleansed from all your filthiness . . . And I will give you a new heart, and put a new spirit within you . . . And I will put my Spirit in the midst of you: and I will cause you to walk in my commandments" (Ezech. 36.25-7).

Zacharias was later to see the fountain of the Spirit springing up in the centre of Jerusalem, as Ezechiel had seen the river flowing from the Temple: "In that day there shall be a fountain open to the house of David, and to the inhabitants of Jerusalem, for the washing of the sinner" (Zach. 13.1). "I will pour out upon the house of David, and upon the inhabitants of Jerusalem, the spirit of grace and of prayers" (Zach. 12.10).

God's gift which will characterize the messianic era will be this: an abundance of water, life-giving water. It is in these terms that the prophets promise an outpouring of the Spirit.

When the time of God's generosity came, and he was giving his Spirit to mankind, Christ and the Apostles used these same terms to speak of the Spirit: "Unless a man be born again of water and the Holy Ghost . . ." (John 3.5). To enter the Kingdom, we must be born of the Holy Spirit, and of the water that symbolizes him. St. Paul declares: "You are born by the laver of regeneration, and renovation of the Holy Ghost" (Tit. 3.5).

There could be no better image for the Spirit than living water, which symbolizes his springing up amid God's people and his miraculous activity. Water from a spring is holy and pure, bringing life and joy. Water begets to life and, even in its gentleness, it is powerful. Its origins are mysterious, rising as it does from deep in the earth, or falling from the skies.

Yet this water symbolism is of fairly recent origin. For a long time it was the wind passing across the earth like the breath of God that was used as the image for the Spirit. It was that wind, that breath, which gave the Spirit his name (in Hebrew, Greek and Latin, the word "Spirit" has this sense). He comes from the mouth of God, an emanation and a sign of his life, just as breathing is the sign that a man is alive. Passing over the waters at the genesis of the world, that divine breath brought life to them; entering man's nostrils, he made him "a living soul"; wherever God sent him he made life abound (Ps. 104.30; *Vulgate* 103).

The whirlwind, though still a sign of life, is also a sign of irresistible power. Throughout the Old Testament, the Spirit of God is the agent in all works of divine power. It is he who carries out the sovereign will of Yahweh; he enables men to fight, to conquer, to achieve, to raise themselves to the vision of the things of God. The strong sea-wind is his image.

Even in the New Testament, the wind remains a sign of the Spirit, remains the reality of this world by whose name he is called. "The power from on high" (Luke 24.49) will beat like a whirlwind upon the assembly of Pentecost, taking possession of the Apostles, and breathing into them that power of which Christ said: "All power is given to me . . . Going therefore, teach ye all nations" (Matt. 28.18-19).

But now the sweetness of the wellspring is added to the force of the whirlwind. As in the concept of God himself, a development has taken place: from transcendence to intimacy, from power to love. Not that the second idea has become a substitute for the first, love for power; the development is one of deepening and interiorization, and the final idea appears as the principle and explanation of the first. God's power, the words of the prophets and the proclamation of the Apostles, all the charismata and the outward works, all come from the silence deep down in the wellspring, the love which is the Holy Spirit.

This progressive revelation of the Spirit runs parallel with the saving history of the world which moves from the fringe of reality to its fullness, from the shadow to the body (Col. 2.17), from the first creation to the heavenly creation. The Spirit, the total reality, from whom everything receives being and life, is the principle of both creations. The first one was created by the breath of God, the second by the activity within God, surging up from the fullness of his being, from the womb of God who is Love: it is "born of water and the Holy Ghost."

The redeeming history of creation moves from a power God exercises outside himself towards the love which holds that power. The action, the power, was what appeared first, but at its origin is the wellspring, the divine charity which becomes manifest at the end. In the New Testament every labour of creation begins within us, in charity, and for an apostle to make external activity more important is to fall back into the Old Testament.

This, then, is the water that flows out from the Temple, from the right-hand side, below the door. But what is the Temple?

II. *THE TEMPLE AND THE DOOR ON THE RIGHT-HAND SIDE*

The prophet Nathan told David: "I will raise up thy seed after thee, which shall proceed out of thy bowels, and I will establish his kingdom . . . I will be to him a father, and he shall be to me a son . . . He shall build a house to my Name" (2 Sam. 7.12,14,13; *Douai* 2 Kings).

From thenceforward, the Temple was part of Israel's hope. When God came to rule, he must have his house, a dwelling whose ideal dimensions are given by Ezechiel (40-47), and his throne "in the midst of the Cherubims." Then Sion would be lifted up above the highest mountains, and the cloud of glory would rest upon the holy hill all the year round (Is. 2.2;4.5).

When the return from exile came to prefigure the salvation God planned for his people, the prophet Zacharias (2.8; 6.12) bestowed messianic praises on Zorobabel, because he raised the sanctuary from its ruins. Daniel saw the anointing of the Holy of Holies as coinciding with the establishment of the Kingdom of God: "Seventy weeks . . . and everlasting justice may be brought; and vision and prophecy may be fulfilled; and the saint of saints may be anointed" (9.24).

When the Jews demanded to know by what right Christ drove the sellers from the Temple, his reply was: "Destroy it, this Temple, and in three days I will rebuild it" (John 2.18-19).

When the veil of the Temple had been rent, when the Temple had been, to all intents and purposes, destroyed, Christ would, in three days, build the Temple of the last times; in his risen body, he is the Temple of the true religion.

And from the right side of that Temple flow the rivers of the Holy Spirit; our Lord foretold some months before his death that they would.

They were celebrating the feast of the Tabernacles, that feast which was, more than any other, a messianic one, "great and holy,"[1] the most joyful of all the feasts. It began as an agricultural festival whose purpose was to ensure rain for the autumn sowing. Later, it was used to celebrate the great works of God, saving his people from Egypt and bringing water for them out of the rock on Sinai. But by Christ's day, the feast of the Tabernacles was still more devoted to that other rock, that more miraculous spring, which were to appear with the Messiah.

Every morning the people celebrated "the feast of the water." A priest, attended by Levites, went down to the pool of Siloe and brought some water from it in a golden jug; the trumpets sounded three times to recall the promise of salvation: "You shall draw waters with joy out of the saviour's fountain" (Is. 12.3), and all the people waved palms and cried, "Hosanna, blessed is he that cometh in the name of the Lord!"

The feast lasted seven days. On the last day, the feast and the joy were so great that it used to be said: "Who has not seen the

---

[1] Flavius Josephus, *Antiquities* 8,4,1.

joy of [the feast of] the water, has never seen joy in his life"
(Mishna).

Every morning, then, the Jews had celebrated the feast of the
water. On the seventh day, "the last, and great day of the festivity"
(John 7.37), a loud voice was suddenly heard above the rustling
of palms and shouting: "If any man thirst let him come to me,
and let him that believeth in me drink! As the scripture saith,
Out of his belly [the Messiah's belly] *shall flow rivers of living
water!*" (John 7.37-8).

As the people were hailing the rock and the water gushing from
it, Christ stood up in the Temple and called to them: the rock
was there, and the water soon to gush out.

"This," the evangelist explains, "he said of the Spirit which
they should receive who believed in him: for as yet the Spirit
was not given, because Jesus was not yet glorified" (7.39).

The rivers spoken of in Scripture were a prophecy of the outpouring of the Spirit. The rock from which they would come was
a man's body, the pierced side of Christ on the day of his
glorification. The disciples must approach by faith, and drink the
rivers of the Spirit from their very source.

When he promised the Eucharist, Christ had foretold that whoever should eat his body should never hunger or thirst again, for
from that body a river would spring up into everlasting life. "I am
the bread of life: he that cometh to me will not hunger: and he
that believeth in me shall never thirst" (John 6.35).

All this was still only a promise. Christ on earth did not give
the Spirit: "As yet the Spirit was not given, because Jesus was
not yet glorified." The hour had not yet struck at which Christ
was to be exalted by his cross into glory. The sacred body was
not yet a source of everlasting life; the rock in the desert still
waited to receive the blow; it was from the Lamb's wound and
from his glory that the rivers of life were to flow together with
the blood of immolation.

Some time later, our Lord again foretold the coming of the Holy
Spirit, and himself as the source of that coming. There was singing
and dancing in the Temple, brightly lit to prolong "the joy of the

water" into the night of the last day of the Tabernacles. The people almost certainly saw themselves as dancing by the light of the pillar of fire that showed the way to the exodus: "I am the light of the world," declared Christ. "He that followeth me walketh not in darkness" (John 8.12). It was at this same period that the man born blind asked for light, and our Lord put clay on his eyes and sent him to wash in Siloe, the messianic pool—"Siloe, which is interpreted, Sent" (John 9.7)—from which the priest had taken water during the feast. He sent him to Siloe, he sent him to the Christ[2] to find the water of light and purification.

The instant Christ died, the veil of the Temple was rent, to proclaim the end of the old Temple and the opening of a new. Then a soldier came up, and struck Christ's side with his lance, and there came out blood and water.

Till the end of time, mankind "will look on him whom they pierced," and those who believe will rejoice at the sight: *"Vidi aquam,"* they will cry: "I have seen the water coming out of the Temple, from the right hand side." "I saw it," St. John tells us, "I have given testimony, and he [Christ] knoweth that my testimony is true" (cf. 19.35). From the wound in his side there came out the water of the Spirit with the blood of the immolation. Christ died in order that the rivers of the Spirit might flow from his sacrificed body. Again, this was but an image, the promise of a reality. The Spirit was to be given by Christ in his paschal perfection, slain and risen.

Why must Christ wait to have died and risen before giving the Spirit? "As yet the Spirit was not given, because Jesus was not yet glorified" (John 7.39). "It is expedient to you that I go, for if I go not, the Paraclete will not come to you. But if I go, I will send him to you" (John 16.7). He had to go to the Father in order to enter, with his human body, into the glory of heaven. For the Spirit flows only in the heights of the Father, and for men he flows only from the body of Christ.

The Spirit is the reality from above, the fullness of reality which

---

[2] St. Augustine, *In Joh.*, tract 44,2; *PL*,35(1714): "He washed his eyes in the pool whose name meant 'the Sent'; he was baptised in Christ."

is in God. Christ said we must be born from above (John 3.3) to signify that we must be born of the Spirit. It is in the divine heights that the Spirit flows forth, from the Father and from the Son who is in the Father's bosom. Only he who dwells in the heights with the Father can give the Spirit. That is why Christ said he must go to the Father.

Of course he dwelt in those heights from the first, but that was in his divinity, whereas our salvation had to be worked out in Christ's earthly humanity, by which he was in our fallen world, and for which he had to win the life all men needed. That is the place of our salvation, the point of contact between God and men: in the body of this man. If the rivers of the Spirit are to flow for us, it must be there; if those who believe can drink at the spring, it must be in Christ's body. "From his belly shall flow rivers of living water." That is why the Spirit was not given until Jesus was glorified. The Christ of this world had to ascend, in his body, to the Father, to become the source of the Spirit for us.

The Holy Spirit rested visibly upon Christ at the time of his baptism in the Jordan; he dwelt in him from the beginning of his life in the world. But the consecration of the Temple dates from Easter, when Christ was raised by the Spirit (cf. Rom. 8.11), by the flowing into him of all the life of God. Then was the Temple filled with glory—by the Spirit who is the glory and the holiness of God—then was its door flung open, and the rivers of the Spirit flowed forth to delight the city of God!

On Easter Day Christ appeared to his disciples, breathed upon them and said: "Receive ye the Holy Ghost" (John 20.22).

III. BY THAT WATER ALL ARE SAVED

The water that flows from the Temple is a water of salvation, a life-giving water. Christ died simply in order to give it to us, in order that it might flow together with his blood; he died to give us the Holy Spirit.

For the Spirit is our eternal salvation, the spring at the heart of God, the divine principle of all things.

The mystery of God's being is in him, he sums it up and expresses it. The God who, in Scripture, is defined by his omnipotence, holiness and transcendence, by his eternal fullness of being and life, who "is spirit" (John 4.24) and who "is love" (1 John 4.8), that God is wholly expressed in the Holy Spirit. Scripture shows him as the personification of divine power, the personification of holiness, of life and of perfection; he is *the* Spirit *par excellence*, the Love of God poured out in our hearts. That is why Scripture calls him "the Spirit of God," because he is the expression of God's secret, the exhalation from the depths of the godhead, the Spirit.[3] He is the personal definition of God's being.

Thus, if God wills to reveal himself, it will be through him. In him it is God, our salvation, who is communicated to us.

He is, therefore, the divine mystery in all its depth communicating itself to us, as mystery and communication at the same time, and he remains always the unknown God, close as he is to our heart; he is perfectly symbolised by the "Glory of Yahweh" which lay over the Tabernacle in the Old Testament, which was at once light and darkness.[4]

Because he is the fullness of being and of life, all that is and all that lives has its source in him, is born of water, is born of the Spirit. The Spirit of God moved over the waters of Genesis (Gen. 1.2), and life came to them; the Spirit was sent and all things were created (Ps. 104.30; *Douai* 103). All creation shares to some degree in his being and his life.

Following upon a first creation whose being was imperfect and whose life so frail that it succumbed to sin and death, man's salvation consists in entering henceforth a fullness of being and of life, through the gift of the Spirit in person.

All who are touched by those powerful waters are created anew,

[3] Cf. R. Asting, *Die Heiligkeit im Urchristentum*, pp. 90, 94, 98.
[4] In the New Testament, Scripture in fact identifies the *Doxa*, the Glory of God, with the Holy Spirit (cf. F. Durrwell, *The Resurrection*, pp. 94-7).

born again, "saved by the laver of regeneration and renovation of the Holy Spirit" (Tit. 3.5). They are saved in an eternal birth.

To find these waters of divine birth, man must come, by faith, close to the Saviour, and drink from their very source at the right side of the Temple: "Let him come, and let him that believeth in me drink, for from the belly of the Messiah will flow rivers . . ."

If we are to drink, we must come to that sacred body which is the only point at which those divine waters flow for us, the only point at which we can make contact with the heights of heaven. We must approach the gaping wound, for the Spirit only flows from the wounds in that body—in other words, from that body in its immolation; and we can only touch that body where its wounds are—in other words by our union with Christ in his death. And it is from the wound in the side that the rivers flow, from that centre, that deepest point of his being that we call the heart, from the exact point where the immolation took place. That is why the Church comes from all sides to ascend Calvary, to eat the paschal Lamb, and continuously to celebrate an inner Pentecost.

Blessed are those saints who have had the glorious experience of satisfying their souls at the stream from that open Heart! Blessed are all those who believe, for the source is open to all who dwell in Jerusalem (Zach. 13.1), to all the Church joined to Christ in his sacred body. He has risen for all men (2 Cor. 5.15); he submitted, for us all, to the glorifying action of the Father, that single action that remains ever actual. And that action is the entry into the man Jesus of the fullness of the Spirit. Whoever unites himself to Christ's body is caught up in the action that raises Christ, is invaded by the eternal Spirit of God: he becomes "one spirit with him" at the same time as one body (1 Cor. 6.17); he enters into the salvation which is in Christ Jesus.

These are the good things that shall be given to the man who comes to the Heart of the Lord.

17

Divine Childhood: A Meditation for Christmas Night

There is only one Christian feast, round which all the other feasts cluster—Easter, the feast of the king. Yet there are many of these other feasts, and it could not be otherwise, for Easter is too rich a feast to be embraced fully in a single celebration. We need a special day for Maundy Thursday, for Good Friday, we need the Ascension and Pentecost, we need the Assumption and All Saints'. For even though we have been admitted to the mystery of Easter, our mind could not take in in a single day the whole mystery of our redemption, a single reality with so many various aspects, and the wealth of grace that spills over from it. Because our mind is too small and our heart too narrow, we celebrate as a separate feast one most important aspect of the paschal mystery—the divine and saving birth of Christ. Christmas is a paschal feast which picks out and sets in relief one aspect of this too-rich paschal mystery by recalling Christ's birth into this world: Christmas celebrates our Lord's birth to save us.

I. CHRISTMAS, A FEAST OF THE PASCH AND THE PAROUSIA

Before he left this world, our Lord said: "I go away, and I come unto you" (John 14.28). He has gone, and his going does

not take him away from us, nor is it followed by a return; he goes
away in order to "come." For, despite all appearance to the
contrary, Scripture knows of only one "coming" of Christ, and his
death did not interrupt but "accomplished" it. There is but one
messianic coming, begun with no display of glory and with only a
limited manifestation of the Spirit in the world, and then suddenly,
at the end of Christ's life on earth, made complete and clear in a
flash of glory and the omnipotent fullness of the Spirit.

Christ "comes" seated on the clouds at the right hand of God
from Easter onwards, judge of the world and founder of the
Kingdom of Heaven, as the Synoptics' Jesus told the Sanhedrin.
He "comes" on "that day" in the hidden life of the Church, where
he dwells by the power of the Spirit, judging this world and driving
out its prince, raising up the dead, as the Johannine Jesus declared.
What is the coming referred to by these texts, what the resurrection,
what the judgement? It is the great messianic coming for the
salvation of all who believe in God, and the resurrection and the
judgement which bring the world's history to its close.

The glorification of Easter instantly bears Christ to the final
point of "his coming," to the high point of his redeeming activity
and manifestation. All the mystery of "the coming" is from that
moment accomplished in him personally: the Kingdom of God has
come, fully, in the man Jesus; God wholly reigns in this man and
imposes upon him his will and his power which is the Holy Spirit;
he gives him the salvation of the Last Day, making him live in the
eternal power of life which is the Holy Spirit. On that day Christ
becomes the eschatological "Lord," in whom all the fullness of God
dwells (Col. 1.19) for the world to come, the Saviour of all who
open their hearts to be saved, a condemnation to all who reject
him. He is the judge who divides, for he is the Saviour who sets up
the kingdom of God's justice, of holiness, in other words, in the
midst of the sinful world. Easter is God's eschatological intervention acting fully in the man Jesus and through him, affecting all
mankind.

It is for the Church to travel towards this Last Day which is present at the centre of her own history, to let herself be transformed into this Christ of Easter, to become more and more his body. In dying to herself, and in the life-giving love of the Holy Spirit, she accepts that the victory of the parousia, which is complete in Christ, be pronounced in her, and show itself gloriously. Every year Christmas celebrates and makes present to us in mystery Christ's "coming"—an event belonging both to the parousia and the pasch—in order that it may be proclaimed and fulfilled in us. Christmas it a feast of the parousia.

II. *CHRISTMAS CELEBRATES A BIRTH*

However, what the Church feels at Christmas in such a mixture of tenderness and love is not the parousia as it presents itself to our minds at Easter—the triumphal exaltation of the Kyrios, coming upon the clouds, condemning the powers of death and of hell; it is a parousia effected by a divine birth. The joy of Christmas is a paschal joy, the same joy evoked by the words of the angel beside the empty tomb, but at Christmas the angel of the Resurrection borrows the words of the angel of Bethlehem: "I bring you tidings of great joy: This day is born to you a Saviour" (Luke 2.10). We are contemplating the Lord of glory and his mystery by way of his birth into the world, thus restricting our perspective, stripping the paschal mystery of a complexity too rich for us, and isolating a single element upon which to concentrate all our attention: our Lord's birth.

Christ's coming for which we have prepared in the four weeks of waiting, that final coming over which we may feel some apprehension for the judgement it brings, that coming takes place, to our great joy, in a divine birth. The successive texts of the liturgy describe the speed with which this parousia comes: "Behold the Lord cometh upon the clouds of heaven with great power. . . . On the fifth day the Lord will come to you . . . Tomorrow will the wickedness of the earth be destroyed . . . Tomorrow you will see his glory." And on that morrow of wonder, that day of his coming, Christ is ushered into our midst with the words: "Thou art my Son: this day have I begotten thee" (Introit for Midnight Mass). On this "great and dreadful day" (Mal. 3.23; *Douai* 4.5), God intervenes in the world by a divine begetting; the salvation of the last days comes to us through a birth; the coming of the King of glory is a nativity; and the joy of the parousia which fills the heart of Christendom to overflowing is that supreme joy that a man feels at the birth of his first-born: "Thou hast made great the joy . . . for a child is born to us, and a son is given to us" (Is. 9.3,6).

When the Liturgy proclaims, *Puer natus est nobis,* "A son is born to us," it is recalling a memory, the birth of our Saviour in the flesh; but it remains a memory, not something made present to us, for the past can no more be brought back than the future brought forward.[1] Yet we believe that the birth of our Saviour is real now. Because of it we hear that majestic phrase rising from the sombre darkness: "Thou art my Son, this day have I begotten thee," without trying to make any subtle interpretations of these words about the eternal generation of the pre-existent Word, for to the Church, the Son who is born is Jesus her Saviour: "The Lord is born unto us today, and he shall be called the wonderful . . ."

---

[1] We speak of the Liturgy re-presenting events of the past, such as Christ's death and resurrection, and anticipating the parousia. Yet we must remember that a historical event cannot be cut out of the past or the future to be introduced into our present time. In their historical reality, Christ's death and the parousia belong one to the past, the other to the future. That the parousia is present in the world now in the Church, that it is manifest to the view of those who believe under the sign of the Eucharist, is because the end of time, judgement and the resurrection, all the reality of the parousia, are present in the risen Christ, and because Christ is present in the Church. Similarly, that Christ's death is present in the Church under the sign of the Eucharist and in the death of the faithful, is because the death of Christ is made eternal in its full reality in his glorification, and forms with it the one and eternal paschal mystery. Thus Christ's death is present wherever his body is present: in the Church and in the Eucharist. But Christ's earthly birth belongs purely to the past, and cannot be made present any more.

says the Introit for the Mass at dawn. It is the birth of the man-God, of the Saviour, that we await with such impatience in Advent.[2] As in other feasts, as daily in the Eucharist, the Liturgy commemorates an event of the past, and makes present a mystery of eternity. At Christmas it commemorates the birth into the world of Christ, and introduces into our present time the *hodie* of the birth into eternity of the man Jesus, Son of God.

III. *CHRIST'S BIRTH IN ETERNITY*

For there is in this man a mystery of eternal birth, a mystery of infancy, which the Church senses overwhelmingly on Christmas night and which is the mystery of our salvation. Christ used to call the disciples of the Kingdom "these little ones" (Matt. 10.42; 18.6; Mark 9.41; Luke 17.2); he gave them this title of humility and love because they were all like children; the Evangelists realized this, and linked these words addressed to the "little ones" with the texts that speak of children. One day he set a child in the middle of his disciples, and proposed him as the necessary model for all who want to belong to the Kingdom. "Unless you become as little children . . ." (Matt. 18.3). Now Christ knew that he was himself the Kingdom come into the world, and the form of all the disciples of the Kingdom. St. Paul tells us that it is Christ we must put on, and to do so accords with what he himself asks of us, for the child he set among us, whom we must imitate in all humility (Matt. 18.4), is the child of God, Jesus "meek and humble of heart" (Matt. 11.29).

Christ always preserved something of the child's attitude towards the Father. He spoke of "his" Father; he spoke of his power with a son's pride: "That which the Father hath given me . . . no one can snatch out of the hand of my Father" (John 10.29). He showed

---

[2] *Exspectata unigeniti Filii tui nova nativitate liberemur*, "We shall be set free by the new birth of thy only-begotten Son which we await," says the second Collect for Ember Saturday in Advent.

utter confidence in him: "Father . . . I knew that thou hearest me always" (John 11.42). On the Cross his tone is one of sorrowful surprise: "Why hast thou forsaken me?" (Matt. 27.46). With his last breath, most filial of all, he puts his life into his Father's hands. He never ceased to be God's Son, and in the early Church he was lovingly called *pais Theou,* a name combining a reminder of the Servant of Yahweh with an affectionate allusion to the Child of God.

Then the Father took him to himself, and introducing him totally into the secret of his divine being, into that embrace which confers sonship, he abolished in him the "condition of a slave" and brought his whole, once mortal, humanity into the eternal origins of the life of sonship, into the instant of divine generation. He generated him as Son of God in his entire being, saying in the act of glorifying him: "Thou art my Son, this day have I begotten thee" (Acts 13.33).

Christ was the Son from the moment of his conception, yet his form of life was not then the Son's. He lived the existence of a slave (Phil. 2.7; Gal. 4.4), a life away from his Father, the life of the men he was to save. He cannot have been living in the bosom of his Father all those years on earth, because he had to "go to the Father," who was separated from him by a distance that could only be crossed in bloodshed, because he had to renounce the life of this world to put himself wholly into the Father's hands. He was living the life of the sons of men, subject to the reckoning of days and hours, a life of weakness extending over successive years, a life growing towards old age and always liable to death.

But now, in his resurrection, he is forever young—younger even than at the moment of his birth into the world. His whole humanity it alive once more with a wholly new principle of life, fixed at the very source of all life, in the eternal generation of the Son of God: "He was established Son of God in power by the resurrection from the dead" (Rom. 1.4). The Father's action in raising him is of the order of the eternal generation; it is the extending to his frail humanity of all the power and glory of divine generation: the man Christ is born divinely in the generating action of the Father—an action whose object he had always been, but of which he now enjoys the fullest effects: "This day have I begotten thee." The mystery of the Christ of Easter is the mystery of the Incarnation come to its perfect development.

Christ will never pass on from this moment of divine birth; he will remain with his whole human being at that prime moment, in that beatifying acceptance of his divine existence. The first Adam grew ever older, and he is continuing to grow even more decrepit in us; in Christ man is young and new, living as he does at the very source of his newness, being today and forever begotten by God.

God received his Son, whose human love was so great that he wanted no existence other than in him; he caught Christ into his own love, which is the Spirit, enveloped, filled and vivified him with the Holy Spirit (cf. 1 Cor. 15.45), and thus raised him to life (Rom. 8.11). To be in the Spirit is to be born of God. The Old Testament saw in the Spirit the divine principle of fruitfulness, and in the New he is seen as the source of all filial life. It is he who caused the Virgin of Nazareth to become Mother of God: "Therefore the Holy which shall be born of thee shall be called the Son of God" (Luke 1.35). At his baptism in the Jordan, a presage and symbol of his death and resurrection, the Spirit descended upon him as he came out of the waters of penance, just as he was to descend upon him when he underwent the baptism of the Passion; and it was the fact of the Spirit's presence that caused God to say: "This is my Son." Everyone who wants to be born as a son of God must be immersed in that Spirit and the water that symbolises him: "Unless a man be born again of water and the Holy Ghost . . ." (John 3.5). The Spirit is the womb of God in which the sons of God are born, that womb of the Father which Christ entered in order to be "established Son of God in power by the resurrection from the dead" (Rom. 1.4).

It is to him that the risen Christ owes the freshness of his eternal youth, for the Spirit is the youth of God, the personal expression of his irresistible power; he is the definition of the divine mystery. After all, is he not the Spirit of life (Rom. 8.2), while God is he who lives? Is he not, throughout Scripture, the effective omnipotence of God, while it is his power that has given God his name? (cf. Matt. 26.64). God is holiness and transcendence, too, and the Spirit appears in Scripture as the Spirit of holiness, the expression of the being who is apart. God is love, and the Spirit is the Love of God poured out in our hearts (Rom. 5.5). "God is a spirit" (John 4.24) and he is the personal Spirit of God. Because he is the expression of the divine nature, every man he gives life to possesses the youth of God, bears the features of God, becomes a son who resembles his Father.

This youth of surging power is still, in Christ, a youth of innocence and loveliness. For the Spirit is divine joy, the smile of God reflected in all in whom the Spirit dwells. He is the all-powerful liberty of God, of whom "thou knowest not whence he cometh nor whither he goeth" (John 3.8), the divine fantasy that makes nonsense of all our calculations. There is, too, in him, something we can only call innocence and naïvete, for it is said of the charity which is the Spirit given to man that it "believeth all things, hopeth all things, thinketh no evil" (1 Cor. 14.5-7). The Apocalypse betrays a most powerful sense of the mystery of this divine childhood. The "lion of Juda," the conqueror, the fearful judge, is given a surprisingly gracious and tender name—he is "the little Lamb"; later he appears at either end of his life, in his birth in the world, and in his exaltation in heaven, as something essentially childlike (Apoc. 12.5).

Of course, in his resurrection, Christ became Kyrios, Lord of the last days, before whom the universe—angels, men, demons— bend the knee. But for us who believe, he is "our" Lord, he belongs to us, for it is for us that he is risen (2 Cor. 5.15; Rom. 4.25), for us that God begets this man divinely. On Christmas night, the Christian people know that the Lord is theirs, as in childhood alone a man can belong to another. In this divine newness, Christ is wholly something communicated to his people, and we sense that his goodness is not simply something he shows for us, but is what he is, that to the very roots of his being he *is* a gift. The Holy Spirit, love and principle of openness, in whom the divine Persons open out to each other and penetrate each other, has broken the bonds of his earthly narrowness and made him communicable. The risen Saviour "has become a quickening spirit" (1 Cor. 15.45), a being wholly animated by the Holy Spirit, who gives life to others by giving them himself. Whereas the first Adam grew old because of the limits that shut him in upon himself, God is forever young because absolutely open, because his whole being is transparent; therefore Christ is fixed both in the newness of his youth, and in love.

His joy in being continually thus born, in living in the Spirit of love, is far beyond our conceiving. And what must be the delight we can find in his youth? Whereas we soon exhaust our study of another human being, in Christ our love will never lose the charm of mystery, of a novelty ever new, and we shall forever remain at the beginning of the happiness of loving.

IV. *OUR SALVATION IS IN THIS BIRTH*

Christ's divine nativity is the parousia promised in Advent, and the Son's generation among men is God's eschatological intervention in their midst, the salvation which redeems man from old age and failing strength. This divine action which begets Christ to the glorious fullness of his filial life, is for our benefit, for Christ is risen for us. In our union with Christ, we become subject to that same divine generation, lifted out of the decrepitude of the old man and fixed at the source of life, at the moment of eternal birth, the moment of Christ's glorification—for we "are raised with" him. In Christ, all who believe are children, born of God in the Holy Spirit, and the holier they are the more sublime their childhood. True, as long as they live in the world, they are a wholly new creation only at the root of their new being, only in Christ their life-principle, while, in as much of the old man as they have not yet stripped away, they remain subject to the demands of age (2 Cor. 4.16). As they go on drawing closer to that principle and being transformed into him, they grow ever younger, sharing ever more fully in the divine birth that is in Christ. When the day comes for the mystery of their birth which now takes place in secret, to be perfected as a glorious parousia, they will be wholly and forever raised up to the moment of the divine birth, through the unique and eternal action of the Father's that glorifies Christ.

Then all creation will become filial, having its share in the youth of the children of God (Rom. 8.21). It is with a lively sense of the repercussions of Christ's divine birth throughout the cosmos that the Christian people, at Christmas, link with their own joy the splendour of the stars and the winter countryside, the praise of beasts and the hymn of the angels. At the beginning, there is the old man, "sin and death"; salvation comes at the end, in a divine childhood, in Christ, "the new man" whom God begets for us. This is what the grace of the parousia means, this is God's intervention in the "last days," this the grace of Christmas. God saves man from growing old by begetting him in his Son, Jesus.

Christmas is a paschal feast and a feast of parousia, a feast of glorification and of redemptive coming, and supremely so, because it is the feast of that divine birth which is the foundation of the mystery of the Easter coming and its glory.[3] Christmas recalls

[3] People sometimes ask whether Advent and Christmas are the beginning or the end of the liturgical year, and the tendency now is to place them at the end. In fact, the liturgy for these feasts does seek to realize in the Church the mystery of the redemptive coming, which is the mystery of the end of time.

If this question had been put in this form to thinkers in the early Church they would certainly have answered: Christmas is both the beginning and the end. In the same way they used to say that Sunday was the first and the eighth day of the week, for Easter, which we celebrate every Sunday, is the eschatological mystery which we shall only reach at the end of time, yet also comes at the beginning of all Christian life. Christmas is a feast

the birth in this world which inaugurated our Saviour's coming; it makes Christ present in the fullness of his divine birth, that is to say in his Easter glory, in which the grace of the Incarnation is consummated, and the coming of the Redeemer complete. On that day, Jesus is born divinely among us and communicates to us the life to which the Father begets him for us, and which raises us in our turn.

A birthday, both by the memory it recalls and the reality it makes present to us, Christmas is a family feast for the Christian people, and impresses its own special character on the piety of the faithful: the joy of adoration mingles with a sense of intimacy, and our love of Christ takes on a human tenderness. God is pleased that his Son should be loved in such a way on that day, for having implanted in us a tenderness that responds to the gaze of a child, he wills that this, like all our other powers, should respond to his Son. And it is the tenderness of virility and strength, devoid of any sentimentality. For the body of the Child of God is stained with blood. "I saw standing in the midst of the throne . . . a Lamb as it were slain" (Apoc. 5.6). Nothing affects us more strongly, nothing calls for a firmer resolve in us, than these mortal wounds from which he will never recover, these signs of his heroic love and the death he had to pass through to be born to God. The Child bears, too, the heavy sceptre of the Kingdom, and his place is at the right hand of the Father, upon the clouds of heaven. In his divine birth he is "the Son of God in power" (Rom. 1.4), who bears the title King of kings (Apoc. 19.16), and who judges the living and the dead.

The violence of these contrasts, and yet their mysterious harmony, this birth to life in the death of a man, this universality of power in a divine babyhood, this love of a son in such tragic

---

of redemption, the feast of the Easter mystery considered under one of its most important aspects. Christmas is the first of the Last Day when Christ "will come" to save us by being divinely born in his Church. Yet it is in this very mystery that the Church is unceasingly born.

majesty—all these combine to give our picture of Christ splendour and depth, as well as an inexpressible tenderness; they provoke in the heart of the Church a perfectly proportioned mixture of trusting and affectionate love, and total adoration.

PART V

MARY AMONGST US

18

Mary Amongst Us

The Christian religion bears a deeply personal imprint. Before being a doctrine it is a person—Christ—to whom we attach ourselves. And even the doctrine is simply giving conceptual expression to that person, to the Christ who is the incarnate Word of God. The institution in which the Christian religion unfolds, the Church, also bears that imprint. The Church is not merely a collection of people. She is the bride, loving and beloved, the mother of the faithful. She is realized in persons, individualized in them, and exists wholly in every believer, though in varying degrees of perfection. Tradition tells us that there is one Christian in whom the Church is realized in her full perfection, in whom she is concentrated and summed up—our Lady, Mary ever virgin.

We may recall the evidence from that tradition, both of the early Fathers and of the Middle Ages, and also of the "French School" which had so profound and sure a sense of the Christian mystery. "I am not surprised," said M. Olier, "that St. John understood the holy and glorious mystery of God's Church, for he had always before his eyes the Blessed Virgin Mary, in whom he saw the whole Church summarized and concluded."[1]

St. John did, indeed, realize this concretization of the Church in Christ's Mother. In a triptych—the woman with the twelve stars,

[1] *La Vie Intérieure de la Très Sainte Vierge Marie,* Ed. Faillon, vol. II, p. 127.

Mary at Cana, Mary beneath the Cross—he shows us Mary and the Church in their role of Saviour's mother, of associate in the Redemption, of mother of the faithful.

I. *MOTHER OF CHRIST ACCORDING TO THE FLESH*

1. THE CHURCH

"A great sign appeared in heaven. A woman clothed with the sun, and the moon under her feet, and on her head a crown of twelve stars: And being with child, she cried travailing in birth. . . . And she brought forth a man child" (Apoc. 12.1,2,5).

This sign in the sky of history, this woman, is the Church; all the writers in the early centuries agree to that, and if further proof were needed, the number of stars in her crown provides it.[2] Before he came into the world, Christ already had his Church in the people of God from which he was to be born. In this first form, the Church was constituted by an ethnic group, by a single race from which the Christ was to come: a maternal Church, a fleshly Church who bore Christ in its womb for an Advent lasting thousands of years, and then brought him into the world: "A great sign appeared in heaven: a woman . . . with child, travailing in birth."

This maternal Church, Christian according to the flesh, found her first personification in the woman of Genesis: this one woman, Eve, bore in her flesh the messianic seed, for God had declared an enmity between woman and the serpent, with the victory to go to the woman's offspring. The Church, belonging to Christ by her maternity, was in preparation, was already realized in this distant unique ancestress of Christ's; and it was in the guise of the

[2] In the Apocalypse the number 12 and all multiples of it signify the Church.

first woman that the Church appeared to the prophet of the Apocalypse: the mother of the Messiah was confronted by "a great red dragon . . . that old serpent, who is called the devil and Satan" (Apoc. 12.3-9), to whom God had said, "I will put enmity between thee and the woman."

All the Old Testament confirms the definition given in the Apocalypse: the people of God is an ethnic group from whom Christ will be born, a maternal Church in whose flesh seed has been sown by the promise of the Messiah. It is not all Eve's children who make up the people of God, but only those to whom the promise has been given; not to all the descendants of Noe, but only to Shem, was that promise made (Gen. 4.26). Of Shem's descendants, only the family of Abraham, then of Isaac, received the promise and were the people of God. Of Jacob's sons, the Bible sets Juda apart from the rest: it is his privilege to be the nucleus of the people of God, and his power too, for it is he who holds the promise; and the other tribes, who broke away from his, withered away, until the people of God was almost entirely made up of Judeans, of "Jews."

The whole reason for Israel's existence lay in the end in which its generations were to conclude; here lay its life, and its salvation, in this fruit that was ripening in its flesh by God's promise; it lived by the Messianic seed deposited in its flesh. The blessing given to Abraham lay in his offspring (Gen. 15.4-6; 22.16-18), in his seed which is Christ (Gal. 3.16), in whom even then he rejoiced (John 8.56). Sara's laughter was caused by the child born in her old age. It is always through accounts of offspring that the Prophets proclaimed salvation to Israel. "Behold a virgin shall conceive" (Is. 7.14). "I will raise up thy seed after thee, which shall proceed out of thy bowels" (2 Kings 7.12). "I will raise up to David a just branch" (Jer. 23.5). And so on, until the announcement came to a virgin in Israel: "The Holy which shall be born of thee shall be called the Son of God" (Luke 1.35).

The Church of God in the Old Testament is essentially maternal; it exists through its maternity, for it is made up of a union of those who are by their flesh united to the flesh of Christ who is to come. But though Israel begets according to the flesh, it is by God that its begetting is Messianic. Sometimes its births are miraculous indeed. For Israel is the spouse of Yahweh, the virgin of Sion dedicated to God, and it is the word of the Lord which has implanted the seed in her from the first. Sara, also a figure of the Old Testament Church which, for one moment, she alone represented, conceived by the word of God and by faith.

To the law of the flesh, to racial relationship, there must be added faith in the salvation that comes from God, and to refuse that faith is to be excluded from the Messianic blessing: "The just shall live in his faith" (Hab. 2.4). St. Paul was later to say that even in Old Testament times the true sons of Abraham were the "sons of the promise" who, though born of the flesh, were "born after the spirit" (Gal. 4.28-9). The maternity of Israel was among those things that are of the order of the Holy Spirit.

2. MARY

The pregnant woman of the Apocalypse, mother of Christ and symbol of the Church, can, and does in fact, receive a Marian interpretation: "That the dragon signifies the devil," wrote a fourth century deacon, "you are all aware, as also that this woman signifies the Virgin Mary who, in perfect integrity, brought into the world our head, and who also expresses in herself the image of the Church."[3] If the image of a woman bearing Christ in her womb, and giving birth to him, expresses the reality of the Church of the Old Testament, it is because that Church was wholly realized in Mary, was accomplished in her, Christ's mother. All of Israel's role, the significance of its innumerable births, were taken up by this one virgin of Israel and accomplished by her. The Church of the Old Testament flowed together, culminated, and attained its perfection in Mary.

The prophecies of the Old Testament have been called a

[3] Ps.-Augustine, De symbolo ad catechumenos, 3,1. PL,40(661).

"Messianic pyramid." At its base, Messianic prophecy extended to the whole human race, as represented by its first ancestors. As the promise drew towards fulfilment, it became the privilege of an ever smaller group. Noah alone held the promise, and of his three sons, the prophecy singled out Shem and his offspring (Gen. 9.26). Of all the Semites, only Abraham and his offspring received God's Messianic word. Even among those offspring there was a choice: only Isaac and his descendants were chosen, and of them only Jacob and his twelve sons. Even then, the promise became the privilege of one tribe, Juda's, and in that tribe, it was concentrated upon the family of David (Gen. 49.8-10; 2 Kings 7.16). Mankind as a whole, one race, one people, one tribe, one family, and lastly one person who received the final message: "Thou shalt conceive!" Gabriel, whose name means "God is strong," the angel who announces the times of fullness and consummation when vision and prophecy are fulfilled (Dan. 9.24), Gabriel, the last of the Messianic prophets who spoke in the name of the Saviour of Israel, was sent to one of the daughters of David, and said: "Thou shalt conceive!"

Messianic humanity, bearing the salvation of God in its womb, climbed the steps of innumerable generations until it reached its summit in this one woman. All the mounting lines of the Old Testament, all its history and prophecy, all its people, converged and found their fulfillment in Mary, as a pyramid rises towards its top and is concentrated in it. Gabriel, in his message, recalled the Messianic thread—the announcement made to Jacob, made to David, made by Isaiah (Luke 1.31-2). He foretold how in Mary the grace of Israel would find its fullness and perfection, and urged her to rejoice at it:[4] "Rejoice, thou full of grace, the Lord is with thee."

[4] The word the Vulgate translates as *ave* is the Greek word *chaire* which means, *Rejoice,* and which the Greek also used as a greeting. If Luke had wished to ascribe a word of greeting to the angel, he would, in this completely Semitic account, have translated into Greek the Hebrew form of greeting: "Peace be with you," as he does in far less Semitic contexts. His use here of the word *chaire* certainly bears its original sense, as it does

"Rejoice!" cries Gabriel, taking up the injunction so often given the daughter of Sion, the people dwelling in the holy city, inviting them to have joy in their Messianic salvation. For three centuries there had been no prophets, and it had not been heard. Gabriel once more takes it up, and brings it to the true daughter of Sion, she who is full of grace, in whom dwells all the Messianic grace of the people of God. "Sing praise and rejoice, O daughter of Sion, for behold I come, and will dwell in the midst of thee," proclaims the prophet Zacharias (2.10). And the angel says to Mary: "Rejoice, thou full of grace, the Lord is with thee." "Rejoice greatly, O daughter of Sion. Behold, thy King will come to thee," says the same prophecy again (9.9). And the angel's words are: "Rejoice, the Lord is with thee."

> Give praise, O Daughter of Sion!
> shout, O Israel!
> be glad, and rejoice with all thy heart,
> O daughter of Jerusalem!
> The Lord hath taken away thy judgement . . .
> thou shalt fear evil no more.
> In that day it shall be said to Jerusalem:
> "Fear not, Sion" (Soph. 3.14-17).

And the angel says to Mary, "Rejoice, thou full of grace, the Lord is with thee. Fear not, Mary, for thou hast found grace with God."

"Rejoice!" Yahweh's heralds made this injunction their signal, a trumpet-sound to herald the approaching coming of God and the time of the end when the promise was to be fulfilled. Now the announcement is made to Mary, and the promise is to be fulfilled in her. The daughter of Sion in whom God is to dwell is wholly personified in Mary. "But how shall this be done?" she asks. And the angel replies: "The Holy Ghost shall come upon thee, and the power of the Most High shall overshadow thee."

In the past "the glory of God" was revealed amid the people,

---

elsewhere in the Septuagint: "Rejoice!" Cf. S. Lyonnet, *Biblica*, 20 (1939), pp. 131-141.

and covered the tabernacle with a luminous cloud. This glory was simply God's holiness as it was manifest to sight, in contact with the Spirit of Yahweh in whom the majesty of God is revealed. In the New Testament, the two concepts of Spirit and glory run together, for the Holy Spirit is the glory of the Most High, the expression of the divinity, the intimate secret of the Most High revealing himself. Isaiah had declared that in the last times the cloud of glory would rest upon Mount Sion, upon the whole Messianic people.

"The Lord will create upon every place of mount Sion and upon all the assemblies a cloud by day and a smoke and the brightness of a flaming fire in the night" (Is. 4.5).

Today, Mary is Mount Sion, she is the whole people of Israel upon whom this burning holiness comes down. Christ, the fruit of the long, hard pregnancy of the maternal Church, is the fruit of Mary's womb. And it is by the word of God and her faith in that word that she is a mother, just as it was by God that Eve's maternity was Messianic, and by their faith in God that Abraham and Sara had a son. But more than in any of her forbears, was the word of God effective in her, was her conception miraculous, far more than they, Mary was the mother of Christ. And Mary had to believe in God more than the others: all the faith of the Old Testament came to fill her: "Blessed art thou that hast believed."

The whole Church of the Old Testament, whose vocation it was to beget in faith, which found its purpose and its meaning in bearing the Messiah, in its womb all this Church is incarnate in the daughter of Israel who said: "Be it done unto me according to thy word." Instinctively, Christians have put a Marian interpretation on many of the texts referring to the whole people. They thought that the singers of Israel, though they did not know her, were singing of this daughter of David who in herself was Israel incarnate. When God put an enmity between the serpent and Eve, Christ's far off ancestress, his words referred far more to Mary and have a far deeper fulfilment in her, for she, far more than Eve, is the mother of the Messiah. All the perfections of the Old Testament foreshadow those of Christ's true mother. The Liturgy attributes to her the praises of the bride in the Song of Songs, whom the Jews had interpreted as being the people of Sion. The praise given to Judith, the national heroine whose name (meaning "the Jewess") suggested the whole nation, is applied by the Church to our Lady: "Thou art the glory of Jerusalem, thou art the joy of Israel!" (Jud. 15.10). We call her Queen of Patriarchs, for it is through her that they are Christ's ancestors at all; Queen of prophets, for it was the fruit of her womb that the prophets foretold.

If the Old Testament Church was a prefiguring of Christ, it is because it was his mother, and every mother prefigures her son. Mary who was, literally, his mother, is the perfect figure of Christ. Like the people of the Old Testament, but far more so, she is the beginning of salvation.

She did not make this glory a cause for self-glorification. Did she even fully recognize it? Even had she realized it to the fullest, she would not have been able to take pride in it, for it was wholly grace and mercy. She was the representative of mankind in need of redemption, whom grace saves; she personified that nation, that child of the desert, born by the dusty roadside, whom God found, washed and fed and adorned, and made his bride (cf. Ezech. 16). She was Eve saved by God, mankind not as they were before they sinned, nor yet in sin and pride, but in the moment of grace and mercy when God said: "I will put enmity between thee and the woman." This humanity's merit was to believe in the word of God who saves, to accept his salvation. And Mary said: "Behold the handmaid of the Lord; be it done unto me according to thy word."

II. *ASSOCIATED IN THE REDEMPTION*

1. CO-OPERATING WITH THE REDEEMING CHRIST

"She cried travailing in birth . . . And she brought forth a man child, who was to rule all the nations with an iron rod. And her son was taken up to God, and to his throne" (Apoc. 12.2,5). Here Scripture condenses the work of redemption into a brief account of a painful birth into this world and an ascent to God. By being born of woman, Christ accepted an existence "according to the flesh" (Rom. 1.3), the existence of a slave rather than of a son (Phil. 2.7), in which he lived at a distance from his Father (John 14.28: "I go to my Father"), in a world of sin and of death (2 Cor. 5.21). Through his flesh, he belonged to an earthly people, was subject to its law (Gal. 4.4), and put himself completely within the world of sin that needed salvation. The work of redemption was achieved by the man Jesus, born into "this world," leaving it by a triumphal death; he entered the immortal holiness of divine life, and thenceforth draws along with him all those who put their faith in him.

A. THE CHURCH

The Church of the Old Testament needed Redemption

Though it bore within itself the seeds of salvation the Old Testament Church was a carnal reality, an earthly city, a "kingdom of this world." By its flesh it was united to Christ, to Christ according to the flesh—for it was made up of carnal men related to the flesh of Christ. But the flesh cannot give life. The Christ of this world, the Christ of flesh, had not yet himself attained the goal of the immortal life of the Spirit in which the salvation of men lay.

When, by his triumphal death, Christ left the world of the flesh, the Church of the Old Testament ceased to exist. In Christ there is neither Jew nor Greek (Gal. 3.28); all the limitations, all the bonds of the flesh are destroyed in him. The Church whose reason for existence was Christ according to the flesh, which was Christian by the flesh that united it to the flesh of Christ, died on the Cross. "Destroy this Temple," said Christ. The Temple of Jerusalem, symbol of the old dispensation, was destroyed by the Jewish priests when they put Christ's body to death. At that moment, the veil of the Temple was rent, to proclaim the end of the old regime. The mystery had gone out of the building. Israel was emptied of substance: "Behold your house is left to you desolate" (Matt. 23.38). For the substance of that people was Christ.[5]

The new Church

With Christ, raised up into the life of the Spirit, the Church is born afresh, united as was the old Church to the body of Christ, but with a union governed by different laws: not now in the flesh, but in the Holy Spirit. She is no longer Christ's mother according to the flesh, but his bride in the Holy Spirit. Even in her body, in the body of every one of her faithful, she is united to the risen body of Christ, like the wife who is one body with her husband. This union is more real than any other according to the flesh, for the Spirit is the Reality[6] and the bond of a divine union. Thus, once again, the Church is made up of the totality of those who are united to Christ's body, but this time united in the Holy Spirit to Christ's body vivified by the Holy Spirit.

In order to celebrate her union with the body of her Saviour in the heights of heaven, the Church must take part in Christ's pasch, in his passage from this world into the glory of the Father.

---

[5] St. Augustine, *The City of God*, 17,11.

[6] In Scripture, the spirit is called truth primarily in the sense of total reality, compared with which the things of this world are merely shadows.

She must die to the flesh with her Bridegroom, and rise with him in the Spirit, for with this Christ forever dead to the world, there can be no relationship other than in the Holy Spirit. She unites herself to him at the same time as she associates herself in the act of redemption; she becomes a single body with him, by forever sleeping with him in death, and waking with him into life.

The Church takes part in the act of redemption for her own salvation, passing with her Saviour from existence according to the flesh into the immortal life of the Spirit. And she takes part in it for the benefit of all those whose salvation is entrusted to her: "We always bear about in our body the death of Jesus, that the life also of Jesus may be made manifest in our bodies . . . So then the death of Jesus worketh in us, and the life of Jesus in you" (2 Cor. 4.10, 12).

B. MARY, ASSOCIATE IN THE REDEMPTION

The Fourth Gospel makes clear from the first Mary's role as associate in the salvation effected by Christ. The story of the marriage feast of Cana is of major importance in St. John. The evangelist carefully notes the chronology of the events which preceded this first manifestation of Christ's glory. On the first day, John the Baptist bears witness before the priests and Levites. The next day he points out him who is the Lamb of God. The next day two of his disciples, John and Andrew, set out to follow Christ . . . and so on. On the seventh day, "there was a marriage in Cana of Galilee, and the mother of Jesus was there."

In the Bible, and especially in the Fourth Gospel, seven is the number of completion, of the fullness of time. Upon this seventh day the Messianic era opened, the era of the miracle of water changed to wine. Our Lord travelled rapidly to reach Cana from the Jordan. He wanted to inaugurate his public life during a marriage feast, for his own marriage was the beginning.

In the evangelist's mind, and in Christ's own eyes, especially the Christ described to us by St. John, the things of this world have a message for us; they are prophecies of the heavenly realities which are to be accomplished. With a speed and force of intuition that astound us, our Lord saw with total clarity the events of the end. Thus, when on Palm Sunday he was told that there were pagans who wanted to come to him, he immediately thought of his approaching Hour, the hour of his exaltation when he was to draw all the nations to himself (John 12.32). But that hour had two facets, one of glory and one of agony; it was through the Cross that he was to be lifted up into divine glory. And this cross suddenly arose before his mind so vividly that he groaned, and begged, "Father, save me from this hour" (John 12.27).

Now, at Cana, on this first day of Messianic activity, everything combined to bring the reality of the Last Day before his eyes. Beside this earthly couple was he whom St. John the Baptist had so recently hailed as the true and long awaited bridegroom (John 3.29); he was there with mother and disciples—making seven in all—that mother who was to be present at the foot of his cross along with one of those disciples, at the Hour of the solemn marriage ceremony. It was a majestic moment in which the Hour that was still to come was made present by our Lord's vision of it. And then his mother came to him and said: "They have no wine." Whether she intended it or not, Mary was in fact asking for a miracle; and the changing of water into wine, in this gospel which speaks so much of passage and of transformation, is deeply symbolic. It proclaims the passage of the old dispensation into the New Testament, the great passover of Christ. This was the interpretation put upon it in the early Church, and modern exegesis has brought it back into favour.

Our Lord, in astonishment, replied: "Woman, what is that to thee and to me? My hour is not yet come." He was refusing his mother: "What is that to thee and to me?" He called her "Woman," which was not a name a son would call his mother. He was calling her by the name of her function, which was to be Woman. Because "my hour is not yet come," Christ's Hour, the hour of his pasch, in which all things were to be transformed in him, was not yet come. As though surprised by his mother's intervention, in those prophetic moments when the situation itself was a foretelling of the supreme events to come, Christ answered, "My hour is not yet come." He refused. He would, of course, perform the miracle on the plane of prefiguration: he would change the water into wine. But on the plane of total reality with which his mind was occupied the true miracle must wait for the Hour to strike. Then, he would no longer say to his mother, "Woman, what is that to thee and to me?"

When the Hour struck, and the Messianic marriage was celebrated, once again "the mother of Jesus was there." She was present at the foot of the cross in the role of Christ's mother. Whether or no she was conscious of the fact, as Christ's mother according to the flesh, she was the personification of the Church as it was then, whose essence was to give birth to Christ. In Mary the whole faithful people was there, what Paul Claudel calls "the vertical Church," at the foot of the Cross. Mary gave her consent to Christ's death, giving up the fruit of her womb, for such was God's saving will. And the whole Old Testament Church, in Mary, consented to its own death; she sacrificed what was the whole cause of her existence, her very essence, her possession of Christ according to the flesh. Israel according to the flesh, in Mary, accepted death.

The other Jews were obstinate; they refused to enter the crucible of the Cross, and clung on to all that was carnal and this-worldly in the Old Testament. But in Mary at least, Israel sacrificed its hopes of an earthly Messiah; in her Israel put its faith in God who saves through death, and was faithful to God even unto death. What all those who believe in Christ, who form the New Testament Church were to do, Mary did first, and she did it as personifying the Church: she died with Christ. Thus the whole Church was present in Calvary in her; the Church of the Old Testament and of the New, Christ's mother according to the flesh, and she who, with Christ, dies to the flesh.

Immediately after his death, Christ was once again united to Mary, in the more intimate relationship, which made him more profoundly present to her, of union in the Spirit: "At the moment of his resurrection, Christ unites himself to the Blessed Virgin in his divine splendour . . . and he dwells in her and she in him . . . As Father of the world to come, and therefore as glorious bridegroom, he unites himself to her by choice."[7]

2. THE MOST HOLY BRIDE

A. THE CHURCH

The Church is holy because Christ is her bridegroom, the Christ who is dead to the flesh of sin and risen in the fullness of divine holiness. He has taken the Church and united her to himself and made her his own body—that body that is immolated to the flesh and raised in the Spirit. With her bridegroom, she rises from the tomb, "all glorious, not having spot or wrinkle, or any such thing, but holy and without blemish" (Eph. 5.27). She could hardly be the body of the risen Christ without herself being holy. "In him dwelleth all the fullness of the Godhead, and you are filled in him" (Col. 2.9-10). She is bride and virgin. She is virgin in regard to this world to which she is dead, and virgin in her union with the body of Christ which is a union made not by the flesh, but by the Spirit and his holy charity.

The Church does not attain to the full holiness of her Saviour all at once. Her sanctification progresses "from faith unto faith" (Rom. 1.17), from an initial gift of self to a total transformation into her Saviour. For every believer it is a progress from baptism to death; for the Church as a whole, from Christ's pasch to the parousia of the last resurrection. This holiness will reach its peak when she becomes totally identified with Christ's body, when the Church is the perfect pleroma of the redeeming Christ, wholly

[7] J. J. Olier, *La vie intérieure* . . ., vol. II, pp. 124–6.

filled with the glory of her risen Lord: "Until we all come unto the measure of the fullness of Christ" (Eph. 4.13) on the day of the parousia. When St. Paul describes her as wholly "glorious, having no spot or wrinkle," he is anticipating history; he is gazing upon her in the pure youth of her eschatological splendour, "sitting in the heavenly places" (Eph. 2.6), after the resurrection of the dead.

B. MARY

Mary contains in herself the whole of the Church's holiness, and her short life spanned the whole history of the Church's sanctification. She is associated with Christ in death as his mother, personifying the whole Church dying with its Saviour. That is why, since then, she has lived in the ecclesial fullness of grace of the risen Christ. She is *the* Christian full of redemptive grace, the perfect pleroma, open to the fullness of the Resurrection because associated with the fullness of the Death: "The special quality of the Virgin is . . . to be wholly a capacity for Jesus, filled with Jesus."[8]

Having enabled us to see in Mary the representative of the whole Church as associated in the work of redemption, Scripture says no more of the fullness of ecclesial grace which is the natural result of this. But the Church herself has recognized with the sureness of her children's instinct, that the grace which is in them all is already totally present in Mary: "O Wonder of wonders! All that Christ was to achieve from the first moment of the Church's formation until the judgement, he has done in his Mother."[9]

We call her the Blessed Virgin, the virgin above all others, for she most fully realizes death to the world of sin and union with our Saviour in the charity of the Holy Spirit. Whereas in believers as a whole, the grace of the Church moves gradually towards its completion and will attain it only at the end of centuries, it became

[8] Bérulle, *Vie de Jésus.* Complete works, Migne, p. 501.
[9] J. J. Olier, *op. cit.,* p. 126.

complete in Mary by the end of her own lifetime. Grace covers its whole trajectory in her; its action, measured in thousands of years, which leads the Church to final resurrection, has already reached its goal in Mary. In her the history of the Church is already complete.

3. MOTHER OF THE FAITHFUL

A. THE CHURCH

Having brought her man-child into the world, the woman in the Apocalypse gives birth to many; she brings forth all the brethren of Christ (Apoc. 12.17). The psalmist had seen the Messianic Jerusalem as the city of all the nations converted to Yahweh:

The Lord loveth the gates of Sion above all the tabernacles of Jacob . . .
I will be mindful of Rahab and of Babylon knowing me.
Behold the foreigners, and Tyre, and the people of the Ethiopians, these were there.
Shall not Sion say: This man and that man is born in her?
. . . The Lord shall tell in his writings of peoples and of princes, of them that have been in her (Ps. 87; *Douai* 86).

This then is the Church, "that Jerusalem which is above . . . which is our mother" (Gal. 4.26), the Church called simply by the first Christians "the Virgin Mary," and which we in our turn call "Mother Church." She is really our mother. Our only redemption and divine life are in the dead and risen body of Christ; there alone rise the rivers of the Holy Spirit,[10] and the Church is the bride associated with Christ in the act of redemption, his body which makes that act still present in the world. The Redemption becomes effective in the Church, and becomes so in so far as it is

[10] John 7.37-9. Since the river of the Spirit rises in the body of Christ, St. Irenaeus concludes that it is accessible to us only in the Church which alone is the body of Christ. *Adv. Haer.* III,24,1.

present in the Church; it is by this Mother of the living that the second Adam begets the new humanity. The Church's motherhood begins with baptism, when we are born from her fertile womb;[11] it is completed in the final resurrection when the faithful will be born even in their bodies into the life of grace which is in the Church. This motherhood is realized in every believer in so far as he participates in the act of redemption. Everyone is in labour to redeem himself and others, for the mystery of Christ, in which believers participate in order to be saved, is valid universally, and the grace of each one flows over the rest in proportion to its power for individual sanctification.[12]

B. MARY

"Woman, what is that to thee and to me? My hour is not yet come," so Christ once said. But once the Hour had struck, he said, with his eyes indicating the disciple, "Woman, behold thy son." Christ's redeeming grace is present in Mary in its fullness, and it produces in her the life of all who believe. For Mary took part in Christ's death in the name of the whole Church, and it was the ecclesial fullness of the new life that was being attributed to her: the fruitfulness of the whole Church was hers:

"Jesus Christ, as Father of the world to come, and thus as glorious bridegroom, chooses to unite himself with her . . . and become with her . . . a principle of divine generation. Thus, having been made by God in his resurrection to have life in order to give it to all men . . . he takes the Blessed Virgin as a new Eve, and in the moment of doing so, makes her participate in everything he has received from his Father, to make her Mother of the living."[13]

---

[11] The first Christians saw the baptismal font as a symbol of the Church's womb.

[12] In the parable of the pounds (Luke 19.17), the servant whose pound had earned ten more, found himself placed over ten cities. Each believer can say with Christ, in whom he is sanctified: "I sanctify myself, that they too may be sanctified."

[13] J. J. Olier, *op. cit.*, p. 126.

Mary's universal motherhood, which we describe in terms of universal mediation, is simply the mystery of the communion of saints as perfectly realized in all its effects in her. To sanctify his mother, Christ gives her the full grace of redemption. He gives it to Mary and he gives it to the Church as a whole; and to each of the faithful the Church gives it in small, to all those who are united to Mary by faith and charity, and live in the Church.

Every grace is an ecclesial grace, a social grace. The grace in us flows out to our brothers in proportion to the power of sanctification it possesses in ourselves. Mary has received grace in the fullness of its power, and we call Mary what we call the Church: "Our blessed mother."

When the sanctification of the Last Day comes, when the dead are raised up in the Holy Spirit, the Church's motherhood, which is the same as Mary's, will be perfected in its effects. The faithful will be brought into life, even in their bodies, by that grace which works in the Church, and which works wholly in Mary. In his loving union with the Church, and in his union with Mary upon whom he concentrates all his love for the Church, Christ raises up the children of God to glory. Even in their bodies, they will be the children of their mother the Church and their mother Mary. That day may be a long way off, but it is coming. More and more clearly is "the sign of the Son of man" appearing in heaven (Matt. 24.30)—that sign which can only be the Church, Christ's body, his sign set above all nations. More and more glorious, also, shines in the heaven of the nations she who personifies Christ's Church. "A great sign appeared in heaven: a woman clothed with the sun."

Thus the whole history of God's people has been lived by Mary. The beginning of her life belongs to the first moment of sacred history, and its end coincides with the final hour of that history; and every stage between these two poles has been covered by Mary. For sacred history began not with man's first sin, but in the moment of redemptive mercy and the first promise of salvation

—and it was in that moment that Mary was born, when God put an enmity between the woman and the serpent. Sacred history will be complete when man is saved by grace even in his body; and at the end of her life Mary attained this final salvation. All the events which mark out the way from these two opposite ends are found summed up in the life of Mary: like the people as a whole, she bore in her flesh the seed of salvation, she gave birth to Christ, and was associated in the work of redemption, for her own salvation and the salvation of the world. Yet she only sums up the history of the Church under one aspect. All life tells us of sin and of grace. Mary is the image of humanity only in the history of its salvation, a sacred icon, as it were, of the Church.

She is not just a figure of the Church, its perfect representative; she is its personification. While the Church becomes an individual reality in each believer, in different degrees, Mary's grace is to incarnate it wholly in herself in its perfection. Through her the Church has brought Christ into the world, and in her it dies with Christ on the Cross. That is why Mary still sings: "My soul doth magnify the Lord, and my spirit doth rejoice in God my saviour. For he that is mighty hath done great things to me."

III. CHURCH LIFE AND MARIAN LIFE

We live in the Church, in her fruitful womb; we draw from her all our Christian substance. We do not live in the Church as we live "in Christ." He is the principle of life, whereas the Church is its environment and means. The Saviour gives his glory to the whole Church, and gives it in miniature to every one of us in the Church. We live in the communion of saints and of holy things; the author of all the saints, and the source of all the holy things, is Christ.

Whoever lives in this communion is assured of salvation: he belongs to Christ's body in which salvation is an effective reality, in which death to the world and resurrection in the Holy Spirit are realized. If a man separates himself from it deliberately, he cuts himself off from grace, for grace is to be found nowhere outside this communion. Similarly we must live in communion with Christ's mother. This life "in Mary," as many other writers have pointed out, must not be taken in the Pauline sense of life "in Christ," for Mary is not the principle of grace. But since the grace of the Church is wholly bestowed upon her, anyone who refuses to live in communion with her has no access to grace. Instinctively, the Christian people have always known that love of Christ's mother is a pledge of salvation.[14]

She is what the whole Church is for us: open to salvation, and receiving it for all. It is up to every believer to work out his own salvation, in the power of God. But what would have happened to the African rhetor Aurelius Augustinus, if his mother Monica had not borne him for thirty years in her maternal love? Happy the man for whom another Christian sanctifies himself, who is borne and nourished in another's love. Happy all who live in communion with our Lady. She is for them what the Church is: a mother, in whom Christ begets us to eternal life. Some Christians have had a mystical experience of this life "in Mary." They have been conscious of her all-pervading love, of a community of life with her in the same grace. If a man lives in this communion of charity with Mary, he is secure in salvation, for all the salvation that Christ gives his Church he gives his mother.

It is not merely that the believer is surrounded by grace in this close union with Christ's mother, but he becomes more and more disposed to open his heart to that grace. He realizes in himself the vocation of the Church, which is to be the pleroma of Christ, to be the receptacle of redeeming grace. Why does God save man

---

[14] This certainty is expressed in the liturgy of several Marian feasts, which applies to our Lady the text from Proverbs "Who findeth me findeth life," in Marian literature from the beginning, and in the writings of the pontiffs (cf. for instance, the Letter Apostolic *Sacro Vergente Anno* 1952: "It is clear to us that wherever the Mother of God is venerated with ardent and genuine piety, the hope of salvation cannot be lacking"). Cf. P. Hitz, *Maria und unser heil,* Limburg-Lahn, 1951.

in the community of the Church, and not in isolation? Among the many reasons, there is one psychological one: belonging to the Church disposes man towards grace. It creates in him humility, an openness of the soul to God's influence; it confirms his faith by the faith of others; it supports his hope, whereas solitude with God would terrify him; it opens his heart to a longing for the things of heaven, for in the Church man is already living in heaven (Eph. 2.6), is already a fellow-citizen of the saints and a friend of God (Eph. 2.19); and the Church's love draws man's heart to love as well.

Even now, this man is rooted in salvation. He cannot lose salvation any more than can the man who is small as a child before God (Matt. 18.3), who thirsts for the things of God (Matt. 5.6), who hopes in God (Rom. 5.5), and the man in whose heart divine charity is poured out (Rom. 5.5).

Communion of life with Christ's mother produces these same effects in the believer. Pride disappears, for pride can no more love Mary than it can the Church. The heart turns away from carnal longings and sets its sights on the reality of heaven; however strongly tempted to despair, it will not lose its trust in God, because of our Lady; it will be opened to the divine *agape* by the force of her maternal tenderness.

All this the Church does in this world through the centuries. Scripture, of course, does not tell us so, for it stops at the moment when the history of the Church starts. But the inspiration of the spirit is still at work in the hearts of the saints.

The faithful love to unite themselves to the whole Church when they pray, as the Liturgy does. It is hardly surprising that they also love to pray with Christ's mother, to add value to their own prayer. By praying with Mary, we pray with the whole Church, and since she is not a collection of people, but one person whom we are drawn to love, this communion is easier and is fraught with charity. For the priest, it is a great strength to know that he is celebrating the *mysterium tremendum* in the name of all holy Church, and of her who personifies that Church fully: *Communicantes et memoriam venerantes in primis gloriosae semper Virginis Mariae, Genitricis Dei et Domini nostri Jesu Christi.*[15]

M. Olier tells how one day he felt that he was being asked to celebrate Mass for the intentions of our Lady. More than one saint, and some of the greatest theologians, such as Bérulle and Père de Condren, have had this rather naïve-seeming piety of offering the sacrifice which we offer for the intentions of the whole Church for the intentions of our Lady.

We must pray and suffer for the Church, and all her needs; we must thank God for the Church, and all the gifts she has been given. But our Lady has been blessed with all the riches of the Church, and in her heart she bears all the Church's needs, for the history of the Church is her own. To pray for her intentions, and give thanks in her name, is to pray for the Church and give thanks for every grace that we and our brothers have received.

If our Lady is the personification of the Church, it is only right that the faithful shall fulfill towards her the duties they have to the Church, and that the fraternal love that is poured into the heart of each one of us for the good of all, should be wholly concentrated upon her: "And the disciple took her to himself" (John 19.27).

[15] From the Canon of the Mass: "In communion with, and venerating the memory in the first place of the glorious Mary, ever virgin, mother of our God and Lord Jesus Christ."